LITERARY CRITICISM:
A SHORT HISTORY

Volume 4

MODERN CRITICISM

LITERARY CRITICISM: A SHORT HISTORY
Modern Criticism

WILLIAM K. WIMSATT, JR. AND CLEANTH BROOKS

Routledge
Taylor & Francis Group

LONDON AND NEW YORK

First published in 1957
First published in this format 1970

This edition first published in 2021
by Routledge
4 Park Square, Milton Park, Abingdon, Oxon OX14 4RN

and by Routledge
605 Third Avenue, New York, NY 10017

Routledge is an imprint of the Taylor & Francis Group, an informa business

British Library Cataloguing in Publication Data
A catalogue record for this book is available from the British Library

ISBN: 978-0-367-69387-9 (Set)
ISBN: 978-1-00-314162-4 (Set) (ebk)
ISBN: 978-0-367-69230-8 (Volume 4) (hbk)
ISBN: 978-0-367-69229-2 (pbk)
ISBN: 978-1-00-314101-3 (Volume 4) (ebk)

Publisher's Note
The publisher has gone to great lengths to ensure the quality of this reprint but points out that some imperfections in the original copies may be apparent.

Disclaimer
The publisher has made every effort to trace copyright holders and would welcome correspondence from those they have been unable to trace.

TO RENÉ WELLEK

INTRODUCTION

I T IS NOT LIKELY THAT A PERSON WHO ENTERTAINS EVEN A MODEST
prejudice against the kind of history writing which appears in this
book will have his mind changed by introductory apologetics. Still
some preliminary advertisement of aims may be only fair—and may even
be generally helpful to a receptive reading. The first principle on which
we would insist is that of continuity and intelligibility in the history of
literary argument. Plato has a bearing on Croce and Freud, and vice
versa. Or, all three of these theorists are engaged with a common reality
and hence engage one another through the medium of that reality and
either come to terms or disagree. Literary problems occur not just because history produces them, but because literature is a thing of such and
such a sort, showing such and such a relation to the rest of human experience. True, languages and cultures, times and places, differ widely.
The literary historian will always do well to nurse a certain skepticism
about the thoroughness with which he may be penetrating the secret
of his documents. But then he has to worry too about an opposite danger
of being merely and overly skeptical. There are techniques of caution
and neutrality which put the historian somewhat in the position of the
student who, having his difficulties with a Latin or German reading examination, is content to put down a translation that does not make sense.
He writes as if he is not convinced that the foreign language does make
sense. Our own notion of how to write a history of literary ideas is just
the opposite of that. The history is bound to be an interpretation, in part
even a translation. In part it will even be built on reasonable guesses. The
least it can do is make sense.

And that connects closely with a second of our main notions about
method; namely, that a history of literary ideas can scarcely escape being
written from a point of view. It seems to us that on a strictly neutral plan
there can be in fact no history of literary ideas at all, nor, for that matter,
any direct history of literature. At least not any history that hangs together. This book, we hope and believe, both grows out of and illustrates
and contributes to a certain distinct point of view. It is the history of one
kind of thinking about values, and hence it could not have been written
relativistically, or indifferently, or at random. It contains much praise and
blame, both implicit and explicit. There are even senses, complimentary
we believe, in which it could be called "polemic" or "argumentative." It
is nevertheless, we contend, a true history. Call it *An Argumentative
History of Literary Argument in the West.*

The reader will now readily conceive yet another of our notions:
namely, that in a history of this sort the critical *idea* has priority over all

other kinds of material. The present "short" history does not attempt a grand assemblage of information (though information of the right kind and in the right amount, we believe, is here). Neither encyclopedism nor the Saintsburyan gigantically conversational range has been our purpose, but a series of narrative focusses precisely on ideas. In some chapters, especially in those concerning the neo-classic age, the argument runs directly along thematic lines. Other chapters, especially those concerning classical antiquity, are developed around certain heroic figures—Plato, or Aristotle, or Longinus. Still even in these chapters, the idea, not the hero, is always paramount. Hence it happens that we have attempted no complete account of any one philosopher or literary man (much less any complete survey of disciples or other minor figures). We have used the little figures, and even the great figures, as they came in handy to our narrative. Hence also we have been little interested in proving the consistency, we have been little dismayed by the frequent inconsistencies, of our great literary theorists. Where we have here and there noticed inconsistencies (as, let us say, in Addison's account of imagination, or in Arnold's account of classic grandeur and the "touchstones"), the point has been made not so much against the author as against a collection of ideas which have often been credited with more coherence than they actually exhibit. Or it has been made simply for the sake of gaining the expository advantage of contrast. By and large, as notably with Plato in the first chapter, we have preferred the idea in full bloom and have made no attempt to harmonize the smaller contradictions, real or apparent, which are always to be found in the canon of a prolific author. When the main ideas of an author have been leveled off or averaged in with all the marginal variations, the result is not a story with parts, contours, accents, climaxes, but a dead level of neutrality—the melted wax doll. The principle applies with equal force to themes and eras in intellectual history. Statistical scrupulosity in the study of "ideas" tends of course toward a smudge. This truth was never more clearly betrayed than in the following recommendation of minute history by a late distinguished American scholar:

> One of the surest evidences of a better understanding of an individual or a period is that sharp lines disappear, strong lights and shadows are modified, uniqueness and isolation melt away, the man is seen to be more like other men, the age like other ages.[1]

The present writers, despite their confidence in the continuity and real community of human experience through the ages,[2] are confident also

[1] R. D. Havens, "Changing Taste in the Eighteenth Century," *PMLA*, XLIV (June, 1929), 534-5.
[2] Some variations on the theme of the "universal" perhaps relevant to the present paradox are to be found near the end of Chapter 15.

of differences—of levels, depressions, and eminences—of the difference between Elizabethan England and Augustan Rome, of that between Chaucer and Pope, and of that between Pope and Blackmore, Dryden and Rymer.

The examples just mentioned invite allusion to one further methodological notion and one which is perhaps not very immediately entailed by what we have so far been saying. We have finally to confess what may seem to some of our more severely idealist friends a principle of distinct impurity in our method. Our book is not a history of general aesthetics (though a few quite limited excursions into the aesthetic ambient have been ventured). On the other hand, it is not a history of literary technicalities or techniques, of prosody or grammar. Yet if we had had to make a choice between a more markedly aesthetic direction and a more grammatical, it is the latter (in the full classical sense of the term "grammatical") which we should have chosen. That is, we have written a history of ideas about verbal art and about its elucidation and criticism. The ultimate object of our regard then, though seen at a remove, through the eyes of the critic and the theorist of criticism, has been poetry or literature. So much literary criticism and theory and so much of the best has been written by the men of letters. Often, whether consciously or not, they have written their general theories as a comment on their own best performances in poetry, and on the *kinds* of poetry which were most dear to them. The theory, furthermore, has been both stated and exemplified by the poems, and undoubtedly both poetry and theory have interacted in several ways. To show that the history of literary theory has been no more than a series of temporary explanations directed toward poetic vogues of the moment and hence that the name of "poetry" enjoys only a long record of equivocality, would be the final triumph of the neutrally and pluralistically minded investigator. Such (need it be said?) has scarcely been our aspiration. On the other hand, to show that through all the ambiguous weave and dialectical play of the successive concrete situations which make the history of poems and theory, the sustaining truth continues and may be discerned and its history written—this would seem to be an appropriate enough goal for the historian who believes that he has in fact a coherent, a real and unequivocal subject matter. To tell the story pure, as a series of internally driven developments of ideas or patterns of abstractly significant oppositions and resolutions, will have advantages for the philosopher. But to tell it more or less impurely, bringing in the colors of the literary milieu and allowing critical episodes to take shape out of the milieu, will have some advantages for the student of literature. In a few sentences of the Epilogue which concludes this book we have tried to sketch a view of how the several literary genre conceptions dominant in several ages—dramatic, epistolary, heroic, burlesque, and lyric—will if studied carefully open up not so many diverse views into multiplicity and chaos but so many complementary insights into the one deeply rooted and perennial human truth which is the poetic principle.

As our chapter titles will suggest, the substance of the book includes Greek and Roman classicism, Renaissance, Augustan, romantic, and Victorian English criticism, and 20th-century English and American. In addition, there are excursions or inter-chapters or sections of chapters dealing with the Middle Ages and with main episodes in modern Italian, French, German, and Russian criticism. The book tries to follow the main lines of the critical heritage and then draw in the story toward the end to the immediate arena of the modern English-speaking world.

Any history of any subject has to begin somewhere—a matter perhaps of some embarrassment. Where it begins will be determined not only by the availability of certain documents but by the views of the author concerning the real nature of his subject. The present history might have lingered longer near its beginning than it actually does with certain proto-glimpses of literary critical consciousness in the Western tradition—invocations by the early Greek poets Homer and Hesiod to the Muses and assertions of an aim to teach or to charm, phrases of some pith and relevance concerning craft and genius or the fate of man, from early and all but lost lyric poets, from law-givers, dramatists, and pre-Socratic philosophers. The history as it actually begins, in our first chapter, plunges immediately, with only a few preliminary words, into an early Platonic dialogue, the *Ion*. This is the earliest extant Western writing that addresses itself deliberately, formally, and exclusively to the general matter of literary criticism. Furthermore this dialogue treats the topic of literary criticism in a way which the present writers conceive to be the correct way—that is, by asking a difficult question about the kind of knowledge which a criticism of a poem, or a poem itself, can lay claim to. What does a poem say that is worth listening to? What does criticism say? The entire course of literary theory and criticism, from the time of Plato to the present, has in effect been occupied with producing more or less acute versions of those questions and more or less accurate and telling answers. Plato's *Ion* is a thoroughgoing, radically naive, inquiry into the nature of poetic composition as a department of verbal meaning and power. It has also the advantage to the historian that it is a dialogue—that is, its arguments are put not purely and schematically but in dramatic form. There are two speakers and at least two points of view. The historian of critical ideas who takes such ideas in any degree tentatively, yet seriously, could scarcely find himself beginning on more congenial ground.

The supplementary passages which appear after most of the chapters in the book are intended to supply in part historical and theoretical dimensions which could not be conveniently handled in the narrative and in part illustrations or problems (some of them comic) which the meditative reader may enjoy placing for himself in relation to the themes of the narrative. Passages following a given chapter may stand either in harmony with one another or in opposition, and in various relations to the content of the chapter.

Quotations from Greek and Latin and from modern foreign languages appear for the most part in already available translations, which are appropriately acknowledged. But here and there the authors have for one reason or another attempted their own, perhaps rather free, translations. These appear for the most part without further advertisement.

This book would perhaps never have been begun except for a suggestion made to the authors a few years back by two friends, George W. Stewart and John Nerber. The authors wish to record their debt and express their gratitude.

The whole work has been written by a method of fairly close collaboration not only in the general plan but in the execution of each part. The authors have read and criticized each other's work closely and repeatedly at various stages. The substantial responsibility for the chapters is, however, to be divided as follows: Chapters 1–24, and 32, W. K. Wimsatt, Jr.; Chapters 25–31, Cleanth Brooks.

The parts of the book by W. K. Wimsatt, Jr., owe an obvious large debt to a Yale graduate English seminar, Theories of Poetry, inaugurated many years ago by Albert S. Cook, and conducted subsequently by F. A. Pottle and T. W. Copeland. To those founders, and especially to F. A. Pottle, and to the students in the course since 1942 and to those in its more recent undergraduate parallel, Introduction to Criticism, the author makes a grateful acknowledgement.

Cleanth Brooks did part of his work on the book while holding a Fellowship of The John Simon Guggenheim Memorial Foundation. He wishes to acknowledge the kindness of the Foundation and to express his thanks.

For various kinds of assistance in research and preparation of typescript, the authors express their thanks to Robert B. Brown, Richard J. Browne, James Cook, Harold Cogger, Mrs. D. W. Gordon, John Oates, Michael Pertschuk, Mrs. David Underdown, and Donald Wheeler.

A more or less pervasive debt in several chapters to a manuscript book by H. M. McLuhan concerning the ancient war between dialecticians and rhetoricians is here gratefully acknowledged and is underscored by the quotation, following Chapter 4, of two substantial excerpts from published essays by Mr. McLuhan.

To their colleagues Bernard Knox, Maynard Mack, John Palmer,

John Smith, and René Wellek, the authors are indebted for reading and criticism of various chapters in early drafts, and to Charles Feidelson, Charles C. Walcutt, and Father Walter J. Ong, S.J., for various kinds of critical advice. More than to any other single scholar, they are indebted for general theoretical and historical help to René Wellek. Not only his published but his yet unpublished works and his advice in conversation have done much to promote the writing of the modern chapters.

To Margaret and Tinkum, for labors expert, various, and unremitting, the authors join in affectionate expression of gratitude.

To Marshall Waingrow the authors owe special thanks for a skillful reading of the entire page proof. Alfred Stiernotte made the index.

Two fairly extended passages of Chapter 32, the Epilogue, follow an essay "Criticism Today: A Report from America," published by W. K. Wimsatt, Jr., in *Essays in Criticism*, VI (January, 1956), 1–21. Our thanks are due to F. W. Bateson, the editor.

ANNOTATIONS AND SOURCES

This book is annotated lightly. The notes aim at giving a guide to verifying our treatment of sources and a minimal clue to further reading. Certain works which have general relevance for the whole book or for major sections of it are brought together in the following list. At various places in the annotation, some of these works are cited by abbreviated titles or simply by names of their authors. The reader will easily understand such references on consulting the list.

Meyer H. Abrams, *The Mirror and the Lamp*. New York: Oxford University Press, 1953

Raymond M. Alden, ed., *Critical Essays of the Early Nineteenth Century*. New York: Charles Scribner's Sons, 1921

J. W. H. Atkins, *English Literary Criticism*. I, *The Medieval Phase*. Cambridge: At the University Press, 1943; II, *The Renascence*. London: Methuen & Co. 1947; III, *The Seventeenth and Eighteenth Centuries*. London: Methuen & Co., 1951

J. W. H. Atkins, *Literary Criticism in Antiquity*, vols. I and II. Cambridge: At the University Press, 1934

Charles S. Baldwin, *Ancient Rhetoric and Poetic*. New York: The Macmillan Company, 1924

Medieval Rhetoric and Poetic. New York: The Macmillan Company, 1928

Renaissance Literary Theory and Practice. New York: Columbia University Press, 1939

Walter J. Bate, *From Classic to Romantic, Premises of Taste in Eighteenth-Century England*. Cambridge, Mass.: Harvard University Press, 1946

Walter J. Bate, ed., *Criticism: The Major Texts*. New York: Harcourt, Brace and Company, 1948

Albert C. Baugh, *A History of the English Language*. New York: D. Appleton-Century Company, 1935

Albert C. Baugh *et al.*, *A Literary History of England*. New York: Appleton-Century-Crofts, 1948

Bernard Bosanquet, *A History of Aesthetic*. London: Swan Sonnenschein & Co.; New York: Macmillan & Co., 1892

Aisso Bosker, *Literary Criticism in the Age of Johnson*. Groningen: J. B. Wolters' Uitgevers-Maatschappij, 1930; revised edition, 1953

René Bray, *La Formation de la doctrine classique en France*. Dijon: Maurice Darantière, 1927

Edgar de Bruyne, *Études d'esthétique médiévale*, vols. I, II, III. Brugge (België): "De Tempel," 1946

E. F. Carritt, *Philosophies of Beauty from Socrates to Robert Bridges*. Oxford: Oxford University Press, 1931

Alexander F. B. Clark, *Boileau and the French Classical Critics in England (1660–1830)*. Paris: Librairie Ancienne Édouard Champion, 1925

Ronald S. Crane *et al.*, *Critics and Criticism Ancient and Modern*. Chicago: The University of Chicago Press, 1952

Benedetto Croce, *Aesthetic as Science of Expression and General Linguistic*, trans. Douglas Ainslie, 2nd ed. London: Macmillan and Co., 1922

John F. D'Alton, *Roman Literary Theory and Criticism*. London and New York: Longmans, Green and Co., 1931

Willard H. Durham, ed., *Critical Essays of the Eighteenth Century*. New Haven: Yale University Press, 1915

T. S. Eliot, *The Use of Poetry and the Use of Criticism, Studies in the Relation of Criticism to Poetry in England*. Cambridge, Mass.: Harvard University Press, 1933

Allan H. Gilbert, ed., *Literary Criticism Plato to Dryden*. New York: American Book Company, 1940

Katharine E. Gilbert and Helmut Kuhn, *A History of Esthetics*. New York: The Macmillan Company, 1939; Bloomington: Indiana University Press, 1953

Theodore M. Greene, *The Arts and the Art of Criticism*, 2nd ed. Princeton: Princeton University Press, 1947

Werner Jaeger, *Paideia: The Ideals of Greek Culture*, trans. Gilbert Highet, vols. I, II, III. New York: Oxford University Press, 1939–44

Leah Jonas, *The Divine Science, The Aesthetic of Some Representative Seventeenth-Century English Poets*. New York: Columbia University Press, 1940

Thomas Munro, *The Arts and Their Interrelations*. New York: The Liberal Arts Press, 1949

William V. O'Connor, *An Age of Criticism 1900–1950*. Chicago: Henry Regnery Company, 1952

Melvin Rader, ed., *A Modern Book of Esthetics, An Anthology*. New York: Henry Holt and Company, 1935, 1952

William Rhys Roberts, *Greek Rhetoric and Literary Theory*. New York: Longmans, Green and Co., 1928

George Saintsbury, *A History of Criticism and Literary Taste in Europe*, vols. I, II, III, 4th ed. Edinburgh and London: William Blackwood & Sons, 1949

Mark Schorer *et al.*, eds., *Criticism: The Foundations of Modern Literary Judgment*. New York: Harcourt, Brace and Company, 1948

Joseph T. Shipley, ed., *Dictionary of World Literature: Criticism—Forms—Technique*. New York: The Philosophical Library, 1943

G. Gregory Smith, ed., *Elizabethan Critical Essays*, vols. I and II. Oxford: Oxford University Press, 1937

James H. Smith and Edd W. Parks, eds., *The Great Critics, An Anthology of Literary Criticism*. New York: W. W. Norton & Company, 1951

Joel E. Spingarn, ed., *Critical Essays of the Seventeenth Century*, vols. I, II, III. Oxford: At the Clarendon Press, 1908–9

Joel E. Spingarn, *A History of Literary Criticism in the Renaissance*. New York: Columbia University Press, 1899

Robert W. Stallman, *Critiques and Essays in Criticism, 1920–1948, Representing the Achievement of Modern British and American Critics*. New York: The Ronald Press Company, 1949

Alba H. Warren, Jr., *English Poetic Theory, 1825–1865*. Princeton: Princeton University Press, 1950

René Wellek, *A History of Modern Criticism: 1750–1950*. I, *The Later Eighteenth Century*; II, *The Romantic Age*. New Haven: Yale University Press, 1955

René Wellek, *The Rise of English Literary History*. Chapel Hill: The University of North Carolina Press, 1941

René Wellek and Austin Warren, *Theory of Literature*. New York: Harcourt, Brace and Company, 1949

Morton D. Zabel, ed., *Literary Opinion in America*. New York: Harper & Brothers, 1951

Titles of learned and critical journals are sometimes abbreviated in the notes, as follows:

AJP   *The American Journal of Philology*
ELH   *ELH: A Journal of English Literary History*
JEGP   *The Journal of English and Germanic Philology*
JHI   *Journal of the History of Ideas*

MLN   *Modern Language Notes*
MLQ   *Modern Language Quarterly*
MLR   *The Modern Language Review*
MP   *Modern Philology*
PQ   *Philological Quarterly*
SP   *Studies in Philology*
PMLA   *Publications of the Modern Language Association of America*
RES   *The Review of English Studies*
TLS   *The Times Literary Supplement*

CONTENTS

Contents

MODERN CRITICISM

A SHORT HISTORY

CHAPTER 25

TRAGEDY AND COMEDY: THE INTERNAL FOCUS

§ *Hegel's "lyrical" conception of tragedy: the ethical problem, conflict between rival "goods"—II. some modern variants of the Hegelian conception: A. C. Bradley and spiritual waste, Prosser Frye and the hero's guilt, J. W. Krutch and faith in the "greatness of man"—Arthur Schopenhauer's influence upon modern conceptions of tragedy: tragedy as affording insight into the blind striving of the Will—III. Nietzsche's "Musical" conception of tragedy: his distinction between an Apollonian and a Dionysian art: the origin of Greek tragedy in the festival of Dionysus, the union of the two gods in tragedy, Apollo speaks Dionysian wisdom—IV. tragedy as a harmonizing of discords: Nietzsche's stress upon the joyful wisdom of tragedy, upon tension in art generally—V. parallels and contrasts between Nietzsche's conception of tragedy and Bergson's conception of comedy: Bergson's notion that laughter springs from the discrepancy between the mechanical and the natural: sources of the comic in repetition, inversion, and reciprocal interference of series—Bergson's views on the social function of comedy, his relation to the "classical" view of comedy, his denial that comedy is a genuine art —VI. other psychological theories of laughter and the comic, Shaftesbury, Penjon, Kline, Kallen—VII. Freud's conception of wit as a device for conserving psychic energy: its aim to recover the lost euphoria of the child— VIII. the witty, the comical, and the humorous as distinguished by Freud: laughter as the sudden discharge of the conserved energy—IX. criticisms of Freud made by Max Eastman, and by Arthur Koestler: Freud's failure to distinguish the self-assertive and the self-transcending, integrative emotions—Koestler's view of the "bisociative" treatment*

of phenomena: his argument that comedy, tragedy, and
the process of scientific discovery all involve bisociative
treatment of phenomena, and that since comedy and
tragedy have the same "cognitive layout," they differ only
in their specific emotional "charges" §

E ACH AGE TENDS TO FIND IN SOME ONE OF THE LITERARY GENRES THE
norm of all literary art. The 17th century, we have seen, found the
highest poetry to be embodied in the epic. The later 18th century
saw in the lyric the "most poetic kind of poetry," [1] for men's interests had shifted, with the burgeoning Romantic movement, from an externally known world to the knowing and expressive self. Georg Wilhelm Hegel illustrates the new emphasis, not only in his philosophy of
history, which is the story of spirit expressing itself through successive
partial revelations until it finally achieves complete self-consciousness,
but in his history of art as well. The first stage finds spirit almost over-
borne by matter, as in Egyptian art; then there comes the perfect balance between spirit and matter, as in Greek sculpture; and finally in
modern art, spirit overflows and envelops matter.[2]

When men's minds are dominated by a lyric norm, their conceptions
of the other genres are affected. Like metamorphosed rocks, the other
genres, under the heat and pressure of lyricism, change their structure
and appearance. Tragedy, for example, may be said to have become
"internalized," even "lyricized." Terms like "struggle," "tension," and
"resolution" shifted their meanings with the new conception of the problem. Consider, for example, how Aristotle characteristically handled the
tragic protagonist's power of choice and his responsibility for that choice.
The act that precipitated the downfall of the hero had to be more than
a simple misadventure—an accident that simply "happened" to him; on
the other hand, it had to be less than a calculated crime. The tragic protagonist could be neither passive victim nor obvious criminal. The problem of guilt and responsibility was thus a matter of central importance;
but it is characteristic of Aristotle that this ethical problem is treated in
the *Poetics* as a function of the plot. That is, the complicated play that
Aristotle called for, a play that includes a *peripeteia* and an *anagnōrisis*,
demands an action by the hero of a certain seriousness and a certain
responsibility. Aristotle's approach was to the total action that the tragedy
presents—not directly to the ethical standards of the hero.

But Hegel's view of tragedy begins—and, one is inclined to say, ends
—with the ethical problem. Whereas Aristotle was content to make

[1] Cf. *ante* Chapter 17, pp. 372–3.
[2] Cf. *ante* Chapter 17.

hamartia a partly responsible act of error without attempting to define the degree of culpability precisely, Hegel defines the hero's error very precisely: the good chosen by the hero is only a partial good though the hero treats it as though it were an absolute good. The characteristic struggle in tragedy is between rival ethical claims: good is set up against good; and the choice is not between good and evil, but between one good and another.[3]

Hegel considered *Antigone* to be the ideal example of Greek tragedy, probably because in this play we have the maximum of ethical tension. Both Creon and Antigone are right in the sense that the ethical loyalties that they acknowledge are valid. But each is wrong in assuming that the ethical principle exerts an *absolute* claim upon his loyalty. The reconciliation comes in our realization that the claims are but partial and that catastrophe has occurred through the human failure of mistaking the part for the whole. But it is well to notice that the reconciliation as envisaged by Hegel occurs in the mind of the spectator or auditor—not necessarily in the mind of the protagonist. Antigone, one has to suppose, goes to her death without ever realizing that she has mistaken a limited ideal for an absolute ideal.

The spectator perceives that though the conflict is dreadful for the human antagonists caught up in it, it is after all simply a stage in the dialectic through which spirit eternally expresses itself. Indeed, the tragic conflict as Hegel defines it fits comfortably into his massive philosophical system. Tragic conflict proves to be simply another instance of the contradiction of thesis by antithesis, a contradiction to be resolved only in a higher synthesis, where the counter claims of thesis and antithesis are admitted, yet any ultimate contradiction between them is shown to be illusory.

Hegel's is a philosopher's definition of tragedy—not necessarily the worse for that, to be sure—but it has provoked the reaction that it is too "intellectual," and it is certainly part and parcel of a theory of art which regards literature as a primitive, and therefore for the mature mind a limited and defective, kind of philosophy. Benedetto Croce, certainly not the least sympathetic critic of Hegelianism, has put this criticism decisively:

> In a greater degree than any of his predecessors Hegel emphasized the cognitive character of art. But this very merit brought him into a difficulty more easily avoided by the rest. Art being placed in the sphere of absolute Spirit, in company with Religion and Philosophy, how will she be able to hold her own in such powerful and aggressive company, especially in that of Philosophy, which in the Hegelian system stands at the summit

[3] See *The Philosophy of Fine Art*, trans. F. P. B. Osmaston (London, 1920), Vol. IV.

of all spiritual evolution? If Art and Religion fulfilled functions other than the knowledge of the Absolute, they would be inferior levels of the Spirit, but yet necessary and indispensable. But if they have in view the same end as Philosophy and are allowed to compete with it, what value can they retain? None whatever; or, at the very most, they may have that sort of value which attaches to transitory historical phases in the life of humanity. The principles of Hegel's system are at bottom rationalistic and hostile to religion, and hostile no less to art.[4]

Hegel's concept of tragedy does not fit all the extant Greek tragedies. *Oedipus Rex*, Aristotle's ideal tragedy, would have to be pulled and twisted more than a bit to make it answer to Hegel's definition: where in that play, for instance, is an ethical good set over against a rival good? Hegel himself admits that practically none of Euripides' tragedies conform to his notion, a matter which he explains by regarding Euripidean tragedy as "modern" in its concern for character and in its ethical laxity.

II

YET Hegel's concept of tragedy, in spite of its forbidding austerity, has had great and lasting influence. A. C. Bradley, for example, in his *Shakespearean Tragedy* (1904) and in his *Lectures on Poetry* (1909) gave us a somewhat softened, though distinctly Hegelian, view. In setting this forth for the English-speaking reader, Bradley was at some pains to defend Hegel against charges of inflexibility. He maintained that Hegel

> does not teach, as he is often said to do, that tragedy portrays only the conflict of such ethical powers as the family and the state. He adds to these . . . others, such as love and honour, together with various universal ends; and it may even be maintained that he has provided in his general statement for those numerous cases where . . . no substantial or universal ends collide, but the interest is centred on "personalities." [5]

But Bradley conceded that Hegel's treatment of the aspect of reconciliation was inadequate. Hegel did not sufficiently notice that more is involved than acquiescence. As spectators of tragedy we feel a positive exultation along with, and indeed because of, our awareness of the fact that "the hero has never shown himself so great or noble as in the death which seals his failure." [6] Our solace at the fall of the hero is, then, not

---

[4] *Aesthetic* (1901), trans. Douglas Ainslie (London, 1922), p. 301.
[5] *Lectures* (London, 1909), p. 85, by permission of Macmillan & Company, Ltd., and St. Martin's Press.
[6] *Lectures*, p. 84.

so much a reaffirmation of the moral structure of the universe as a heightened awareness of the greatness of man. Though not every tragedy shows ethical powers in conflict with each other, every tragedy does show, so Bradley argued, "a self-division and self-waste of spirit." [7] We see Macbeth's courage and imagination wasted in his defeat—yet their true grandeur is revealed only by his defeat. Thus, Bradley would broaden Hegel's definition: the typical and essential conflict to be found in tragedy is not that of good against good, but rather a conflict within the self: "*any* spiritual conflict involving spiritual waste is tragic." [8]

Bradley's definition has the merit of fixing attention upon an element that is found in a great deal of literature: not only in a tragedy like *Macbeth*, but in *Don Quixote*, in "Sir Patrick Spens," and even in "An Ode to a Nightingale." But the definition will scarcely help us distinguish tragedy as a genre. The tragic conflict is within the soul: tragedy manifests itself in our sense of spiritual waste. In this essentially "lyric" definition, the tragic becomes a personal and subjective quality.

In rejecting, as a ground for tragedy, Hegel's austere idealism in favor of a milder humanism, Bradley certainly acted in the spirit of the age. He praised tragedy for bringing home to us the spiritual qualities of the hero—his self-assertion, his noble endurance, his magnificent vitality—and nearly all recent writers on the subject have joined Bradley in this emphasis. Bonamy Dobrée, for example, regards tragedy as our prime means for testing man's ultimate strength. "Tragedy," he writes, "is man's trial of his individual strength, a trial becoming increasingly unpopular, indeed incomprehensible, with the advance of democracy." [9]

Prosser Frye's *Romance and Tragedy* (1922) also presented a Hegelian view of tragedy, but Frye retained, as the very center of tragedy, Hegel's insistence upon a problem of ethical choice. Like Hegel, Frye found in Greek tragedy the very type of tragedy, and he refused to soften the edges of his definition to admit more comfortably the Shakespearian masterpieces. Shakespeare, great poet though Frye admitted him to be, was dangerously committed to a modern and "Euripidean" interest in character—to the consequent blurring of a proper ethical focus.

Tragedy, as Frye defined it, rests upon the assertion of a universal moral order. The fall of the hero momentarily disturbs that order: the auditor or the reader is shocked. So great is the disproportion between what we feel ought to happen and what actually does happen that we experience a kind of giddiness—what Frye calls "the moral qualm." In genuine tragedy, however, that qualm is overcome: the very fall of the hero confirms the moral order which it had at first shock seemed to call in question. The tragic writer must stress this ultimate stability of the

[7] *Lectures*, p. 86.
[8] *Lectures*, p. 87.
[9] *Restoration Tragedy* (Oxford, 1929), p. 9.

moral order, for he is interested as a writer, not in a psychological, but in a metaphysical problem. The question that he must put is this: why does evil occur?

Shakespeare's alleged failure to put this question causes Frye to deny that he is a typically tragic poet. The question that Shakespeare characteristically puts seems to be: by what steps, through what process, did this apparently powerful and virtuous creature come to grief? And so we have the "tragedies" of Othello or of Hamlet, with their inordinate interest in character and their blurred focus on the metaphysical problem.

Sophocles, on the other hand, shows us that the fall of the hero is not an "accident" but is inevitable, the consequence of a certain blindness on the part of the hero. *Antigone*—which Frye follows Hegel in regarding as the ideal instance of tragedy—will illustrate. Antigone in her entire devotion to one ethical claim denies the other. But to defy the *polis* was a terrible thing, no matter what the motive, and no matter even that the motive be one which, like Antigone's, elicits a pitying response. The Greek audience, Frye insists, would have felt Antigone to be involved in criminality. This tension between terror and pity in our attitude toward the protagonist is for Frye the one necessary tension in tragedy. When this tension is relaxed—when we can view the protagonist with unqualified sympathy, then we are no longer in the presence of tragedy. The downfall of the hero has indeed become merely an unfortunate accident, a matter of unpropitious environment, or of some failure of adjustment. The tragic protagonist has to be responsible for his act; but if he is responsible, then he is in some sense culpable.

To this important point, Frye bears able and effective testimony, but he out-Hegels Hegel in the sternness of his ethical demands. His tragic writer is frankly a teacher; and he argues that literature, in so far as it is "true to itself and its own character," is concerned not to "image life" but to "commemorate some idea about it—or in other words interpret it." The interpretation that Frye demands is of a specific kind: it is not to be an economic or a sociological or an anthropological interpretation. It is to be a "humane" interpretation, and for Frye this depends upon the "new humanism" of Irving Babbitt and Paul Elmer More.[1] Indeed, Frye's *Romance and Tragedy* must be regarded as one of the ablest documents produced by the New Humanists. But, as in so much of the work of this group, there is a certain note of desperation. Frye is carrying out a stubborn rear-guard action. He gloomily notes that almost from the very birth of tragedy there has been a falling off, with no real recoveries. Even the classical Racine did not accomplish a return to genuine tragedy. The neohumanist scholar did not really hope for better days: he was simply keeping the record straight.

[1] Cf. *ante* Chapter 20.

Most modern writers on tragedy, however, have found such a diet too rich for their blood. They have not been interested in ultimate metaphysical questions. They are thoroughly secular and man-centered. What they see in tragedy is primarily a glorification of man's power to endure. We have already mentioned Dobrée's emphasis upon this theme, and other names might be added. Thus, W. V. O'Connor in his *Climates of Tragedy* (1943) refuses to allow that certain modern plays are tragedies on the ground that they do not sufficiently stress "the strength of man," but instead merely "offer consolation in a dogma." And Joseph Wood Krutch in *The Modern Temper* (1929) makes "faith in the greatness of man" a necessary condition for producing tragedy. A tragic writer, he says, does not have to believe in God, but "he must believe in man." Thus, our modern failure to write tragedies springs, not from our loss of faith in the supernatural, but from our loss of faith in the worth of human nature.

Modern writers—Krutch certainly and even A. C. Bradley probably —did not, however, arrive at the theme of noble, tragic endurance by simply expanding Hegel's formula. They borrowed generously from Hegel's German contemporaries and followers. Thus the theme of man's endurance as stated by Krutch reads like a secularization of A. W. Schlegel's treatment of tragic endurance as a form of human self-assertion, a gesture, as Schlegel would have it, made in the face of fate in order to assert the mind's proud claim to a participation in the divine.[2] Among the 19th-century German aestheticians, however, one may point to a much more direct and obvious source in the work of Arthur Schopenhauer. He was "for a long time unread and unknown," but by the end of the 19th century he had become "the most popular and influential of writers. Even in authors, like Gautier or Flaubert, who probably never set eyes on one of his books, we may fancy we feel a kindred spirit."[3]

In *The World as Will and Idea* (1818), Schopenhauer utterly rejected Hegel's notion that the universe manifests the force of spirit, *Geist*, unfolding itself through a self-ordained dialectic and revealing its reasonable nature more and more fully in history. Instead Schopenhauer conceived the ultimate reality to be a blind energy, which in its aimlessness actually belied the term *Will* by which he would name it. This "Will" objectified itself at various levels, in inorganic matter, in the vegetable and the animal kingdoms, and of course, in Man himself. But Man's reason does not represent a coming into consciousness of the Will, a stage in its *self*-realization, for the Will is irrational.

Man's reason is simply one more instrument at the disposal of the Will's blind striving. Yet it lies in Man's power to refuse to be an instru-

[2] Cf. *ante* Chapter 17.
[3] Gilbert and Kuhn, p. 472.

ment of the Will. He is able to free himself of desire, and at least at moments, stand aside from the struggle and simply contemplate serenely the innermost nature of reality.

Scientific knowledge, Schopenhauer insisted, does not reveal that reality. Scientific knowledge is eminently practical: it describes phenomena so as to put them at our service—which really means, at the service of the Will. But the knowledge that art gives is impractical, and that is its glory. Tragedy gives us an insight into the heart of the mystery, into the nature of evil, which is the nature of reality and hence of the Will. But Schopenhauer reserved a special function to the art of music. Music, unlike the other arts, is not tied to any objective representation of the Will but "speaks of the Will itself." "The composer reveals the inner nature of the world, and expresses the deepest wisdom in a language which his reason does not understand; as a person under the influence of mesmerism tells things of which he has no conception when he wakes." [4]

III

TRAGEDY is profoundly "musical" in just this sense, so argued Friedrich Nietzsche in his brilliant essay on *The Birth of Tragedy* (1872). But in doing so, Nietzsche rejected Schopenhauer's notion that tragedy was to be associated with serene contemplation. Tragedy did not arise among the Greeks out of any withdrawal from life, nor were the spectators of the tragedies of Aeschylus and Sophocles "detached" observers. On the contrary, only a formal and artificial barrier separated them from the dancing chorus, with whom emotionally they were at one.

Nietzsche, accordingly, repudiated the notion that Greek tragedy was developed under the auspices of Apollo, the god of the poised, harmonious, "classical" art that we traditionally associate with the Greeks. Nietzsche conceded a role to Apollo in Greek tragedy, but it was a role finally subordinate to that of Dionysus, the god of wild flute music, of wine and intoxication, of the dancing throng and of the orgy in which men as satyrs were connected with their darker, subterranean selves and with the primordial unity of nature.

The luminous order and tranquillity that are traditionally associated with Greek art were not the expression of a naturally Apollonian spirit. The Greek was naturally Dionysian; and his art thus represents a victory won over his own nature. As Nietzsche put it in a later essay:

Extravagance, wildness, and Asiatic tendencies lie at the root of the Greeks. Their courage consists in their struggle with their

[4] *The World as Will and Idea*, trans. R. B. Haldane and J. Kemp (London, n.d.), I, 336.

Asiatic nature: they were not given beauty any more than they were given Logic and moral naturalness: in them these things are victories, they are willed and fought for. . . .[5]

Tragedy was thus, for Nietzsche, the product of a fruitful tension between diverse energies. Certain other forms of art contrive to remain relatively pure. For instance, the painter, the sculptor, and the epic poet are characteristically Apollonian: they work under the special patronage of the god of light, of vision, and of dream. And the actor, the dancer, the musician, and the lyric poet are characteristically devotees of Dionysus. They follow a wilder prompting, and create dynamic patterns out of ecstasy and incantation.

To the modern reader imbued with Freud, Nietzsche's association of *dream* with the Apollonian serenity may appear puzzling, even perverse. For the modern reader will be tempted to regard Nietzsche's Apollonian art as that of the conscious mind and the Dionysian as that of the Freudian unconscious, in which case, dream, with its bold violations of space-order and of logic and its connections with the primordial depths of the mind will seem to be Dionysian rather than Apollonian. But Nietzsche uses *dream* primarily in the sense of the seer's vision, the waking dream, an ideal view which represents phenomena not as they are, but as they ought to be. For this very reason the Apollonian dreaming art demands a Dionysian counterbalance. The idealized representation if *too consciously imposed* degenerates into a flaccid and sterile academicism. The detachment proper to great art can come only after passionate involvement.

The timid German bourgeois, Nietzsche scornfully noted, was eager for ideal schemes that flattered his complacency, for solutions that he had not "earned," for harmonies that were trivial because they avoided the very appearance of dissonance. Such a person, Nietzsche insisted, was quite incapable of conceiving what tragic art meant to the audiences that viewed the drama of Aeschylus and Sophocles. To participate in the experience of genuine tragedy, man must put aside the brittle rigidities of his rationality. Man must lose his petty civic identity and become elemental man; he must, before the vision of the god can be vouchsafed to him, become the satyr, the goat-man.

Indeed, according to Nietzsche, this was just what actually happened in the course of history. Ancient Greek tragedy grew out of the worship of Dionysus. The satyr chorus—originally the band of ecstatic worshippers—was "the womb of dialogue." In the plays before Euripides, all the tragic protagonists were types of Dionysus, seen as such by the chorus in their ecstatic state. When Euripides failed to retain the chorus in its primi-

[5] *The Will to Power* (1896), *Complete Works*, XV (trans. A. M. Ludovici, New York, 1910), 417. This and following passages from Nietzsche's works reprinted by permission of the publishers, George Allen & Unwin Ltd.

tive function, he destroyed tragedy. Nietzsche elaborates the point: the "optimistic dialectic" of Euripides—which Nietzsche associates with that of Socrates—"drove *music* out of tragedy." [6] In the Socratic-Euripidean dispensation, there was a "necessary, visible connection between virtue and knowledge"; hence the tragic protagonist necessarily became a dialectician, the dramatist became essentially "an echo of his own conscious knowledge," and the dark, vital wisdom of the chorus was rendered nugatory. In short, Euripidean "tragedy" had moved toward the Apollonian pole.

True tragedy, on the other hand, Nietzsche asserted, could be interpreted only as "a manifestation and illustration of Dionysian states, as the visible symbolization of music, as the dream-world of Dionysian ecstasy." [7] Such a "dream-world" is, of course, in Nietzsche's terms, Apollonian—but in tragedy, Apollo is made to express "Dionysian knowledge."

> . . . the Apollonian illusion is [in the effect of tragedy] found to be what it really is,—the assiduous veiling during the performance of tragedy of the intrinsically Dionysian effect: which, however, is so powerful, that it finally forces the Apollonian drama itself into a sphere where it begins to talk with Dionysian wisdom, and even denies itself and its Apollonian conspicuousness. Thus then the intricate relation of the Apollonian and the Dionysian in tragedy must really be symbolized by a fraternal union of the two deities: Dionysus speaks the language of Apollo; Apollo, however, finally speaks the language of Dionysus; and so the highest goal of tragedy and of art in general is attained. [8]

The spectator of tragedy sees the hero "in epic clearness and beauty" —the epic, we remember, is an "Apollonian" art—nevertheless, wrought up to Dionysian ecstasy, the spectator "delights in [the hero's] annihilation. . . . He feels the actions of the hero to be justified, and is nevertheless still more elated when these actions annihilate their originator." [9] When Apollo begins to talk with "Dionysian wisdom," he gives us myth, for tragic myth, as Nietzsche defines it, is "a symbolizing of Dionysian wisdom by means of the expedients of Apollonian art." [1] Science, with optimistic belief in "the explicability of nature," destroys myth, and with it, the possibility of tragedy. This notion that tragedy— and by later extension, all art—is grounded in myth was, however, to

---

[6] *The Birth of Tragedy* (1872), *Complete Works*, I (trans. W. A. Haussmann, London, 1910), 111.
[7] *Birth of Tragedy*, p. 111.
[8] *Birth of Tragedy*, pp. 166–7.
[9] *Birth of Tragedy*, p. 168.
[1] *Birth of Tragedy*, p. 168.

make its main fortune in the next century. Its typical 20th-century modes will be discussed later in Chapter 31.

I V

SCIENCE is optimistic, but tragic wisdom is joyful. The zest for life expresses itself through conflict and tension. Though elements of this view were derived from Schopenhauer, Nietzsche, as time went on, attacked with increasing bitterness Schopenhauer's idea that tragedy begot a mood of resignation. Art is "the great stimulus," the "great will to life," [2] and tragedy springs from exultant strength. Nietzsche charged Aristotle with folly in having supposed that the function of tragedy was to purge us of the emotions of pity and fear. Tragedy is not cathartic but tonic. Even a Zola's preoccupation with the ugly and sordid came about because artists like Zola rejoice in the ugly. The ugliness and disorder of the world constitute a challenge to the artist. The artist does not passively record a beauty that he finds rooted in nature. Beauty is not found—it is made by the artist, who imposes it by his own will, and thus wins a victory over disorder. For in beauty, "contrasts are overcome, the highest sign of power thus manifesting itself in the conquest of opposites." [3] The artist creates out of joy and strength—not out of weakness—and the most convincing artists are precisely those "who make harmony ring out of every discord." [4] The great artist is able to acknowledge "the terrible and questionable character of existence" [5] and still affirm the goodness of life. As a poet of our own time has expressed it:

> All perform their tragic play,
> There struts Hamlet, there is Lear,
> That's Ophelia, that's Cordelia;
> Yet they, should the last scene be there,
> The great stage curtain about to drop,
> If worthy their prominent part in the play,
> Do not break up their lines to weep.
> They know that Hamlet and Lear are gay;
> Gaiety transfiguring all that dread. [6]

And again, as he looked out upon the world moving toward the Second World War:

[2] *Will to Power*, p. 285.
[3] *Will to Power*, p. 245.
[4] *Will to Power*, p. 288.
[5] *Will to Power*, p. 291.
[6] W. B. Yeats, "Lapis Lazuli," *Collected Poems* (New York, 1951), p. 292. This and following passages from Yeats's writings are reprinted by permission of The Macmillan Company.

> Irrational streams of blood are staining earth;
> Empedocles has thrown all things about;
> Hector is dead and there's a light in Troy;
> We that look on but laugh in tragic joy.[7]

If all art is an affirmation of life, and if the greatest art is that in which the affirmation is made in the face of the terrible and questionable, then tragic art reveals itself as the greatest art:

> The highest state of Yea-saying to existence is conceived as one from which the greatest pain may not be excluded: the tragico-Dionysian state.[8]

The artist, as Nietzsche conceives him, is a projection of the Nietzschean philosopher. He is a man who is hard and lives dangerously, scorning cowardly generalizations and shop-worn solutions, despising syntheses that he has not "earned," daring to subdue to his purpose the most recalcitrant materials, always "setting his chisel to the hardest stone." Yet the artist does deal in illusion—at least his work can be exploited for the illusory comfort that it may seem to give. And so Nietzsche sometimes praised the artist as the man who truly lives "beyond good and evil," but at other times was moved to reproach the artist because he solaced men with lies. Only a hairline would seem to separate the poet's gift of "metaphysical comfort" from the bogus comfort of soporifics and anodynes.

It is probably idle to try to labor Nietzsche's position into entire consistency: Nietzsche was the deliberate iconoclast, using a rhetoric of overstatement, bold metaphor, exhortation, laconic imperatives, and the like; and moreover his philosophy suffered alteration during the course of his career. In making the value of art depend, not upon the work itself but upon the stress in the soul of the artist who produced it [9] or upon the process, strenuous or easy, by which the spectator apprehended it, Nietzsche provided the basis for endlessly shifting subsequent evaluations.

We have earlier spoken of the pervasive "lyric" quality of the German 19th century: the norm of poetry is consciously or unconsciously sought for in the personal and subjective utterance. The fundamental poetic problem became that of the poet's personal expression, and more

---

[7] "The Gyres," *Collected Poems*, p. 291.

[8] *Will to Power*, p. 291.

[9] Substantially this position is taken in a recent essay by a critic whom one would never think of associating with Nietzsche. Lionel Trilling, at the end of his *Liberal Imagination* (New York, 1950), p. 297, writes: "The aesthetic effect which I have in mind can be suggested by a word that I have used before—activity. We feel that Hemingway and Faulkner [as contrasted with Dos Passos, O'Neill, and Wolfe] are intensely at work upon the recalcitrant stuff of life; when they are at their best they give us the sense that the amount and intensity of their activity are in a satisfying proportion to the recalcitrance of their material."

specifically, the problem of how he might, in the midst of a hostile world, preserve his own individuality and set the seal of his own personality upon the pattern of words that he makes. Tragedy, because of the authority of classical Greek literature, was still spoken of by the Germans as the highest of the literary arts. But the soul of tragedy was no longer to be sought in the plot: it was to be sought in the dramatist's own soul. Nietzsche, as we have seen, conceived of tragedy as "musical": it was the greatest of the arts because it involved a "harmonization" of the greatest possible tensions.

The assimilation of tragedy to a "lyric" form through conceiving of it as a pattern of tensions that are "resolved" or of discords that are ultimately "harmonized" suggests a counterdevelopment that was to appear in later criticism; that is, the tendency to see in even the tiniest lyric a kind of "drama," a pattern of conflicts set up, developed, and then resolved. The "musical" structure of poetry, of which the French symbolists were to make so much, is "musical" in something like this Nietzschean sense. Here again Nietzsche proved himself a forerunner. He anticipated brilliantly the course that the age was to take.

V

TRAGEDY and comedy have always been bracketed together, if only in simple opposition—the laughing mask set off by the weeping mask. Nietzsche's conception of tragedy as a pattern of tensions obviously provides a means for bringing tragedy and comedy much closer together. In German romantic theory we have already [1] called attention to the strong concern to provide a rationale for the comic and to dignify it as an integral side of the serious. Nietzsche's theorizing provides, from the side of tragedy, a powerful answering tendency. By boldly asserting that tragedy is "Dionysian," Nietzsche roots it in impulses immemorially assigned to the comic—that is, in the natural and instinctive impulses which reach their apogee in intoxication, revelry, and wild exuberance.

The celebrated essay *Le Rire* (1900) by Henri Bergson yields a sufficiency of parallels to *The Birth of Tragedy*. Bergson found the basis for the comic in the contrast between the mechanical and the organic. It is intelligence that treats everything mechanically; it is instinct that has an affinity for the organic. Like Nietzsche, Bergson traced art ultimately to the dark, instinctive side of the mind.

He asserts in his *Évolution Créatrice* that it is instinct, not intelligence, that is molded on the very form

> of life. While intelligence treats everything mechanically, instinct proceeds, so to speak, organically. If the consciousness

[1] Cf. *ante* Chapter 17.

that slumbers in it should awake, if it were wound up into
knowledge instead of being wound off into action, if we could
ask and it could reply, it would give up to us the most intimate
secrets of life.[2]

The intellect deals with what Bergson terms "extensive manifolds";
thus the intellect produces science and all the systematizations of knowledge that are so useful to us for the practical ordering of our lives. But
the intellect distorts reality—freezes it into abstract patterns—breaks it
up into discrete data—and so falsifies the essentially dynamic and changing thing that is reality; that is, the intellect is incapable of dealing with
an "intensive manifold." For this we require the more subtle instrument
of art. Like Schopenhauer, Bergson finds in art, not in science, the
means to the knowledge of reality.

Life presents itself to us, Bergson says, as "evolution in time and
complexity in space. . . . [There is a] continual change of aspect, the
irreversibility of the order of phenomena, [and] the perfect individuality of a perfectly contained series. . . ."[3] Since such are the characteristic traits that distinguish what is alive from what is mere mechanism, their
antitheses—*repetition, inversion,* and *reciprocal interference of series*—
are the characteristic patterns of the mechanical; and it is the mechanical that prompts our laughter. We laugh at the failure of human response:
the man acting like an automaton, mindlessly following a pattern when
the situation calls for change (repetition); the man allowing himself to
be victimized by mere things (inversion); the man clumsily falling over
himself instead of acting gracefully and effectively (reciprocal interference of series).

Bergson valiantly strove to relate every instance of the comic to
one of these three categories of the mechanical. Disguise, for example,
was to be regarded as comic because the disguising clothes (as distinguished from our "normal" clothing, which seems at one with the body)
appear to us to be a "rigid envelope round the living suppleness of the
body." Disguise, in other words, constitutes another instance of the im-
pingement of the mechanical upon the vital and organic. Having
stretched his theory sufficiently to make disguise an instance of mechanization, Bergson then stretched the category of disguise:

A man in disguise is comic. A man we regard as disguised is also
comic. So, by analogy, all disguise is seen to become comic, not
only that of a man, but that of society also, and even the disguise of nature.[4]

[2] *Creative Evolution* (1907), trans. Arthur Mitchell (New York, 1937), p. 165.
[3] From: *Comedy,* "Laughter" by Henri Bergson, "An Essay on Comedy" by
George Meredith, introduction and appendix by Wylie Sypher. Copyright 1956 by
Wylie Sypher, reprinted by permission of Doubleday & Company, Inc.
[4] *Laughter,* p. 42.

Though maintaining that every comic incongruity is an instance of mechanization, Bergson was aware that not every such mechanization produces a comic effect. We do not laugh, for example, at the automatism of a crippled man, even though his hobbling gait is to the last degree mechanical. The comic response demands that we suppress our sympathies: there must be, in Bergson's phrase, an "anesthesia of the heart." Where, as with the crippled man, we cannot suppress our sympathies, there will be no laughter.

The writer of comedy realizes this. He plays down our sympathy for the individual; he appeals to the assumptions of society; he engages our intelligence rather than our emotions. Thus, he achieves the necessary anesthesia. For the function of comedy is corrective; society punishes by laughter the individual's deviation from the social norms.

Bergson's account of the social function of comedy is substantially the orthodox, "classical" account—quite as much as George Meredith's.[5] But Bergson achieved his orthodoxy by a kind of *tour de force*. For comedy's very commitment to society and its association with the play of intelligence forced Bergson to deny that comedy was a genuine art. He denied it in so many words: comedy, he wrote,

> is not disinterested as genuine art is. By *organising* laughter, comedy accepts social life as a *natural* environment, it even obeys an impulse of social life. And in this respect it turns its back upon art, which is *a breaking away from society and a return to pure nature.*[6]

In such a passage, Bergson's romantic bias is fully declared: genuine art is natural and instinctive. Comedy makes the deviations from social life seem mechanical as if they were deviations from nature and therefore comic in their own right. The parallel with Nietzsche's view of tragedy again invites attention. One might say that whereas Nietzsche's tragedy represents the dark and instinctive (the Dionysian) drawing the luminous and rational (the Apollonian) into its orbit, Bergson's comedy represents a countermovement: our ultimate commitment to the instinctive and natural is drawn into the orbit of the self-conscious and artificial.

Bergson makes his case against the aberrancy of comedy from "genuine art" by exhibiting typical comic characters. Though genuine art is always concerned with what is uniquely individual, the characters that appear in comedies are types. A comic character is generality personified—which is why we can so readily speak of "a Tartuffe," Bergson

---

[5] In Chapter 11 *ante*, we have observed that Meredith's essay—one has to remind oneself of its date, 1877—was a kind of anachronism. It is a brilliant summation of an earlier ideal of comedy—French classical comedy of the great period.

[6] *Laughter*, pp. 170-1. The italics are ours.

says, but never of "a Phèdre" or "a Polyeucte." [7] Plausible as this statement sounds, perhaps we may wonder whether it constitutes a decisive
test: it is not altogether clear that we cannot with propriety speak of "a
Hamlet," tragic character though he be; and the great comic character
Falstaff has appeared to many readers to be anything but mere generality personified. Be that as it may, Bergson has called down upon himself
reproaches for what have impressed some critics as strained manipula-
tions of the facts, the better to make them answer to his special theory.
Even his basic tenet that all laughter springs from the contrast between what is mechanical and what is natural has been criticized as much
too narrow and rigid. Yet it must be conceded that Bergson's conception
of the comic as closely connected with the natural and instinctive is fully
in the current of 19th-century ideas.

VI

MUCH earlier, in 1709, Lord Shaftesbury, in an essay significantly entitled *"Sensus Communis:* an Essay on the Freedom of Wit and Humor"
(I, iv), had observed that

> the natural free spirits of ingenious men, if imprisoned or con-
> trolled, will find out other ways of motion to relieve themselves
> in their constraint; and whether it be in burlesque, mimicry, or
> buffoonery, they will be glad at any rate to vent themselves, and
> be revenged on their constrainers. . . .

During the 19th century, the psychologist Bain, whom Bergson quotes,
developed the theory of laughter as "the rebound of hilarity," a sudden
deliverance from emotional and moral constraints. Charles Renouvier
added the notion that laughter was also a deliverance from the constraints
of rationality itself. And Auguste Penjon published in 1893, several years
before the appearance of Bergson's *Le Rire*, an essay entitled *"Le Rire
et la Liberté"* in which laughter is interpreted as the sudden surging up
of the sense of freedom. Penjon's theory of humor was summed up by
an American psychologist, L. W. Kline, in the following terms:

> The humor stimulus gives glimpses of the world of uncertain-
> ties, of spontaneities and of life, and in so doing creates the sense
> of freedom of which the sense of humor is the obverse side. [8]

The function of humor is to rest and relax the mind. Humor is said to
cut "the surface tension of consciousness" and to increase "the pliancy

[7] *Laughter*, p. 163.
[8] "The Psychology of Humor," *American Journal of Psychology*, XVIII (July,
1907), 437.

of [the mind's] structure to the end that it may proceed on a new and strengthened basis." It "spells" the mind, as Kline put it; it permits it a breathing space on "an uphill pull."

How humor accomplishes this ministry is stated in terms reminiscent of Schopenhauer: humor detaches us "from our world of good and evil, of loss and gain and enable[s] us to see it in proper perspective." And Kline's account of how humor has promoted the very evolution of the race seems to echo Bergson:

> Influences that tend to check mechanization and to incline the mind to grapple with the new and with the ideal prolong the possibilities of spiritual development. Humor and play are two such processes, with the honors in favor of humor. It stands guard at the dividing line between free and mechanized mind, to check mechanization and to preserve and fan the sparks of genius.[9]

The sense in which laughter betokens a freedom from constraint has been interpreted more literally and brutally by Horace Kallen.[1] All laughter reflects a sense of triumph and self-enhancement which may or may not also involve the degradation of an enemy. Having conquered its enemy, "the organism," riding on a tide of released energies, finding itself "again in possession of itself," and now apprehending the "lapsed situation," laughs "spontaneously, instinctively." Kallen remarks that the facial expression at the laughable as in smiling bears "a startling resemblance to [that of] an animal about to rend and devour its prey." But he is able to trace the first dawn of humor to a period before even the teeth appear. For he can find a semblance of the "apprehension of the comic" in "the replete child, repeating the pleasurable act of sucking."[2]

The notion of laughter as the expression of triumphant well-being is as old as the speculations of Thomas Hobbes—as old indeed as the Platonic dialogues; and some readers will prefer Hobbes's account of it to Kallen's, finding Hobbes's brand of behaviorism handled with more dignity and with somewhat less facial contortion.

> *Sudden Glory* [Hobbes writes in his *Leviathan*, I, vi] is the passion which maketh those *Grimaces* called LAUGHTER; and is caused either by some sudden act of their own, that pleaseth them; or by the apprehension of some deformed thing in another, in comparison whereof they suddenly applaud themselves.[3]

[9] Kline, *American Journal of Psychology*, XVIII, 439.
[1] "The Aesthetic Principle in Comedy," *American Journal of Psychology*, XXII (April, 1911), 137–57.
[2] Kallen, *American Journal of Psychology*, XXII, 156.
[3] *Leviathan* (1651).

But perhaps one should not dismiss the facial contortions too summarily. Because of the marked physiological reactions that occur in laughter, comedy has from an early date attracted to itself far more affective theorizing than has tragedy. The development of laboratory techniques in the 19th century produced hundreds of physiological studies bearing on the phenomenon of laughter. Even psychologists not notably behavioristic in approach have been interested in and influenced by the physiological character of laughter. For example, Sigmund Freud writes in a passage that anticipates the phraseology of Kallen, "the grimaces and contortions of the corners of the mouth that characterize laughter appear first in the satisfied and satiated nursling when he drowsily quits the breast." But his *Wit and Its Relations to the Unconscious* (1905) elaborates a far more complex theory of the comic than this particular quotation might suggest.[4] Indeed, Freud will not allow that the "sudden glory" of triumphant well-being is comic laughter at all, insisting that children do not have a sense of the comic. Nevertheless, it is in the happiness of the replete child that Freud finds the key to the pleasure that adults take in the comic. Indeed, his monumental essay concludes with the statement that the methods of wit, comedy, and humor all attempt to return us to the state of the child. They

> strive to bring back from the psychic activity a pleasure which has really been lost in the development of this activity. For the euphoria which we are thus striving to obtain is nothing but the state of a bygone time, in which we were wont to defray our psychic work with slight expenditure. It is the state of our childhood in which we did not know the comic, were incapable of wit, and did not need humor to make us happy.[5]

But to understand why the state of euphoria experienced by the child is characterized by a "slight expenditure" of psychic energy requires further examination of Freud's views on the subject.

VII

EARLY in his study Freud remarks that brevity is indeed the soul of wit, quoting Shakespeare's statement and that of the psychologist Theodor Lipps.[6] The brevity manifests itself through various devices of condensation such as "mixed word-formation" and "double meaning with allu-

---

[4] The passages quoted here and on pp. 573–6 and 611 are taken from *The Basic Writings of Sigmund Freud*, trans. and ed. by A. A. Brill, copyright, 1938, by Random House, Inc. Reprinted by permission of the Trustees of the Brill Estate.

[5] *Basic Writings*, p. 803.

[6] Freud writes: " 'Brevity alone is the body and soul of wit,' declares Jean Paul (*Vorschule der Ästhetik* [1804], I, 45). . . . Lipps' description of the brevity of

sion." Freud distinguishes eleven such devices, all of which he regards as simply variant forms of the principle of condensation. What is common to wit, in Freud's conception, is a principle of parsimony in the expenditure of psychic energy. The verbal economy observable in witty expressions—the "use of few or possibly the same words"—points toward a more important kind of economy, this saving of psychic energy.

What is actually saved and how the saving is effected is most easily illustrated by taking our examples from what Freud calls "tendency" wit, that is, wit that is aggressive, whether hostile or obscene. (Freud holds that all obscene wit represents an act of sexual aggression.)

How such wit serves to economize psychic energy, Freud illustrates in this fashion: When circumstances forbid any direct attack upon an enemy or even directly abusive language, as in retort to superior authority, "wit . . . serves as a resistance against such authority and as an escape from its pressure." For wit provides a means for getting around whatever hinders directly hostile expression and thus allows us to express ourselves after all. Such hindrances to expression need not be outward; they may be inward. "Repressions," for example, forbid the civilized man's enjoyment of the obscene. But a witty obscenity allows him to elude the repression and to enjoy what, if expressed directly, would not be tolerated.

> The only difference between the cases of outer and inner hindrances consists in the fact that here an already existing inhibition is removed, while there the formation of a new inhibition is avoided. . . . a *"psychic expenditure"* is required for the formation as well as the retention of a psychic inhibition. Now if we find that in both cases the use of tendency-wit produces pleasure, then it may be assumed *that such resultant pleasure corresponds to the economy of psychic expenditure.*[7]

So much for the pleasure of wit that has a hostile or obscene tendency. The pleasure that we take in "harmless wit" also arises from an economy of psychic expenditure. The reason is not far to seek. All thinking requires effort: it is "easier to mix up things than to distinguish them; and it is particularly easier to travel over modes of reasoning unsanctioned by logic." Children delight, for example, in word play and nonsense games. One of the pleasures of alcohol is that under its influence the adult can become again a "child who derives pleasure from the free

---

wit is also significant. He states that '. . . [wit] expresses itself in words that will not stand the test of strict logic or of the ordinary mode of thought and expression. In fine, it can express itself by leaving the thing unsaid' [*Komik und Humor*, 1898, *Beiträge zur Ästhetik*, VI, p. 90]." *Basic Writings*, p. 636.

[7] *Basic Writings*, p. 712.

disposal of his mental stream without being restricted by the pressure of logic." [8]

> Ale, man, ale's the stuff to drink
> For fellows whom it hurts to think.

But all of us, Freud would argue, plausibly enough, are fellows whom it hurts to think. Alcohol protects our childish pleasure by dulling the censorship of reason. In harmless wit, the wit-work circumvents this obstacle by offering a sop to reason; that is, the wit-work sees to it that the "senseless combination of words or the absurd linking of thoughts" does "make sense after all." Thus, just as tendency wit circumvents the hindrances set up by suppressions and inhibitions, harmless wit circumvents the hindrances set up by reason and critical judgment. As Freud summarizes the matter, wit

> begins as play in order to obtain pleasure from the free use of words and thoughts. As soon as the growing reason forbids this senseless play . . . , it turns to the jest or joke in order to hold to these sources of pleasure and in order to be able to gain new pleasure from the liberation of the absurd. In the rôle of harmless wit it assists the thoughts and fortifies them against the impugnment of the critical judgment. . . . Finally, it enters into the great struggling suppressed tendencies in order to remove inner inhibitions. . . . Reason, critical judgment, and suppression, these are the forces which it combats in turn. [9]

The semi-automatic reaction of laughter is easily fitted into Freud's scheme, for if wit always involves an economy of psychic energy, it is that "saved" or "gained" energy that is discharged as laughter. Freud borrows, and in the process modifies, Herbert Spencer's view of laughter as the discharge of psychic *irritation*. [1]

VIII

FREUD carefully distinguishes the witty from the comical and the humorous. All three, to be sure, involve a "saving" of psychic energy, and all three discharge the gained energy in laughter. But Freud seeks through a rather intricate argument to differentiate the several ways in which the gain in energy is made and to specify in each case the form of psychic energy that is conserved. In wit, as we have seen, Freud argues that our gain in psychic energy comes about through our not having to expend our energy in sustaining an inhibition. In contemplating the comic, how-

[8] *Basic Writings*, p. 719.
[9] *Basic Writings*, p. 726.
[1] Freud also mentions L. M. Dugas's description of laughter as a release from tension and Bain's conception of laughter as a "freedom from restraint."

ever, our gain comes from finding that we have built up expectative tensions that are redundant. For example, we see someone straining to lift a heavy basket and laugh when the basket proves to be unexpectedly light. We compare the expected effort with the actual effort as we imaginatively project ourselves into the lifter's situation. Such a comparison occurs, Freud insists, in all instances of the comic. We always compare, if only unconsciously, the effort that the fumbling clown or the clumsy child makes in order to perform some action with the effort which we should need to exert. Thus Freud's theory of the comic at some points resembles Bergson's, the clumsily wasteful expenditure of energy reminding one of Bergson's stiffly mechanical actions. Like Bergson too, Freud attempts some remarkable extensions of what he regards as the basic comic situation. The comic, he tells us, is always found first in *persons* and is then transferred to objects, situations, and the like.

In dealing with the third member of his triad, humor, Freud is much less intricate and consequently may seem less strained. The psychic energy that we "save" in the humorous situation is the energy that would otherwise go into feelings of sympathy. The most obvious instance is that furnished by "gallows-humor." The prisoner on the way to execution pretends to worry about catching cold, and we laugh. If "he who is most concerned is quite indifferent to the situation," [2] then we can save our sympathy, and it is this sympathy that we expected to expend but did not expend that we discharge pleasurably in laughter.

Freud assigns humor and the comic to the foreconscious, but wit, to the unconscious. Indeed, at one point Freud describes wit as "the contribution to the comic from the sphere of the unconscious." The techniques used in dream work—displacement, representation by opposite, absurdity, indirect expression, and so forth—are the techniques used in wit. Since the aim of the dream is simply to preserve our sleep, the dream does not need to be intelligible. It is an asocial product. Wit, however, has to be intelligible; we feel the need to impart wit. Hence in wit the amount of distortion through displacement and condensation has its limit. Dream serves "preponderantly to guard against pain," but wit serves "to acquire pleasure"; and that pleasure, as Freud has described it in the passage that we quoted earlier, is an approximation to the euphoria of childhood.

IX

ONE of the most vigorous attacks upon Freud's theory of the comic has been made by Max Eastman.[3] Eastman finds it incomprehensible that Freud should deny a sense of the comic to children, who are, of course,

[2] *Basic Writings*, p. 799.
[3] *The Enjoyment of Laughter* (New York, 1936).

the "greatest laughers of all." But, of course, Freud does not deny that
children laugh. The child laughs, and his motives for laughter, Freud
says, are "clear and assignable." Someone slips and falls, and the child
laughs "out of a feeling of superiority or out of joy over the calamity of
others. [His laughter] amounts to saying: 'You fell, but I did not.' " [4] In
short, the child's laughter is an instance of Hobbes's "sudden glory." (And
this is precisely why Freud denies that it has a part in the comic.) Balzac
can be quoted: "As children only do we laugh, and as we travel onward
laughter sinks down and dies out like the light of the oil-lit lamp." So
true is this, Eastman goes on to say, that most adults will rarely laugh at
"a mere nothing . . . unless it is reinforced and sanctioned by some
meaning. . . . They demand, in short, that jokes should have a point." [5]
But in writing this, Eastman has blundered squarely upon Freud's central idea. Indeed, when Freud writes that "Certain pleasure motives of
the child seem to be lost for us grown-ups . . . ," he might be echoing
Balzac. His *Wit and Its Relation to the Unconscious* could be fairly described as a study of the manoeuvers by which the adult endeavors to
recover the lost infantile laughter.

A much more competent and informed criticism of Freud's theory
of the comic is made by Arthur Koestler in his *Insight and Outlook*
(1949). Koestler is able to accept most of what Freud has to say about
wit, but he finds Freud's comments upon the comic needlessly intricate.
Freud attempts to "reduce differences in the quality of the behaviour patterns involved in a comic situation to differences in quantity." Koestler
finds that this preoccupation with mere quantitative difference on occasion leads to absurdities, as when Freud writes: "Chance exposures of the
body . . . affect us as comic, because we compare this easy way of en-
joying what is offered to the eye with the great effort which would otherwise be necessary to attain the same aim." [6] As if, comments Koestler, this
were the way to account for our laughter when the dignified gentleman
rips his trouser seat as he executes a sweeping bow.

Koestler locates the principal defect of Freud's theory in what he
calls a failure to distinguish between the self-assertive and the self-
transcending emotions. Neither Bergson [7] nor Freud recognizes the existence of a self-transcending emotion, and as a consequence neither of them

---

[4] *Basic Writings*, p. 794.
[5] *The Enjoyment of Laughter*, p. 37.
[6] *Insight and Outlook* (New York, 1949), p. 426. Reprinted by permission of
The Macmillan Company.
[7] Koestler regards Bergson's theory of the comic as too narrow—Bergson's
"comic" is only one sub-category, though a frequently occurring sub-category, of
the comic. Bergson also neglects "the emotional dynamics of laughter," but his is
"the most stimulating work ever written on the subject" (*Insight and Outlook*, p.
421).

is able to see "the direct connection between the comic and the tragic, between laughter and crying, between humour and art." [8]

In *Insight and Outlook*, Koestler boldly undertakes to demonstrate just these relationships. He would connect not only the comic with the tragic, but the mental processes involved in the creation of wit with those involved in making a scientific discovery. The key to these connections lies in what Koestler calls the "bisociative" treatment of a phenomenon. The comic contrast is bisociative: we see the phenomenon in question under two contrasting aspects. It is linked to two different fields of interest. The phenomenon is regarded as an habitual member of one of these fields, but its affinities with the second field "have hitherto been regarded as adventitious, or have passed unnoticed." [9] This bisociative treatment may be illustrated by the simplest joke ("One swallow does not make a summer, nor quench the thirst"); but it is also illustrated by Archimedes' action when, lying in his bath, he suddenly connected the immersion of a body in water with the problem of measuring the volume of the crown. The pun on "swallow" links two quite different fields through a trivial sound connection; the discovery that sent Archimedes rushing from his bath shouting "Eureka" also connected different fields —and again through a trivial and unimportant link, though the consequences were to be most important. Both wit and the "eureka process" have, as Koestler puts it, the same "intellectual geometry." Metaphor also employs this intellectual geometry: metaphor links up two fields not ordinarily connected and allows us to view the "link" in the perspective of two fields—"bisociatively."

Koestler regards laughter as the discharge of nervous tension, but he gives this notion a twist not to be found in Freud. Emotional processes have greater inertia than cognitive processes. When one line of logic or one chain of association is suddenly intersected by another, our understanding

> does jump from the first field to the second, whereas our emotion, incapable of performing the sudden jump, is spilled. This difference in behaviour implies that emotion tends to persist in the direction of a straight line, like a bull, whereas thought can dance about like a matador; in other words, that emotion has a greater mass momentum. [1]

Laughter is the discharge of the emotion "spilled" when the understanding makes one of its sudden hair-pin turns in traversing the course of the witticism. The emotion suddenly becomes excessive—or to use Freud's

[8] *Insight and Outlook*, p. 430.
[9] *Insight and Outlook*, p. 53.
[1] *Insight and Outlook*, p. 60.

term, there is a sudden "gain"—and the now unneeded emotion can gush out as laughter.

Man alone is capable of laughter; his ability to laugh is a mark of his civilization. "All animals are fanatics," since they cannot emancipate themselves "from the fanaticism of the biological urge."

> The sudden realization that one's own emotional state is "Unreasonable" signalizes the emergence of self-criticism. . . . Thus laughter rings the bell of man's departure from the rails of instinct.[2]

The inert emotions discharged in laughter are the self-assertive, aggressive-defensive emotions. They are to be carefully discriminated from the self-transcending, integrative emotions that underlie tragic art. Any tragedy can be turned into a comedy by altering the emotional charge. "Every story of Boccaccio's" can be transformed into a little tragedy without altering its factual content and "Oedipus Rex can be made to appear as a prize fool who kills his father and marries his mother, all by mistake; the tragedy is turned into a French farce without altering its cognitive layout." [3]

> Unlike the self-asserting emotions, the self-transcending emotions
>
> are capable of following the train of thought round any junctional corner. . . . The emotions of participative sympathy attach themselves like a dog to the narrative and do not become detached from it whatever the surprises, jumps, changes of associative climate through which the narrator leads it. . . . When a bisociation occurs, [they] do not become detached from thought, but follow it loyally to the new field.[4]

Since tragedy, like comedy, makes use of a bisociative technique, Koestler requires some such explanation as this to account for the fact that the emotional charge in tragedy is not also "spilled" en route and discharged in laughter. Koestler frankly would not want it spilled, for the self-transcending emotions have their own value, they are integrative; they move man toward a sympathetic participation in the universe about him. They teach loyalty to the larger whole of which man is a part.

Koestler's position here is that of the modern liberal humanist, with all the appropriate political and social implications. Art is a civilizing influence: through comedy it helps us to jettison the assertive emotions; through tragedy it fosters the integrative emotions; it teaches us to live together; and through its cathartic effects it helps the individual to endure what is otherwise without remedy.

[2] *Insight and Outlook*, pp. 69–70.
[3] *Insight and Outlook*, p. 241.
[4] *Insight and Outlook*, p. 277.

The experience of tragedy is of special therapeutic value for modern man, who is confined "to the arid plane of associative routine," the plane of the trivial. His contacts with tragic reality are so infrequent that, "instead of eliciting original adjustments, [they] throw him completely out of gear. . . . Routine has become man's rusty armour which makes the living flesh rot underneath." [5] Modern man, deadened as he is by "associative routine," stands in special need of viewing himself and his situation "bisociatively." He needs to have the trivial plane on which he lives intersected by the tragic plane.

The prominence that Koestler gives to the self-transcending emotions renders his theory of literature strongly reminiscent of that of 18th-century aestheticians like Shaftesbury and Lord Kames who emphasize sympathy.[6] Koestler's tone is, of course, quite different: he levies upon modern biological and neurological research for evidence, pointing to the basic tendency toward integration in even the most primitive organisms. But his stress upon the affective and his assumption that the greatest and most valuable art civilizes man by extending his sympathies connect him unmistakably with figures like Shaftesbury. Like the 18th-century aestheticians, Koestler holds what is ultimately an optimistic view of man and his arts. The self-transcending emotions, even though they are connected with " 'depersonalization' of consciousness," or with "the self becoming dissolved" or with Freud's "oceanic feeling," are *not* connected with Freud's death-instinct.[7] That, Koestler dismisses as having no biological foundation. ". . . biologically Freud's death-and-destruction drive is a myth—the only one," Koestler somewhat startlingly avers, "which his myth-destroying genius embodied into his system." [8] Cultivation of self-transcendence points, then, not toward death but toward the road of evolution and human progress.

A number of tendencies that have developed through the last seventy-five years seem to culminate in Koestler's *Insight and Outlook:* the stress upon conflict, upon tension, and upon the quality of emotional charge; the drawing together of comedy and tragedy, and their subsumption—along with aesthetic illusion and the "eureka" process—under one pattern, a pattern of bifurcation, of resistances acknowledged but transcended.

Koestler's is an ambitious, and in its promise of neat unification, an attractive scheme. That tragedy and comedy do make use of the same *general* intellectual frame-work—the same "intellectual geometry," in

[5] *Insight and Outlook*, p. 379.
[6] Cf. *ante* Chapter 14.
[7] Koestler writes (p. 216) that the "pessimistic, antihumanistic bias" in Freud's system may have been determined by "Freud's life-long work on neurotic patients with infantile fixations and regressive tendencies, against the background of the decaying civilization of the Austro-Hungarian Empire."
[8] *Insight and Outlook*, p. 153.

Koestler's phrase—may perhaps without too much difficulty be conceded. But the concession tends to throw great weight upon the character of the "emotional charge" in a literary work: for the quality of that charge would seem to be the sole means left by which one may differentiate comedy and tragedy. Thus there are difficulties. How one can alter an emotional charge without also altering the "cognitive layout" may not be altogether apparent. We have already noted Koestler's claim that *Oedipus Rex* could be transformed into a French farce without tampering with the cognitive layout. But Koestler hardly tells us how we can know that Oedipus is a tragic hero and not a "prize fool" apart from what Oedipus says and does—apart, that is, from the action of the play. Koestler takes it for granted that the author could manipulate the reader's attitude toward a character without at the same time altering the presentation of the character. There is obviously some loose and easy sense in which an author can do this; otherwise it would not be possible to produce parodies and ironic paraphrases. But Koestler seems to commit himself to a more questionable proposition—namely, that the emotional charge can in fact be quite sharply and cleanly separated from the cognitive "layout." He says flatly that "other attitudes can be produced [by] altering the stimulus . . . in such a way that its cognitive aspect or ground plan remains unchanged while its emotion-evoking aspects are altered," [9] and he goes on to say that his distinction between the "cognitive aspect" and the "emotion-evoking aspects" corresponds to the distinction made in *The Meaning of Meaning* [1] by C. K. Ogden and I. A. Richards between "two uses of language," the referential and the emotive.

This distinction between the referential and the emotive does play an important part in the theorizing of some of the critics to be discussed in a later chapter. Ogden and Richards, like Koestler, are conversant with modern psychology, and again, like him, their theories show a strong affective bias. But just because they are less ambitious to subsume so many various workings of the mind under one pattern, they will provide us with a more specifically literary focus for our examination of the problem.

SUPPLEMENT

Thus Satan's character, as Milton presents it, cannot but inspire feelings of sympathy and admiration. The traditional motive of Satan's fall was pride. Milton had then to describe the pride of Satan. But, as we have seen, pride

[9] *Insight and Outlook*, p. 240.
[1] *The Meaning of Meaning: a Study of the Influence of Language upon Thought and of the Science of Symbolism* (London, 1923).

was the ruling passion in his own soul. Consequently, the character of Satan is drawn with a power unique in literature. In reality, Milton pours out his own feelings. Satan's first speeches are pure Miltonic lyricism.

—Denis Saurat, *Milton: Man and Thinker* (New York, 1925), p. 214

. . . any real exposition of the Satanic character and the Satanic predicament is likely to provoke the question "Do you, then, regard *Paradise Lost* as a comic poem?" To this I answer, No; but only those will fully understand it who see that it might have been a comic poem. Milton has chosen to treat the Satanic predicament in the epic form and has therefore subordinated the absurdity of Satan to the misery which he suffers and inflicts. Another author, Meredith, has treated it as comedy with consequent subordination of its tragic elements. But *The Egoist* remains, none the less, a pendant to *Paradise Lost*, and just as Meredith cannot exclude all pathos from Sir Willoughby, so Milton cannot exclude all absurdity from Satan, and does not even wish to do so. That is the explanation of the Divine laughter in *Paradise Lost* which has offended some readers. There is a real offence in it because Milton has imprudently made his Divine Persons so anthropomorphic that their laughter arouses legitimately hostile reactions in us—as though we were dealing with an ordinary conflict of wills in which the winner ought not to ridicule the loser. But it is a mistake to demand that Satan, any more than Sir Willoughby, should be able to rant and posture through the whole universe without, sooner or later, awaking the comic spirit. The whole nature of reality would have to be altered in order to give him such immunity, and it is not alterable. At that precise point where Satan or Sir Willoughby meets something real, laughter *must* arise, just as steam must when water meets fire. And no one was less likely than Milton to be ignorant of this necessity. We know from his prose works that he believed everything detestable to be, in the long run, also ridiculous; and mere Christianity commits every Christian to believing that "the Devil is (in the long run) an ass."

—C. S. Lewis, *A Preface to Paradise Lost* (Oxford, 1942), pp. 92–3, by permission of Oxford University Press, Inc.

A serious analysis of literary art [such as this] with only an occasional, passing mention of Shakespeare may have seemed to many readers a curious innovation. The reason for it, however, is simple enough, and has been suggested above: Shakespeare is essentially a dramatist, and drama is not, in the strict sense, "literature."

Yet it is a poetic art, because it creates the primary illusion of all poetry —virtual history. Its substance is an image of human life—ends, means, gains and losses, fulfillment and decline and death. It is a fabric of illusory experience, and that is the essential product of poesis. But drama is not merely a distinct literary form; it is a special poetic mode, as different from genuine literature as sculpture from pictorial art, or either of these from architecture. That is to say, it makes its own basic abstraction, which gives it a way of its own in making the semblance of history.

Literature projects the image of life in the mode of virtual memory; language is its essential material; the sound and meaning of words, their familiar or unusual use and order, even their presentation on the printed page, create the illusion of life as a realm of events—completed, lived, as words formulate them—events that compose a Past. But Drama presents the poetic illusion in a different light: not finished realities, or "events," but immediate, visible responses of human beings, make its semblance of life. Its basic abstraction is the act, which springs from the past, but is directed toward the future, and is always great with things to come.

—Susanne K. Langer, *Feeling and Form* (New York, 1953), p. 306. Reprinted by permission of Charles Scribner's Sons.

I have gone into this scene [I, v of *Hamlet*] at some length, since it illustrates so perfectly the relationship between psychology and form, and so aptly indicates how the one is to be defined in terms of the other. That is, the psychology here is not the psychology of the *hero*, but the psychology of the *audience*. And by that distinction, form would be the psychology of the audience. Or, seen from another angle, form is the creation of an appetite in the mind of the auditor, and the adequate satisfying of that appetite. This satisfaction—so complicated is the human mechanism—at times involves a temporary set of frustrations, but in the end these frustrations prove to be simply a more involved kind of satisfaction, and furthermore serve to make the satisfaction of fulfilment more intense. If, in a work of art, the poet says something, let us say, about a meeting, writes in such a way that we desire to observe that meeting, and then, if he places that meeting before us—that is form. While obviously, that is also the psychology of the audience, since it involves desires and their appeasements.

—Kenneth Burke, *Counter-Statement* (New York, 1931), p. 40; also Hermes Publications, 1953, pp. 30-1. By permission of the author.

If the difference between tragedy and comedy is a difference between the emotions they express, it is not a difference that can be present to the artist's mind when he is beginning his work; if it were, he would know what emotion he was going to express before he had expressed it. No artist, therefore, so far as he is an artist proper, can set out to write a comedy, a tragedy, an elegy, or the like. So far as he is an artist proper, he is just as likely to write any one of these as any other; which is the truth that Socrates was heard expounding towards the dawn, among the sleeping figures in Agathon's dining room.

—R. G. Collingwood, *The Principles of Art* (Oxford: Clarendon Press, 1938), p. 116, by permission of Oxford University Press, Inc.

CHAPTER 26

SYMBOLISM

§ *Coleridge's wish to destroy the antithesis between words and things: its partial fulfillment in certain modern philosophies of symbolic form—II. Emerson's Transcendentalism: its relation to Coleridge and to German philosophers, its strength and its weakness, Whitman's optimism and Melville's disquieting doubts—III. Edgar Allan Poe's concern for lyric intensity: his efforts to "purify" poetry, the implications of these efforts for subject matter and form, poetry analogized to music—the influence of Poe's ideas upon Baudelaire: Baudelaire's system of "correspondences," tendencies in Baudelaire toward the irrational and the occult—IV. Mallarmé's poetry as a refinement of thing or event to a "Platonic idea" of itself, poetry as evocation and poetry as ritual—V. two side developments of French symbolism: Verlaine and lyric impressionism, and Rimbaud and the systematic disordering of the senses, Rimbaud's conception of the poet as voyant—VI. Valéry and his detachment of the poem, as pure meaning, from the realm of reality, his years of silence, the tendency of symbolist poetry to extinguish itself—some attempts to define and summarize the nature of French symbolism—VII. William Butler Yeats as a symbolist poet: his debt to Arthur Symons, the relation of "magic" to poetry, Yeats's attempt to create a personal myth—VIII. Yeats's knowledge of philosophy, his conception of poetry as yielding a peculiar kind of knowledge, parallels between his position and that of R. G. Collingwood—Yeats's saving dualism: his refusal to fall into "angelism"* §

THE DOCTRINE THAT WORDS CREATE KNOWLEDGE IS A PART OF THE romantic theory of the imagination. Coleridge, for example, constantly verges upon such a conception in his speculations upon poetry as a way of mediating between the subject and the object. In a letter to William Godwin (22 September 1800) he writes:

> I wish you to write a book on the power of the words. . . . is *Thinking* impossible without arbitrary signs? And how far is the word "arbitrary" a misnomer? Are not words, etc., parts and germinations of the plant? And what is the law of their growth? In something of this sort I would endeavour to destroy the old antithesis of Words and Things; elevating, as it were, Words into Things and living things too.[1]

Many of the more recent developments in literary theory can be read as attempted answers to the questions which Coleridge puts here to Godwin. Present-day philosophers like Croce, R. G. Collingwood, Ernst Cassirer, and Susanne Langer have concerned themselves with the laws that govern the growth of words and may indeed be said to have gone far to destroy the old antithesis between words and things. Even a theorist like I. A. Richards, who began with the thesis that words were arbitrary signs, in the course of time proceeded toward a correction and modification of that thesis, and in doing so came to argue for a much more organic conception of words, finally arriving at the view that reality itself, as man can know it, is a symbolic construction: "the fabric of our meanings, which is the world," is Richards' way of putting it in 1936.[2] Indeed, the tendency to treat words as things has in our time gone so far as to provoke vehement reactions. Thus, Allen Tate has denounced the

> belief that language itself can be reality, or by incantation can create a reality: a superstition that comes down in French from Lautréamont, Rimbaud, and Mallarmé to the Surrealists, and in English to Hart Crane, Wallace Stevens, and Dylan Thomas.[3]

In Tate's list, the preponderance of French and American names is significant. Though Coleridge prophetically raised the right questions and

---

[1] *Unpublished Letters of S. T. Coleridge*, ed. E. L. Griggs (London, 1932), I, 155-6. A few years later Lord Byron voiced much the same aspiration in his *Childe Harold*.

> I do believe,
> Though I have found them not, that there may be
> Words which are things.
>
> —Canto III, stanza CXIV

[2] Cf. *post* Chapter 28.
[3] *The Forlorn Demon* (Chicago, 1953), p. 61.

even implied some of the answers later to be proposed by the symbolist theoreticians, the most direct line of development does lead through French and American thinkers. Coleridge's American followers, more nearly than his English, entered into direct engagement of the problem of symbolic form. We refer to the American Transcendentalists, Ralph Waldo Emerson, H. D. Thoreau, and Herman Melville.

II

IN HIS essay entitled "The Poet" (1844) Emerson boldly pronounced "Words and deeds" to be "quite indifferent modes of the divine energy. Words are also actions, and actions are a kind of words." [4] The poet is not to be sharply set apart from the "practical" man; nor is his work to be thought of as artful in some sense that cuts it off from nature and the natural. ". . . the poet names the thing because he sees it, or comes one step nearer to it than any other. This expression or naming is not art, but a second nature, grown out of the first, as a leaf out of a tree." [5] The last phrase echoes the metaphor that Coleridge used in his letter to Godwin, and to something like Coleridge's purpose. Emerson is insisting that verbal expression is not a wilful and arbitrary thing—as Coleridge put it elsewhere, not "a pure work of the will"—but natural and organic as the growth of the leaf is organic.

We are not to take too seriously, of course, such parallels of phrasing between Emerson and Coleridge. They may be accidental, and the reader in any case soon learns not to put too much reliance upon the letter of the somewhat rhapsodic language in which Emerson habitually expressed himself. Yet there can be no doubt that Emerson has to be accounted one of the forerunners of the conception of literature as symbolic form. [6]

Emerson drew upon Coleridge's sources in neo-Platonism and German idealistic philosophy, and, of course, he drew directly upon Coleridge himself. But he was apparently affected even more deeply than was Coleridge by a sense of crisis in the problem of knowledge. He was sensitized to feel that problem by a number of circumstances—his provincialism, his lack of a rich and sustaining tradition, his "innocence," and his relatively slight interest in aesthetic forms as such.

The old rationalism in which Emerson had been brought up had been routed. The Cartesian dualism between the objects of the world and the spirit which thought about them had suddenly collapsed. Kant had

[4] *Works* (Fireside Edition, Boston and New York, 1909), III, 14.
[5] *Works*, III, 26.
[6] See the convincing argument made by Charles Feidelson, Jr., in *Symbolism and American Literature* (Chicago, published by The University of Chicago Press, 1953. And copyright 1953 by the University of Chicago.) See especially pp. 119-35.

asserted that the mind was no *tabula rasa* on which external objects scratched their impressions: the mind was an active force, which, by its own forms, moulded our conceptions of reality. Emerson and the other intellectual leaders of his culture, starved after two hundred years of the Puritanic attenuation of symbolism and already more than vaguely dissatisfied with abstractions, were ripe for the discovery that the mind was a transcendental force.[7]

But Emerson was not a thinker systematic enough to work out the implications of the position, either for philosophy or for literary criticism. The fact of the mind's transcendence remained for him a kind of overpowering insight to which he recurred in endless variations in his rather high-pitched and evangelistic essays. Emerson wins his victories of reconciliation over the contradictions of experience a shade too easily. William Butler Yeats might have said of Emerson, as he did say of Shelley, that he lacked the vision of evil. One remembers Carlyle's complaint to Emerson that he took "so little heed of the frightful quantities of *friction* and perverse *impediment* there everywhere are; the reflections upon which in my own poor life made me now and then very sad, as I read you." [8] Emerson reminds one of the protagonist in *The Waste Land*, whose eyes failed him at the vision in the hyacinth garden, and who was neither living nor dead, "Looking into the heart of light, the silence." Emerson's vision of the poem fails under excess of light: he sees little more in any poem than the scintillant fact that it *is* a poem—no mere shadow of external objects and no mere subjective fancy, but a coalescence of man with nature in a union that guarantees the participation of both man and nature in something transcendental.

For Emerson the poetic vision, we may say, is a kind of universal solvent: it brings the most refractory and stubbornly contradictory things into unity. Or, as he put it himself in "The Poet," the poet renders the whole realm of phenomena transparent:

> As the eyes of Lyncæus were said to see through the earth, so the poet turns the world to glass, and shows us all things in their right series and procession. For through that better perception he stands one step nearer to things, and sees the flowing or metamorphosis; perceives that thought is multiform . . . and following with his eyes the life, uses the forms that express that life, and so his speech flows with the flowing of nature.[9]

The difficulty of turning the world to glass, however, is that a really transparent world would be quite invisible. Wishing to see everything,

---

[7] *Symbolism and American Literature*, p. 129.

[8] Carlyle to Emerson, April 6, 1870. *The Correspondence of Carlyle and Emerson* (Boston, 1894), II, 360–1.

[9] "The Poet," *Works*, III, 25.

we should actually see nothing. It would be unfair to the spirit of his essay to bind Emerson rigidly by the terms of his own metaphor. The fact of *some* transparency—"We are symbols and inhabit symbols," [1] he says in the same essay—is evidently all that Emerson really meant to claim. Yet the passage quoted does fairly suggest the weakness in Emerson's conception, and it points to a problem that any thoroughgoing system of symbolism has to face: if there are no fixities and definites at all but only symbolic fluidity, then there would appear to be some danger that everything will disappear into froth and bubbles.

Such is the characteristic weakness of the poetic performance of Walt Whitman, the poet upon whom Emerson's transcendental theory registered with most emphatic force. In Whitman's *Song of Myself* the poet and the universe about him merge so effortlessly that the poem threatens to collapse into tautology. The poet discovers with a kind of jaunty wonder that he is a part of nature and indeed is not to be separated from all those things ordinarily thought of as external to man:

> I find I incorporate gneiss, long-threaded moss, fruits,
>   grains, esculent roots,
> And am stucco'd with quadrupeds and birds all over. . . .

The typical problem raised by Herman Melville's work, however, is not that of too easy reconciliation. With Melville the question is rather whether there is any reconciliation at all. Even more than Emerson, Melville was shaken by the crisis in epistemology. And Melville possessed the vision of evil. That the universe was not merely an external and mechanical framework, but was plastic, "organic," and alive was for Melville something more than an innocently exhilarating discovery. The discovery also held an element of terror, for the evil in the world was not, thereby canceled; indeed, it was rendered more deeply and ineradicably alive. Moreover, to a mind desperate for truth, the very ambiguity of the universe was horrible.

The heroes of Melville's novels are all concerned with the problem of knowledge. Each of them asks whether we can truly *know* anything, or whether we are not actually caught in a quicksand of our own dreams and imaginative projections, a quicksand into which our struggles to reach objective truth can only mire us deeper. In his masterpiece, *Moby Dick* (1851), Melville frankly accepted a "methodological paradox." That is, he accepted the fact that although the "realm of significance" would seem to deny "the dual reality of subject and object," yet in fact the realm of significance rises from and returns to that duality. The realm of significance is allowed to do so in this novel; for example, the whale is "simultaneously the most solid of physical things and the most

[1] *Works*, III, 24.

meaningful of symbols." [2] But in Melville's later novels, the objects are hazy and the heroes become more and more involved in a frustrating struggle with shadows. The failure of Melville's novel *Pierre: or The Ambiguities* (1852) may be imputed to Melville's having become "contemptuous of literary form in general." Melville as author "suspects from the beginning what his hero discovers in the end, that all literature is meretricious." [3]

> He reached not only a personal, but also a technical, impasse.
> The logic of his career was the logic of his aesthetic premises;
> his concept of artistic truth was calculated to lead him into a
> skepticism of art. [4]

Something of the sort seems to have happened to another extreme proponent of symbolist theory, the French poet Arthur Rimbaud. After publishing *Une Saison en Enfer*, Rimbaud apparently came to an impasse, burned his manuscripts, and left Europe to become an ivory-trader and gun-runner in Abyssinia. [5]

III

THERE are good reasons for grouping Edgar Allan Poe with the Transcendentalists, who were, of course, his contemporaries and fellow-countrymen. Poe, to be sure, had some sharp things to say on the topic of Emerson's obscurantism, and he deplored the general bias of New Englanders toward the allegorical and toward the didactic. "We Americans especially," he writes, "have patronised [the heresy of the Didactic]; and we Bostonians, very especially, have developed it in full." [6] But Poe's literary theorizing was in general derived from the same sources as those of the Transcendentalists.

What sets Poe apart from the Transcendentalists is his special aestheticism, aspects of which have already been discussed in our chapter on "Art for Art's Sake." [7] By contrast with Emerson's attitude toward poetry, Poe's is technical and "professional." Poe envisages the poet not as that vague and splendidly democratic creature, "man speaking," but as a craftsman who brings his intelligence fully, and even coldly, to bear upon the problem of organizing words into specific literary struc-

[2] *Symbolism and American Literature*, p. 184.
[3] *Symbolism and American Literature*, p. 201.
[4] *Symbolism and American Literature*, p. 164.
[5] Enid Starkie in her study, *Arthur Rimbaud* (New York, 1947), p. 294, offers among other conjectures, the suggestion that "perhaps [Rimbaud's] new form of poetry led him to a dead end. . . ."
[6] "The Poetic Principle," *Complete Works*, ed. J. A. Harrison (New York, 1902), XIV, 271.
[7] Cf. *ante* Chapter 22.

tures. Poe was prepared to take quite literally Milton's compliment to Lycidas on his knowledge of how "to build the lofty rhyme." A poem had an architecture and it was well built or ill built. Its shape ought not to be a matter of "accident or intuition" but ought to reveal—at least in the ideal case—"the precision and rigid consequence of a mathematical problem." [8] This aspect of Poe's criticism was to prove, as we shall see, most attractive to Baudelaire and the other French symbolist poets. For them it evidently constituted a special way of focusing upon the pure lyric intensity that Poe argued was the essence of poetry.

There could be no such thing as a *long* poem. That phrase, Poe confidently declared, was "simply a flat contradiction in terms." The "degree of excitement" which entitles one to use the term "poem" simply cannot be sustained throughout a long work, for all such excitements are "through a psychal necessity, transient." [9] This stress upon lyric intensity implied a special kind of subject matter and a special kind of form. The subject matter must be an experience of peculiar intensity. The form must be purely functional, with all that is nonfunctional—all that is merely "prose" connective tissue—eliminated. In short a poem should have the intensity that one finds in a waking dream and its elements should contain as little "inert" matter as the notes of a musical composition. It is "in Music, perhaps," Poe writes, "that the soul most nearly attains . . . the creation of supernal Beauty." [1]

Thus dream and music were used by Poe to suggest the special kinds of purity that he demanded of poetry, and this analogizing of poetry to dream and to music was to run all the way through the speculations of the French symbolists. Poe refers in his *Marginalia* to "points of time where the confines of the waking world blend with those of the world of dreams." [2] Nearly a century later, Poe's very phrasing returns to us in a passage of one of W. B. Yeats's last poems, referring to

> . . . forms that are or seem
> When sleepers wake and yet still dream,
> And when it's vanished still declare,
> With only bed and bedstead there,
> That heavens had opened. [3]

This indeed would be to catch a glimpse of the supernal beauty; and if the modern poet's almost aggressive insistence upon the domestic realism of the bedroom furniture seems oddly out of key with the ornate and mannered Gothic decor that Poe usually provides as the setting for

[8] "The Philosophy of Composition," *Works*, XIV, 195.
[9] "The Poetic Principle," *Works*, XIV, 266.
[1] "The Poetic Principle," *Works*, XIV, 274.
[2] *Works*, XVI, 88.
[3] "Under Ben Bulben," *Collected Poems* (New York, 1951), p. 343, by permission of The Macmillan Company

such experiences, the contrast itself makes a point: it testifies to the vitality of Poe's key ideas and to their ability to suffer translation from one realm of sensibility to another. Yeats's version of the waking dream, of course, reveals the impress of his own personality and also reflects the modifications the notion received in passing through the succession of French symbolists and then back into English again. Like most other British and American poets, Yeats accepted very little from Poe directly. The poetry that enchanted Baudelaire left Yeats cold. He observed to a friend: "Analyse the Raven and you find that its subject is a commonplace and its execution a rhythmical trick. Its rhythm never lives for a moment, never once moves with an emotional life. The whole thing seems to me insincere and vulgar." [4]

But upon Baudelaire Poe's empurpled rhetoric registered with very different effect. In 1846 or 1847 Baudelaire read his first French translations of Poe, and felt immediately a powerful sense of spiritual kinship with the American poet. In an ecstasy of discovery, he took over Poe's whole doctrine of pure poetry. The poet, Poe had said, had nothing to do with the good or the true, but only with the beautiful. His prime task was to "reach the Beauty above," [5] of which the beauty of this world is a reflection. In Chapter 22 *ante* we have already considered the implications of this statement for the doctrine of art for art's sake. It remains to relate it more specifically to the theories of the French symbolists.

To assert that the beauty of this world is but a "reflection" of a "Beauty above" is in itself to imply a symbolist aesthetic of sorts. But Poe makes it quite plain that we can attain to this eternal beauty—even if to no more than "a portion" of it—only by making use of "multiform combinations among the things and thoughts of Time." [6] The general recipe is old enough: but in Poe's formulation it is worth noting that "things and thoughts" are made to lie down beside each other as if any invidious distinction between them had been obliterated.

Poe's "multiform combinations" finds its parallel and development in Baudelaire's more celebrated "system of correspondences." As Baudelaire wrote in 1859 in an article on Théophile Gautier: ". . . it is our instinct for beauty which causes us to consider the earth and its visibilia . . . 'comme une *correspondance* du Ciel.' " [7] In *Les Fleurs du Mal*

---

[4] The letter, dated 3 September 1899, is addressed to W. T. Horton. See *The Letters of W. B. Yeats*, ed. Allan Wade (New York, 1955), p. 325. This and following passages from Yeats's writings are reprinted by permission of The Macmillan Company. Aldous Huxley has some acute as well as amusing observations on the fact that French men of letters have so much admired Poe whereas English-speaking readers tend to find him vulgar. See his *Vulgarity in Literature* (London, 1930), pp. 26–36.

[5] "The Poetic Principle," *Works*, XIV, 273.

[6] "The Poetic Principle," *Works*, XIV, 274.

[7] Guy Michaud, *Message Poétique du Symbolisme* (Paris, 1947, 3 vols.), I, 70.

(1857), Baudelaire expresses this conception in a sonnet entitled "*Correspondances*," where all nature is viewed as a temple, a natural temple whose living pillars are the trees. As the wind blows through these "forests of symbols," confused words are now and then breathed forth. The poet, because of his special endowment, is able to apprehend these words, for in all things there is a symbolic sense and every object in nature has its special connection with a spiritual reality.[8]

The correspondences are developed upon several planes. The poet asserts that there are equivalences among the data of the various senses—sounds, colors, odors. ("*Les parfums, les couleurs, et les sons se répondent.*") And he speaks of perfumes "fresh as a child's skin, sweet as oboes, green as meadows."

In the second place,

> Since sensuous data can have "the expansion of infinite things," it follows that a desire, a regret, a thought—things of the mind —can awaken a corresponding symbol in the world of images (and vice versa). . . . From the world of the senses the poet takes the material in which to forge a symbolic vision of himself or of his dream; what he asks of the world of the senses is that it give him the means of expressing his soul.[9]

The neo-Platonic flavor of this conception of poetry is sufficiently evident. In Baudelaire's poetry, this general idealistic tendency reinforces, and is reinforced by, special tendencies toward the irrational and the occult. But Baudelaire showed himself the true disciple of Poe[1] in refusing to be guided by instinct alone. He believed in method; he could even refer to inspiration as "the reward of daily effort." He classed himself among those artists who attempt to "discover the obscure laws by virtue of which they have created, and to draw from this study a number of precepts whose divine goal is the infallibility of poetic production."[2]

IV

PREOCCUPATION with method was, however, far more than with Baudelaire the special concern of Stéphane Mallarmé. Mallarmé took very

[8] Baudelaire's theory of correspondences also derives in part from the notions of the Swedish mystic, Emanuel Swedenborg. In his article on Victor Hugo (1861), Baudelaire writes: "Moreover Swedenborg . . . has already taught us . . . that everything, form, motion, number, color, scents, in the *spiritual* as well as in the *natural* realm, is significant, reciprocal, converse, corresponding. . . ." See Guy Michaud, *La Doctrine Symboliste: Documents* (Paris, 1947), p. 22.

[9] Marcel Raymond, *From Baudelaire to Surrealism* (Paris, 1933, revised 1940); translated into English by "G.M." *Documents of Modern Art Vol. 10*, New York: George Wittenborn, Inc., 1949, p. 18.

[1] Cf. *ante* Chapter 22.

[2] In an article on Richard Wagner. See *From Baudelaire to Surrealism*, p. 21.

seriously Poe's notion of a poem so carefully organized that it possessed "the precision and rigid consequence of a mathematical problem." One finds Mallarmé writing such a passage as the following:

> The further I go, the more faithful I shall be to those severe ideas which my great master, Edgar Poe, has bequeathed me. The wonderful poem *The Raven* was conceived thus, and the soul of the reader enjoys exactly what the poet wanted it to enjoy.[3]

During the 1870's and the 1880's, Mallarmé came to be regarded as the saint and sage of the symbolist movement. He was not a popular poet; he published little; but his Tuesday receptions at which he talked with his friends about poetry became an institution. To his house there came not only the French poets and critics of the period, but writers in English such as Oscar Wilde, Arthur Symons, George Moore, and W. B. Yeats. With Mallarmé, the cultivation of poetry went far toward becoming a ritual and a cult. It also went farthest toward becoming an enterprise engaging all the powers of the mind—not a matter of blind inspiration or of sudden and inexplicable visitations by the Muse, but a problem of craftsmanship and of philosophical theorizing. It is to Mallarmé that one turns, incidentally, for what is probably the most celebrated observation about symbolic methods. In 1891 he wrote:

> . . . the Parnassians, for their part, take the thing as a whole and show it; that's where they are deficient in mystery. They deprive the mind of the delicious joy of believing that it is creating. To name an object is to do away with three-quarters of the enjoyment of the poem which is derived from the satisfaction of guessing little by little; to suggest it, that is the illusion. It is the perfect handling of the mystery that constitutes the symbol: to evoke an object little by little in order to show a state of mind or inversely to choose an object and to disengage from it a state of mind, by a series of unriddlings.[4]

Someone has described Mallarmé's characteristic poetic activity as that of trying to refine and purify any object or event to the "Platonic idea" of that object or event. There was in him a compulsion to reduce to essences by removing the accidental and adventitious. Mallarmé was concerned that nothing in the poem be the effect of mere chance, that the articulation of every part with every other part should be complete,

---

[3] *Message Poétique du Symbolisme*, I, 165.

[4] *Réponse à une Enquête* (1891), quoted in *La Doctrine Symboliste: Documents*, p. 74. Mallarmé's reference to the "delicious joy" that the mind experiences in "believing that it is creating" recalls Coleridge's remark that the reader feels Shakespeare to be a poet "inasmuch as for a time he has made you one—an active creative being." For more recent instances of this view, see *post* Chapter 28.

each part implying every other part, and that the meaning of the poem should be inseparable from its formal structure. In the Mallarmean poem the words acquire something of the bulk and density of things; the poem is treated almost as if it were a plastic object with weight and solidity and with even a certain opacity. For the words are not *signs*, transparently redacting ideas. Instead they have acquired something like bulk and mass. The poems have become little mysterious worlds whose meaning is to be read with only somewhat less difficulty than the meaning of the great world of which the poems are in a sense analogical copies.

Words for Mallarmé were then much more than signs. Used evocatively and ritualistically, they are the means by which we are inducted into an ideal world. "Poetry is," as Mallarmé defined it in 1886, "the expression by means of human language restored to its essential rhythm, of the mysterious sense of the aspects of existence: it endows our sojourn with authenticity and constitutes the sole spiritual task." [5]

V

THE main line of succession of the French symbolist movement, it is generally agreed, runs from Baudelaire to Mallarmé and thence to Paul Valéry.[6] But before taking up Valéry, it will be useful to examine briefly two important side developments. The first of these has to do with the career of Paul Verlaine. We have already had occasion to cite Poe's observation that it is in music that the soul most "nearly attains . . . the creation of supernal Beauty." The symbolist movement may be described as the effort to bring poetry to the condition of music—indeed Valéry did so describe it in 1926. Mallarmé's poetry is clearly musical in this sense, words being organized and orchestrated almost as if they were musical notes. But Verlaine's poetry is "musical" in a more direct and literal sense. In his poetry, the words tend to be emptied of their intellectual content. As Michaud puts it, in Verlaine's poetry "the language is vaporized and is reabsorbed into the melody." [7] Raymond says of Verlaine that he was "born to bring to its perfection the intimate and sentimental lyricism founded by Marceline Desbordes-Valmore and Lamartine." [8] Verlaine represents a temperament, a mood, rather than a technique. It will be more accurate to call his poetry impressionistic than to call it symbolist.

Yet if Verlaine has to be excluded from the circle of genuine symbolist poets, he had, nevertheless, much to do with bringing symbolism

[5] *Message Poétique du Symbolisme*, II, 321.
[6] See, for instance, *From Baudelaire to Surrealism*, p. 5.
[7] *Message Poétique du Symbolisme*, I, 123.
[8] *From Baudelaire to Surrealism*, p. 22.

to public notice. In 1884 Verlaine published his *Les Poètes Maudits*. The "accurst" poets discussed were Mallarmé, Tristan Corbière, and Arthur Rimbaud. It is easy to see why Verlaine applied the adjective to Corbière and Rimbaud, poets clearly repulsed by the society in which they lived; it is less easy to see how it applies to Mallarmé, and a recent writer on Mallarmé doubts whether Verlaine ever understood Mallarmé's poetry "in any profound way." [9]

The case of Verlaine provides an opportunity to render more precise the sense in which symbolist poetry may be said to be "musical"; that of Rimbaud allows one to develop a little further the sense in which the symbolist poet may be said to give over the initiative to the words themselves. Mallarmé, though he may be said to have given words their heads,[1] never, as the Surrealists were to do later, dropped the reins completely, abandoning the poem to the latent energies of language. Whether Rimbaud may be fairly said to have "abandoned" all conscious control is debatable; but Rimbaud is clearly a precursor of Surrealism. He deliberately cultivated the unconventional and the irrational.

In Rimbaud's conception, the poet is essentially a *voyant*, a seer. He applauded, as the "first voyant," Baudelaire, that "King of poets, a real God," even though he lamented the fact that Baudelaire lived in "too artistic a *milieu*" and encumbered himself with old literary forms.[2] For the new discoveries demanded new forms. The *voyant* perceives those images that the unconscious reveals only fitfully and accidentally to the ordinary man. Rimbaud's poetry was to be the systematic exploitation of such images. To this end the poet would make use of drugs, alcohol, debauchery—anything that broke down the control of reason and freed the faculties from their ordinary inhibitions. Rimbaud's famous recipe for the poet's activity reads thus: "The poet makes himself *voyant* by a long, vast, reasoned derangement of all the senses" (*Lettres du Voyant*, 1871).[3]

VI

VERLAINE, as we have seen, called Rimbaud and Mallarmé "poètes maudits" and himself gloried in the term *décadent*. Théophile Gau-

---

[9] Wallace Fowlie, *Mallarmé* (Chicago, 1953. Copyright [1953] by the University of Chicago). Fowlie goes on to say (p. 255): "The essay on Mallarmé was Verlaine's opportunity to cast opprobrium on those critics and readers who had considered him insane and ridiculous. Although Mallarmé's personal life would never place him with Poe, Baudelaire, Rimbaud, and Verlaine himself, his fate as poet was that of revolutionary, one cursed by the existing society."

[1] "A pure work, Mallarmé has written, gives over the initiative to the words themselves. The deliberate rhetoric of the poet disappears in them."—Fowlie, *Mallarmé*, p. 269.

[2] See *Message Poétique du Symbolisme*, I, 138, and Starkie's *Rimbaud*, p. 128.

[3] See Starkie, *Rimbaud*, p. 129.

tier had used *décadent* in his preface to Baudelaire's *Les Fleurs du Mal*, and Paul Bourget would call Baudelaire the "theoretician of decadence." The *décadent* was a seeker after rare sensation, a dandy, perhaps a roué, a cultivated dilettante, and, as one critic has phrased it, decadence came "to signify a kind of moral solitude of an artist, coupled with an exasperated and perverse form of mysticism." [4] The fashion of decadence was a way of protecting oneself from bourgeois triviality and all the dullness of a world increasingly given over to industrialism. So defined, the term has pertinence for Rimbaud and Verlaine, but less for a poet like Mallarmé. (Valéry observes that although "Verlaine and Rimbaud continued Baudelaire in the order of sentiment and sensation, Mallarmé carried his work forward in the province of perfection and poetic purity.") [5] At any rate, in 1885 some of the younger *décadent* writers repudiated that term and chose to call themselves "symbolists." The latter term certainly answered more nearly to the idealism of men like Mallarmé and Valéry, to their stress upon the intellectual construct, and above all to their attitude toward language. The symbolists, having discovered the non-notational aspect of language, proceed to explore the rich possibilities of intimation, suggestion, and all the other modes of linguistic indirection. Thus, one might attempt to summarize the history of the movement.

But "symbolism" was a rather loose and vague term, as Valéry himself was well aware. It was used to cover various and sometimes conflicting conceptions of poetry. What had been baptized Symbolism, Valéry was to write in retrospect in 1920, is summed up simply in an "intention of several groups of poets (not always friendly to one another) to recover from music the heritage due to them." [6] In music, there is no dross, no inert residue. Form and content coalesce. It was to this purified wholeness that symbolist poetry aspired. Valéry remarks in his essay on Baudelaire that Poe

> understood that [poetry] could claim to realize its own object and produce itself, to some degree, in a *pure state*.
>
> Thus, by analysing the requirements of poetic delight and defining *absolute poetry* by *exhaustion*, Poe showed a way and taught a very strict and fascinating doctrine in which he united a sort of mathematics with a sort of mysticism. . . . [7]

In Valéry's own work this aspiration to absolute purity finally led

---

[4] Fowlie, *Mallarmé*, p. 257.

[5] "The Position of Baudelaire" (first published in 1924), *Variety: Second Series*, trans. W. A. Bradley (New York, 1938), p. 98.

[6] Fowlie, *Mallarmé*, p. 268. Valéry's words are: "*Ce qui fut baptisé le Symbolisme, se résume très simplement dans l'intention commune à plusieurs familles de poètes (d'ailleurs ennemies entre elles) de reprendre à la Musique leur bien.*"

[7] *Variety: Second Series*, p. 92.

on past poetry, considered as a realized structure, to a preoccupation with the poetic activity as such. That is why Valéry could say to his friend André Gide: "They take me for a poet! I don't give a damn about poetry. It interests me only by a fluke. It is by accident that I have written verse. It has no importance for me." [8] Poetry, that is, was interesting only in so far as one could make it an exercise in pure creation. Thus symbolist poetry at its apogee threatens to purify itself out of existence. If the pressure for pure meaning is pressed unremittingly, the poem is finally detached from reality and becomes knowledge of *nothing!* Valéry's poetic masterpiece, "*Le Cimitière Marin,*" derives its power from a candidly tragic apprehension of some final dichotomy between knowledge and life. It is the dichotomy tirelessly echoed, though of course with a different inflection, in the later poetry of William Butler Yeats:

> For wisdom is the property of the dead,
> A something incompatible with life. . . . [9]

That symbolist poetry should, in its yearning for purity, extinguish itself was much more than a merely academic possibility. Valéry did remain silent for some twenty years before he resumed the writing of poetry. We have already referred to Rimbaud's abandonment of poetry in favor of a life of action in Africa.

Any attempt to summarize symbolist doctrine exposes the vagueness of the pronouncements of the various symbolists and critics, not to mention their frequent contradictions. One might be forgiven for coming to doubt whether the term "symbolism" has any specific meaning at all, and to conclude that it is, like the term "romanticism," simply the name for a bundle of tendencies, not all of them very closely related. A definition may be attempted as follows:

> Whether a real school of symbolism ever existed, remains a problem of speculation. . . . Each poet developed and represented a single aspect of an aesthetic doctrine that was perhaps too vast for one historical group to incorporate. . . . But more than on any other article of belief, the symbolists united with Mallarmé in his statements about poetic language. The theory of the suggestiveness of words comes from a belief that a primitive language, half-forgotten, half-living, exists in each man. It is language possessing extraordinary affinities with music and dreams.[1]

This is a just appraisal; yet the phrasing, "primitive language, half-forgotten, half-living," could be misleading to a modern reader. It could

[8] *Message Poétique du Symbolisme,* III, 572.
[9] "Blood and the Moon," *Collected Poems,* p. 234.
[1] *Mallarmé,* p. 264.

suggest certain special developments of our own time which scarcely existed for Baudelaire and Mallarmé and to which, as the context shows, the words do not refer: that is, the tremendous contemporary interest in the pre-logical and primitive mind, whether of children or savages or neurotics, and as treated typically in anthropology and in depth psychology. With this interest, there has arisen a powerful new interest in myth as a "primitive language, half-forgotten, half-living," and there have been bold and sometimes extravagant speculations about the relation of myth to poetry. Such developments of symbolist and expressionist theory will be dealt with in a subsequent chapter. Suffice it to say that the French symbolists were interested in the magic of the Rosicrucians rather than that of the Trobriand Islanders, and in the ritual practices of the heretical sects of the Middle Ages rather than in those of the present-day tribes of the Congo and Amazon. In short, their interests were "philosophical" rather than "psychological," and "traditional" rather than "anthropological."

VII

SUCH also were the interests of the English-speaking poets and critics who were most powerfully influenced by the French symbolists, men like T. E. Hulme, Ezra Pound, and T. S. Eliot, whose ideas we shall consider in a later chapter, and even men like William Butler Yeats, whose attempt to construct a personal myth in *A Vision* (1925) might seem to argue a different concern. The affinities between Yeats and the French symbolists are numerous, and some of them have already been suggested by our recourse to Yeats in several earlier pages in order to illustrate symbolist ideas. Yet the direct influence of the French poets upon Yeats was slight. Though as early as 1894 Yeats took with him on a visit to Paris a letter of introduction to Mallarmé, he seems to have learned about symbolist ideas largely from his friend Arthur Symons, who dedicated to Yeats his *Symbolist Movement in Literature* (1899). A letter that he wrote many years later in 1937 indicates how slight the direct influence of Mallarmé had been. Yeats writes that he has just been looking at

> Roger Fry's translation of Mallarmé. . . . I find it exciting, as it shows me the road I and others of my time went for certain furlongs. It is not the way I go now, but one of the legitimate roads.[2]

What Yeats learned from Symons about symbolism comes out most plainly in Yeats's essay on "The Symbolism of Poetry" (1900). He re-

[2] Written, May 4, to Dorothy Wellesley: see *Letters of W. B. Yeats*, p. 887.

marks that the scientific movement had tended to bring into literature "externalities of all kinds," and that as a consequence, literature had been in danger of losing itself in

> opinion, in declamation, in picturesque writing, in word-paint-ing, or in what Mr. Symons has called an attempt "to build in brick and mortar inside the covers of a book." [3]

Now, however, "writers have begun to dwell upon the element of evo-cation, of suggestion." Yeats asserts that "the substance of all style" is a "continuous indefinable symbolism," which he chooses to illustrate, not from one of the new writers, but from one of the 18th-century poets, Robert Burns.

> There are no lines [he writes] with more melancholy beauty than these by Burns—
> "The white moon is setting behind the white wave,
>   And Time is setting with me, O!"
> and these lines are perfectly symbolical. Take from them the whiteness of the moon and of the wave, whose relation to the setting of Time is too subtle for the intellect, and you take from them their beauty. But, when all are together, moon and wave and whiteness and setting Time and the last melancholy cry, they evoke an emotion which cannot be evoked by any other arrangement of colours and sounds and forms. [4]

In the same essay Yeats writes that

> All sounds, all colours, all forms, either because of their pre-ordained energies or because of long association, evoke in-definable and yet precise emotions, or, as I prefer to think, call down among us certain disembodied powers, whose foot-steps over our hearts we call emotions. [5]

Yeats's deliberate invocation of some kind of supernaturalism by refer-ences to "pre-ordained energies" and "disembodied powers" and the general glitter of his rhetoric should not be allowed to distract us from what is the central issue: though the emotions are "indefinable" yet they are nevertheless "precise." That is, the fact that the emotions can-not be defined in logical and scientific terms does not in the least in-validate their claim to precision.

A year later, in an essay entitled "Magic," Yeats trailed his cloak even more vigorously in the face of the naturalist, flaunting his belief

[3] W. B. Yeats, *Ideas of Good and Evil* (London, 1903), p. 240, by permission of The Macmillan Company.
[4] *Ideas of Good and Evil*, pp. 241-2.
[5] *Ideas of Good and Evil*, p. 243.

in the "evocation of spirits" (though he was careful to acknowledge that he did "not know what they are"). He recorded in that essay his belief in three doctrines which have been, he declared, "the foundations of nearly all magical practices." The doctrines were:

(1) That the borders of our minds are ever shifting, and that many minds can flow into one another, as it were, and create or reveal a single mind, a single energy.

(2) That the borders of our memories are as shifting, and that our memories are a part of one great memory, the memory of Nature herself.

(3) That this great mind and great memory can be evoked by symbols.[6]

"To show that past times have believed as I do," Yeats cites Joseph Glanvill's story of the Scholar Gipsy, the story upon which Matthew Arnold founded his poem. Yeats seems to take the Scholar Gipsy's powers quite literally; yet the context makes it plain that what interests him especially is what is summed up in the twice-used phrase, "the power of imagination." Yeats quotes the passage in which the Scholar Gipsy tells his Oxford friends that the gipsies

he went with were not such impostors as they were taken for, but that they had a traditional kind of learning among them and could do wonders by the power of imagination. . . . The scholars . . . earnestly desired him to unriddle the mystery. In which he gave them satisfaction, by telling them that what he did was by the power of imagination, his phantasy leading theirs. . . .[7]

That power, Yeats declares, is alive today, and symbols are still the "greatest of all powers whether they are used consciously by the masters of magic, or half unconsciously by their successors, the poet, the musician and the artist."[8]

The contrast with Arnold could hardly be more complete: the Scholar Gipsy, for the great Victorian critic, is obviously a fabulous creature, part of the folklore of a charmingly naive world toward which the sore-beset modern rationalist can turn back no more than a wistful glance. But for Yeats, the power of imagination possessed by the Gipsy is still valid and is to be claimed to its fullest extent. If to assert one's

[6] *Ideas of Good and Evil*, p. 29.
This conception of the great mind and the great memory sounds like an interesting anticipation of Carl Jung's doctrine of the collective unconscious with its repository of archetypal images which on occasion can well up into individual minds. Jung stated his conception first in 1912.
[7] *Ideas of Good and Evil*, pp. 48-9.
[8] *Ideas of Good and Evil*, p. 64.

belief in this kind of power means to make claims for magic as such, Yeats will do so. But it is worth remarking that Yeats seems to swallow the magic for the sake of possessing the imagination and not the other way around.

Our softening of Yeats's assertions of a literal belief in magic may seem overconfident in view of his membership in organizations boasting such titles as the "Order of the Golden Dawn," his association with Madame Blavatsky, and his lifelong interest in table-rapping, spirit mediums, and clairvoyants. But these more lurid stageprops ought not to distract us from Yeats's other interests—such as the philosophy of history as developed by Vico and Hegel and the epistemology of Plato and Plotinus and Bishop Berkeley. Even *A Vision*, that extravagant attempt to set forth a personal mythology, the substance of which Yeats claimed to have received from the "teaching spirits" through the mediumship of his wife, had an intellectual justification which Yeats could state in sober enough terms. Works like Berkeley's *Principles of Human Knowledge*, Yeats wrote, might prove "to our logical capacity" that there is a "transcendental portion of our being that is timeless and spaceless," and yet "our imagination [may] remain subjected to nature as before." It was otherwise for the ancient philosopher, Yeats maintained, for he "had something to reinforce his thought,—the Gods, the Sacred Dead, Egyptian Theurgy, the Priestess Diotime." * *A Vision* was to furnish to the modern philosopher a like imaginative reinforcement.

VIII

ALL symbolist doctrines seem to rest either upon some kind of idealism or else to deny the dualism of ideality and materialism altogether by considering these opposed concepts to be abstractions out of a prior and deeper reality in which they lie undifferentiated. The latter alternative has proved historically a difficult one to sustain. The position of those philosophers of symbolic form who, like Ernst Cassirer and Susanne Langer, seek to avoid moving into any kind of pure idealism, we shall discuss in a later chapter. Most symbolist poets and critics, including those already discussed in this chapter, tend to be rather pure idealists. And so did Yeats.

In 1926 Yeats wrote to his friend Sturge Moore that because the "teaching spirits" had forbidden it, he did not read philosophy until he had completed *A Vision*. But then, he writes, "I read for months every day Plato and Plotinus. Then I started on Berkeley and Croce and Gentile." [1] One of the topics canvassed at length in this correspond-

* *A Vision* (London, 1925), pp. 251-2.
[1] *W. B. Yeats and T. Sturge Moore: their Correspondence, 1901-1937*, ed. Ursula Bridge (Oxford University Press, Inc.: New York, 1953), p. 83.

ence (published 1953) has to do with the cat that John Ruskin was alleged to have picked up and thrown out of the window with the explanation that it was really a tempting demon. Yeats wanted to know on what basis, if any, the cat could be regarded as "unreal," and specifically how Ruskin could have distinguished the demon cat from the house cat. His choice of the problem is significant. It provided him with an occasion to talk about the topics that had particularly engaged his interest as he read Plato, Berkeley, Kant, Hegel, and Croce. Some of his arguments turn out to be quite fantastic, but, as Yeats wrote to Moore, the "points most of my fantasies and extravagancies were meant to suggest are . . . that images of the mind and images of sense must have a common root . . . and that whatever their cause or substratum that substratum is not fixed at one spot in space." [2]

In general Yeats was a good—if somewhat unconventional—Kantian. He termed "the vast Kantian argument" the "most powerful in philosophy." From it there descended "two great streams of thought," the "philosophy of will in Schopenhauer, Hartmann, Bergsen [sic], James, and that of knowledge in Hegel, Croce, Gentile, Bradley and the like." [3] Of these "two paths to reality," as Yeats elsewhere refers to them, that "of knowledge" proved the more attractive to him.

Poetry yields a special kind of knowledge. Through poetry, man comes to know himself in relation to reality, and thus attains wisdom. On this theme Yeats's own poetry descants tirelessly. The magi seeking the manger in Bethlehem are conceived of as seekers after knowledge, "hoping to find . . . The uncontrollable mystery on the bestial floor." [4] When Yeats imagines the rape of Leda by the swan, the question that he puts is: "Did she put on his knowledge with his power?" [5] In "The Gift of Harun Al-Rashid," the young bride gives unwittingly to her older philosopher husband that precious gift that is "to age what milk is to a child," "A quality of wisdom" which springs from "her love's Particular quality." [6] Even Yeats's account of the fortunes of the soul after death, as detailed in *A Vision*, is the story of a quest for knowledge. The soul must first relive all the passionate experiences of its life until it understands them, and then it must experience the opposite of all that it actually did and suffered in its life so that it may truly complete its knowledge of itself. Only then is it allowed to drink of the cup of Lethe.

The knowledge that poetry confers is obviously something other than a traffic in "opinions," which the poet associates with competition and intellectual hatred. It is not produced by the "levelling, rancorous, ra-

[2] *Yeats and Moore: Correspondence*, p. 92.
[3] *Yeats and Moore: Correspondence*, pp. 122–4.
[4] *Collected Poems*, p. 124.
[5] *Collected Poems*, p. 212.
[6] *Collected Poems*, p. 444.

tional sort of mind That never looked out of the eye of a saint Or out
of a drunkard's eye." [7] It is so completely detached from the life of action
that Yeats says more than once that only the dead have true wisdom; or
else he regards such true wisdom as the living may enjoy to be something
so deep and instinctive that its possessor hardly knows that he possesses
it—

> Considering that, all hatred driven hence,
> The soul recovers radical innocence
> And learns at last that it is self-delighting,
> Self-appeasing, self-affrighting,
> And that its own sweet will is Heaven's will. . . .[8]

Perhaps we shall appreciate these scattered "poetic" utterances if
we set beside them some comparable passages from a systematic aesthetician. The writings of the late R. G. Collingwood, philosopher and one
of the English translators of Croce, will serve our purpose well. Collingwood admired Yeats's poetry, his own position is that of an idealist
and symbolist, and like Yeats he was even interested in "magic" and found
a place for it in his intellectual scheme. In his *Principles of Art*, he comments upon the artist's concern for knowledge as follows:

> Theoretically, the artist is a person who comes to know
> himself, to know his own emotion. This is also knowing his
> world, that is, the sights and sounds and so forth which together
> make up his total imaginative experience. The two knowledges
> are to him one knowledge, because these sights and sounds are
> to him steeped in the emotion with which he contemplates them:
> they are the language in which that emotion utters itself to his
> consciousness. His world is his language. What it says to him it
> says about himself; his imaginative vision of it is his self-knowl-
> edge.[9]

Compare with this passage what Yeats wrote in 1900:

> Solitary men in moments of contemplation receive . . . the
> creative impulse from the lowest of the Nine Hierarchies, and so
> make and unmake mankind, and even the world itself, for does
> not "the eye altering alter all"? [1]

And in one of his earliest poems:

[7] *Collected Poems*, p. 236.
[8] *Collected Poems*, p. 187.
[9] *The Principles of Art* (Oxford, 1938), p. 291, by permission of Oxford University Press, Inc.
[1] "The Symbolism of Poetry," *Ideas of Good and Evil*, pp. 246–7.

. . . words alone are certain good:
Sing, then, for this is also sooth. . . .
Dream, dream, for this is also sooth.[2]

Collingwood goes on to say:

But this knowing of himself [by the artist] is a making of himself. . . . The coming to know his emotions is the coming to dominate them, to assert himself as their master. . . .

Moreover, his knowing of this new world is also the making of the new world which he is coming to know. The world he has come to know is a world consisting of language; a world where everything has the property of expressing emotion. In so far as this world is thus expressive or significant, it is he that has made it so. . . .

The aesthetic experience . . . is a knowing of oneself and of one's world. . . . It is also a making of oneself and of one's world, the self which was psyche being remade in the shape of consciousness, and the world, which was crude sensa, being remade in the shape of language, or sensa converted into imagery and charged with emotional significance.[3]

Beside this passage from the philosopher can be set any number of passages gleaned from the poet, in which he asserts the creative power of man's imagination. Out of "poet's imaginings," out of the "memories of love," out of "Memories of the words of women,"

Man makes a superhuman
Mirror-resembling dream. . . .[4]

From man's blood-sodden heart are sprung
Those branches of the night and day
Where the gaudy moon is hung. . . .[5]

More arrogantly still,

Death and life were not
Till man made up the whole,
Made lock, stock and barrel
Out of his bitter soul,
Aye, sun and moon and star, all.[6]

And of man's rage for knowledge of what he is, the poet declares:

[2] *Collected Poems*, p. 8.
[3] *The Principles of Art*, pp. 291–2.
[4] *Collected Poems*, p. 197.
[5] *Collected Poems*, p. 247.
[6] *Collected Poems*, p. 196.

> man's life is thought,
> And he, despite his terror, cannot cease
> Ravening through century after century,
> Ravening, raging, and uprooting that he may come
> Into the desolation of reality. . . .[7]

But it is to a letter written by Yeats not long before his death that one turns for what is perhaps the best statement of Yeats's yearning for the "concrete" knowledge that poetry can give, of his sense of the part that man's own expression plays in the determination of that knowledge, and of his recognition of man's limitation with regard to the apprehension of any knowledge:

> . . . I know for certain that my time will not be long. I have put away everything that can be put away that I may speak what I have to speak, and I find "expression" is a part of "study." In two or three weeks—I am now idle that I may rest after writing much verse—I will begin to write my most fundamental thoughts and the arrangement of thought which I am convinced will complete my studies. I am happy, and I think full of an energy, of an energy I had despaired of. It seems to me that I have found what I wanted. When I try to put all into a phrase I say, "Man can embody truth but he cannot know it." I must embody it in the completion of my life. The abstract is not life and everywhere draws out its contradictions. You can refute Hegel but not the Saint or the Song of Sixpence. . . .[8]

An argument is subject to refutation. The noble life, the song, the poem, are none of them subject to refutation. For the poem, like the life of the saint, does not state a proposition but embodies a meaning.

Earlier in this chapter we had occasion to speak of the danger inherent in any thorough-going symbolic system, particularly as held by an idealist: if, as Emerson put it, "the poet turns the world to glass," how shall he be able to show us anything? Will not all shapes and outlines simply disappear into one blur of diffused radiance? Yet this danger, Yeats, in spite of the extravagance of some of his idealistic pronouncements, successfully avoided. Indeed, we have had few poets in history who have stressed more powerfully the density and hard particularity of the objects of the external world. In celebrating the power of words, as all proponents of symbolist-expressionist doctrines must, Yeats did not lose thereby his grip upon things. Or, if we were willing to suppose with the symbolists that we could get at things only through language, then we would still have to say that in Yeats's poetry, language is not de-

[7] *Collected Poems*, p. 287.
[8] Written to Lady Elizabeth Pelham, 4 January 1939: see *Letters of W. B. Yeats*, p. 922.

natured and diluted into a common gray "wordiness." Words retain the sharp outlines and individual profiles of "things." Yeats's earliest poetry is indeed vague and dreamy, everything melting imperceptibly into something else; but the poetry of his maturity is angular, precise, and even shockingly realistic. Because this is true, the poet is able to exploit real oppositions. The poetry is filled with tensions between stubbornly recalcitrant contraries. Everywhere Yeats finds the drama of the antinomies.

"Donne," Yeats observes in his *Autobiographies* (1916), "could be as metaphysical as he pleased, and yet never seemed unhuman and hysterical as Shelley often does, because he could be as physical as he pleased." [9] Yeats took the lesson to heart. Even in celebrating his hero Bishop Berkeley, in whose clarifying vision "Everything that is not God" was "consumed with intellectual fire," Yeats remembered the lesson. He gives Berkeley the proud title "God-appointed" because he

> proved all things a dream,
> That this pragmatical, preposterous pig of a world, its farrow
>   that so solid seem,
> Must vanish on the instant if the mind but change its theme.[1]

But the poetry establishes the solidity of the pig. If the intellectual fire emanating from the Bishop's mind promises to consume pig, bishop, and all in a blaze that will leave no ash, the poet is too wise to attempt to portray that holocaust in the poem. In the poem, the pig is as real (and for the poem as necessary) as the bishop.

One can state Yeats's saving physicality in a somewhat different way: a danger endemic to symbolist doctrine is that of "angelism," the "sin of a man who rejects human existence and wants to be like God." Raymond, in his *From Baudelaire to Surrealism*, says that a Catholic would find such a sin in Mallarmé's poem, "*Les Fenêtres*," where the speaker, unwilling to accept his limitations as a man, wishing to extend the domain of his consciousness forever farther, turns his back upon life as a great frustrating force, and facing the casement windows, now "gilded by the chaste morning of the infinite," exclaims, "I look upon myself and see an angel." [2] "Angelism" as a sin incurred by Poe is the subject of Allen Tate's essay entitled "The Angelic Imagination." Tate admits that "strictly speaking, an *angelic imagination* is not possible. Angels by definition have unmediated knowledge of essences." [3] Man, lacking such direct intuition of essences, is committed to the imagination, for he can take hold of essences only through analogy—analogy to the natural world. If in his pride, however, he refuses to look at nature, then Tate says, he is "doomed to see

---

[9] Quoted from *Autobiographies* (New York, 1927), p. 402.
[1] *Collected Poems*, p. 233.
[2] *From Baudelaire to Surrealism*, p. 24.
[3] *The Forlorn Demon*, p. 70.

nothing." Poe "overleaped and cheated the condition of man. The reach of our imaginative enlargement is perhaps no longer than the ladder of analogy. . . . [Poe having kicked the ladder away] sits silent in darkness."[4]

Yeats never scorned the ladder of analogy, and never forgot the relationship of the "masterful images" of his accomplished poetry to the world of "things," even when those images, "because complete," seem to compel the admission that they "Grew in pure mind." In a stanza that is suggestive of Tate's figure of the ladder (and which Tate may unconsciously be recalling), Yeats writes that the "masterful images" began in

> A mound of refuse or the sweepings of a street,
> Old kettles, old bottles, and a broken can,
> Old iron, old bones, old rags, that raving slut
> Who keeps the till. Now that my ladder's gone,
> I must lie down where all the ladders start,
> In the foul rag-and-bone shop of the heart.[5]

These lines may seem too somberly desperate in their acknowledgement of the limitations of the human being. They collide with Yeats's bolder idealistic assertions. They certainly embarrass any attempt to reduce Yeats's critical position to a neat and tidy consistency. But they point to an important fact about Yeats's poetry: there is a real working dualism—real oppositions as distinguished from merely opposed positions in an abstract dialectic. The poetry can aspire to the reduction of all things to "intellectual fire" for the very good reason that the materials to be consumed are not wraiths of uninflammable moonshine. (Like the French symbolists before him, Yeats had learned, in part from Nietzsche, the uses of tension and conflict in art.) The materials that make up the poems have enough substance to resist, and when ignited, to feed, combustion.

SUPPLEMENT

For the poet, language is a structure of the external world. The speaker is *in a situation* in language; he is invested with words. They are prolongations of his meanings, his pincers, his antennae, his eyeglasses. He maneuvers them from within; he feels them as if they were his body; he is surrounded by a verbal body which he is hardly aware of and which extends his action upon the world. The poet is outside of language. He sees words inside out as if he

[4] *The Forlorn Demon,* p. 78.
[5] *Collected Poems,* p. 336.

did not share the human condition, and as if he were first meeting the word as a barrier as he comes toward men. Instead of first knowing things by their name, it seems that first he has a silent contact with them, since, turning toward that other species of thing which for him is the word, touching them, testing them, palping them, he discovers in them a slight luminosity of their own and particular affinities with the earth, the sky, the water, and all created things.

—Jean-Paul Sartre, *What is Literature?*, trans. Bernard Frechtman (New York, 1949), pp. 13–14. Reprinted by permission of the publishers, The Philosophical Library.

It may be well to remind the reader that in the work from which this passage is quoted, Sartre is arguing for an engaged literature—not at all for art-for-art's-sake.

Whereas the Neoclassical writers had been taught to observe particular natural objects carefully and accurately and then abstract the general from them, the Romantics reverse the process. Thus Blake says: "All goodness resides in minute particulars" but "Natural objects always did and now do weaken, deaden and obliterate imagination in me" and Coleridge writes in a letter:

> The further I ascend from animated Nature (i.e., in the embracements of rocks and hills), from men and cattle, and the common birds of the woods and fields, the greater becomes in me the intensity of the feeling of life. Life seems to me then a universal spirit that neither has nor can have an opposite.

As long as images derived from observation of nature had a utility value for decorating the thoughts of the mind, nature could be simply enjoyed, for Nature was not very important by comparison with human reason. But if there is a mysterious relation between them, if

> *La Nature est un temple où de vivants piliers*
> *Laissent parfois sortir de confuses paroles;*
> *L'homme y passe à travers des forêts de symbols*
> *Qui l'observent avec des regards familiers.*
>
> *Comme de longs échos qui de loin se confondent*
> *Dans une ténébreuse et profonde unité,*
> *Vaste comme la nuit et comme la clarté,*
> *Les parfums, les couleurs et les sons se répondent.*

> —Baudelaire (*Correspondances*)

then the merely visual perception is not the important act, but the intuitive vision of the meaning of the object, and also Nature becomes a much more formidable creature, charged with all the joys, griefs, hopes and terrors of the human soul, and therefore arousing very mixed feelings of love and hatred.

On the one hand, the poets long to immerse in the sea of Nature, to enjoy its endless mystery and novelty, on the other, they long to come to port in some transcendent eternal and unchanging reality from which the unexpected is excluded. Nature and Passion are powerful, but they are also full of grief. True happiness would have the calm and order of bourgeois routine without its utilitarian ignobility and boredom.

Thus the same Baudelaire who writes:

> Why is the spectacle of the sea so infinitely and eternally agreeable?

> Because the sea presents at once the idea of immensity and of movement . . . Twelve or fourteen leagues of liquid in movement are enough to convey to man the highest expression of beauty which he can encounter in his transient abode.

(Mon Coeur Mis à Nu)

and identifies human nature with the sea:

> *Vous êtes tous les deux ténébreux et discrets*
> *Homme, nul n'a sondé le fond de tes abîmes,*
> *O mer, nul ne connaît tes richesses intimes*
> *Tant vous êtes jaloux de garder vos secrets!*
> (*L'Homme et la Mer*)

also exclaims:

> *Ah! ne jamais sortir des Nombres et des Êtres*

and likens Beauty to a dream of stone (cp. the stone of Wordsworth's dream):

> *Je hais le mouvement qui déplace les lignes,*
> *Et jamais je ne pleure et jamais je ne ris.*

—From *The Enchafèd Flood* by W. H. Auden, pp. 84–6, copyright 1950 by The Rector and Visitors of the University of Virginia. Reprinted by permission of Random House, Inc.

We have entered a universe that only answers to its own laws, supports itself, internally coheres, and has a new standard of truth. Information is true if it is accurate. A poem is true if it hangs together. Information points to something else. A poem points to nothing but itself. Information is relative. A poem is absolute.

—E. M. Forster, *Anonymity: An Enquiry* (London, 1925), p. 14

Symbolism in one form or another has been used by nearly every great European poet and Baudelaire's definition could without violence be applied to their practice. The use of symbols is simply one aspect of language; the mistake lies in trying to invest them with some sort of transcendental significance instead of regarding them as a technical device of the same order as simile or metaphor. A symbol is nothing more than a vehicle for imaginative experience. What is essential is that it should correspond to the emotion evoked, and a great deal of Mallarmé's obscurity is due to the fact that he tried to use symbols to convey experiences which had not been transmuted into poetry. Baudelaire himself cannot be altogether exonerated from the charge of adding to the confusion and it is unfortunate that his *Correspondances* have been used by critics as a text instead of being treated as a piece of muddled psychology.

This does not mean that Baudelaire and his followers did not extend and develop the use of symbols. They undoubtedly did. Now the term has a variety of meanings. It includes the expanded image in *l'Albatros*, the use of the "sea" as a symbol of liberation in the work of both Baudelaire and Mallarmé and Mallarmé's way of "working" words in the *Swan*. These are straight-forward examples. What is more interesting is Baudelaire's use of the *néant* and the *gouffre* to symbolize the void behind the façade of contemporary civilization.

—Martin Turnell, "The Heirs of Baudelaire," *Scrutiny*, XI (Summer, 1943), 295–6, by permission of the author.

CHAPTER 27

I. A. RICHARDS:
A POETICS OF TENSION

§ *Affective criticism and laboratory techniques—
other forms of psychological criticism: Freud's view of art
as "substitute-gratification"—Max Eastman's concept of
art as "pure realization," and Santayana's hedonism—II.
Richards' evaluation of various psychological views of art:
his rejection of hedonism, of the specifically "aesthetic"
emotion, of empathy, etc., in favor of synaesthesis—III.
synaesthesis defined as the equilibrium of opposed impulses: discriminated from either vacillation on the one
hand or simple resolution on the other—synaesthesis characterized as a readiness to take any action we choose—
this harmonization of impulses related to the principles of
"exclusion" and "inclusion," parallels with Santayana, irony
as a character of this "balanced poise"—IV. Ransom's
criticism of Richards' notion that the poise is in our response and not in the structure of the "stimulating object"
—Ransom's criticism of other art theories that are based
upon some notion of tension and fusion, his criticism of
Eliot—the resemblances and differences between the
theories of Richards and Eliot—V. Richards' series of
cleavages: between two kinds of aesthetic failure, between
evaluative and technical criticism, his later modification of
these views—VI. Richards' separation of two kinds of
"truth," truth of reference and truth of coherence, and his
solution of the problem of the relation of science and
poetry—VII. other dualistic and quasi-dualistic theories of
poetry: Ransom's distinction of structure and texture, his
doctrine of the irrelevance of the texture to the structure,
this notion as criticized by Yvor Winters—Eastman's
parallel doctrine of irrelevance: poetic discourse as "impractical," Ransom's psychologism and his appeal to Freud
—VIII. Freud's general contribution to criticism reassessed
and compared with that of Richards* §*

A FFECTIVE CRITICISM IS, AS WE HAVE SEEN, AS OLD AS CRITICISM ITSELF. It appears, for example, in Plato's view that poetry "feeds and waters the passion" and in Aristotle's doctrine of catharsis. But in the 19th century, the decay of metaphysics and the extraordinary growth of the physical sciences gave a special stress to affective theories. Gustav Fechner, for example, took the problems of aesthetics into the laboratory. Fechner set out to construct an aesthetic theory, not *von oben* but *von unten*. The methods of investigation were to be empirical and inductive. There were to be "controlled" experiments to determine what percentage of human beings find the rectangle a more pleasing shape than the square or what percentage prefer rectangles proportioned to the golden section as compared to rectangles of other proportions. But the future of psychologism in criticism was not to lie with this kind of experimentation, whether carried out by Fechner or by such investigators as Zeising, Wundt, or Helmholtz.[1] The great impact of psychology upon 20th-century criticism was to come through introspective psychologists like Theodor Lipps or through students of abnormal psychology like Sigmund Freud and Carl Jung.

Freud's theory of wit and the comic has been discussed in a preceding chapter. Though Freud did not apply his theory of wit directly to literature, certain parallels clearly suggest themselves. The creation of poetry like the creation of wit draws upon the unconscious; poetry and wit are both in some sense "inspired." Many of the techniques of poetry, like those of wit and dream, are evidently to be subsumed under a principle of condensation. "Rhyme, alliteration, refrain, and other forms of repetition of similar sounding words in poetry" afford us pleasure, Freud writes, for the same reason that "harmless wit" yields us pleasure; and that pleasure, as we have seen in the last chapter, is a pleasure gained through economy of psychic expenditure.[2]

When Freud does address himself directly to the subject, his account of art is disappointingly simple: the pleasure of art is quite baldly reduced to that of a "substitute-gratification." Freud lumps the artist and the neurotic together in their reversion to fantasy. Art represents a vicarious fulfilment of wishes denied to the artist by reality. But the artist differs from the neurotic in several very important ways: [3]

---

[1] Adolf Zeising (*Neue Lehre von den Proportionen des menschlichen Körpers*, 1854) actually preceded Fechner in some of Fechner's characteristic experiments; Fechner's *Vorschule der Asthetik* was published in 1876. Wilhelm Wundt made researches in sensation and feeling. Herman Helmholtz produced works on *Physiological Optics* (1856–66) and *Tone Sensation* (1862).

[2] "Wit and its Relation to the Unconscious," *The Basic Writings*, pp. 712 ff.

[3] From *A General Introduction to Psychoanalysis* by Sigmund Freud, copyright R 1948 Susie Hoch; copyright 1935 Edward L. Bernays, by permission of Liveright Publishers, New York (Permabook Edition, pp. 384–5).

First of all he understands how to elaborate his day-dreams, so that they lose that personal note which grates upon strange ears and become enjoyable to others; he knows too how to modify them sufficiently so that their origin in prohibited sources is not easily detected. Further, he possesses the mysterious ability to mold his particular material until it expresses the ideas of his phantasy faithfully; and then he knows how to attach to this re-flection of his phantasy-life so strong a stream of pleasure that, for a time at least, the repressions are outbalanced and dispelled by it. When he can do all this, he opens out to others the way back to the comfort and consolation of their own unconscious sources of pleasure, and so reaps their gratitude and admiration; then he has won—through his phantasy—what before he could only win in phantasy: honor, power, and the love of women.[4]

Freud makes pleasure a specific means used by the artist ("attach . . . so strong a stream of pleasure") as well as the general end of his art; moreover the closing sentence of the passage indicates that he was willing to lump together, quite indiscriminately, the various kinds of pleasure to which art may conduce, including the quite solid and ma-terial pleasures which financial success may bring. But Freud, as he him-self more than once pointed out, made no pretense to a total literary theory. He was apparently willing to leave the task of discriminating specific aesthetic pleasure or pleasures to the aesthetician and literary critic.

II

BEFORE examining the special positions argued by typical affective critics, however, it may be well to reiterate that the heavy stress upon affectivity in our time is closely related to our preoccupation with science. Thus, a critic like Max Eastman, who regards poetry as a "pure effort to heighten consciousness," [5] counsels the poet "to yield up to science the task of interpreting experience" and "of finding out what we call truth." [6] Eastman instances a poet like Edna St. Vincent Millay as exhibiting the proper stance with reference to science. She is quite well informed about "complexes" and "ductless glands" and yet does not allow that knowledge to inhibit a burning love poetry. She recaptures the language of the Elizabethans, not to recover their "unscientific" world view, but "only to clothe therein her feelings and her fearless will to have them." [7]

[4] Cf. Melvin Rader, *A Modern Book of Esthetics* (1935), pp. 70-2.
[5] *The Literary Mind* (New York, 1932), p. 170, by permission of the publishers, Charles Scribner's Sons.
[6] *The Literary Mind*, p. 239.
[7] *The Literary Mind*, p. 148.

George Santayana had earlier begun with a similar distinction between the emotionally neutral and abstract world as described by science and the emotions that the objects of that world stir within us. The beauty that we attribute to objects is merely, Santayana argued, in *The Sense of Beauty* (1896), the objectification of our own emotions. Though we insist upon regarding beauty as "the quality of a thing," it is really a pleasure within us, and indeed in our normal, common-sense view of the world, it would never occur to us to include in our concept of reality "emotional or passionate elements." This objectification of our feelings in the "sense of beauty" is a survival of an "animistic and mythological habit of thought," once quite universal, as with primitive man, but now banished from the world of pure science and also from "the intermediate realm of vulgar day," where "mechanical science" has influenced our thinking.[8]

> The scientific idea of a thing is a great abstraction from the mass of perceptions and reactions which that thing produces; the esthetic idea is less abstract, since it retains the emotional reaction, the pleasure of the perception, as an integral part of the conceived thing.[9]

The need for clarification of our ideas in this realm was pressed with a special urgency by I. A. Richards, the critic through whose mediation psychology was to make its greatest impact upon literary criticism. Richards asked his readers to purge their critical thinking of all such animistic habits as cause us to make unwarranted connections between our inner feelings and the nature of objective reality. But his specific contribution lay in his account of the way language bears on the problem. He distinguished "two uses of language."

> A statement may be used for the sake of the *reference*, true or false, which it causes. This is the *scientific* use of language. But it may also be used for the sake of the effects in emotion and attitude. . . . This is the *emotive* use of language.[1]

Science makes statements, but poetry makes what Richards calls "pseudo-statements": their referential value is nil. Poetry makes an emotive use of language. That is its specific character. But, of course, not every instance of such emotive use is aesthetically valuable, and Richards indicts both Eastman and Santayana for not discriminating between emotional intensity and valuable emotional experience. Richards' earliest book, *The Foundations of Aesthetics* (1921), written in collaboration with

[8] *The Sense of Beauty* (New York, 1896), p. 47.
[9] *The Sense of Beauty*, p. 48.
[1] *The Principles of Literary Criticism* (London, 1924; 4th impression, 1930), p. 267, by permission of the publishers, Harcourt, Brace and Company, Inc.

C. K. Ogden and James Wood, will provide a convenient scheme for summarizing the more typical affective theories of our century and at the same time setting forth the choices and rejections by which Richards arrived at his own special theory. Richards and his colleagues list sixteen meanings of the term *beauty*, the last seven of which they label "psychological views."

The simplest of these defines the beautiful as anything "which excites Emotions." [2] Such a definition, our authors comment, is much too wide. For "it is not easy to ascribe the highest value to emotions in general, merely as emotions. They may often be experienced without particular significance, and have their place without necessarily being the concern of art." [3]

A somewhat more restricted view specifies pleasurable emotions; that is, "Anything is beautiful—which causes Pleasure." Richards and his colleagues choose to refer this definition of beauty to Santayana, its "most accomplished modern advocate." [4] But the great disadvantage of any pleasure view of art, they point out, "is that it offers us too restricted a vocabulary." [5] Criticism exhausts itself in recording that the art work is indeed pleasing. (Such would indeed seem to be the limitation of a really simple hedonism, but it is a question whether Santayana's hedonism is of this kind. His hedonism, as we shall see, has been subjected to a number of complications and refinements.)

Among the writers who have felt constrained to narrow the field of emotions expressed by art to "some unique emotion," Richards and his colleagues cite Clive Bell and Roger Fry. Bell asserts that the work of art gives us a "peculiar emotion," an "aesthetic emotion" as such. Both Bell and Fry specify that the work of art must possess "significant form." "Significant form," however, can be defined only by the "rather uncommon emotion which it causes." [6]

The difficulty with such a peculiar emotion, Richards points out, is that any attempt to define it is bound to be circular: death-dealing things, for example, do not necessarily have any quality in common except that they all can cause death, and by the same token "beautiful" things need have in common only the fact that they can cause someone to avow that they are beautiful. But if the critic proposes to connect beautiful things by nothing further than the assertion that he feels them all to be beautiful,

---

[2] *Foundations of Aesthetics*, 2nd ed. (New York, 1925), p. 21. The passage refers to what is essentially Eastman's position though Eastman is not mentioned in this book. For Richards's specific comments upon Eastman, see *The Philosophy of Rhetoric* (New York, 1936), pp. 123-4.

[3] *Foundations*, p. 56, by permission of George Allen and Unwin, Ltd., and the authors.

[4] *Foundations*, p. 52.

[5] *Foundations*, p. 53.

[6] *Foundations*, p. 61.

he has not advanced beyond his original assertion: namely, that they provoke in him that "peculiar" emotion.

Richards and his colleagues mention further attempts to characterize
the art emotion. The beautiful has been defined as anything that involves
the processes of *empathy*. Empathy (*Einfühlung*) was the name that
Theodor Lipps gave to a process which he described as "feeling something, namely, oneself, into the esthetic object." [7] In this activity, "the
antithesis between myself and the object disappears, or rather does not yet
exist." [8]

Vernon Lee (Violet Paget) independently formulated much the
same account as that of Lipps. When we say, for example, that the
mountain rises, we are transferring from ourselves to the looked-at shape
of the mountain the idea of rising and the emotions that accompany it.

> . . . it is this complex mental process, by which we (all unsus-
> pectingly) invest that inert mountain, that bodiless shape, with
> the stored up and averaged and essential modes of our activity—
> it is this process whereby we make the mountain *raise itself*,
> which constitutes what . . . I have called *Empathy*. [9]

But since experiences involving empathy are part of the day-by-day experiences of our lives and are by no means confined to aesthetic experiences, Richards points out that we shall have to limit empathic experiences
further if we are to distinguish those which are beautiful. Vernon Lee
limits the beautiful to those objects which allow empathic projection *and*
in which the projection is pleasurable because the process facilitates our
vitality. But such a formula is still too vague to represent any real advance over the usual hedonistic account of art. [1]

This review of various affective theories, though not exhaustive, will
suggest some of the reasons for Richards' choice of *synaesthesis* as the one
affective theory that seemed to him fit to serve as the foundation of an
aesthetic. Even projective theories like empathy apply to so much non-
artistic experience that they fail to isolate the specific values of art. The
element constant to all experiences that have the characteristic of beauty,
concludes Richards, is *synaesthesis*—a harmony and equilibrium of our
impulses.

[7] "*Einfühlung, innere Nachahmung, und Organempfindungen*," *Archiv für die
gesamte Psychologie*, Vol. I (1903): quoted from Melvin Rader, *A Modern Book of
Esthetics* (1935), p. 302.
[8] Rader, p. 294. Here we are evidently dealing with a psychological version of
the metaphysics of Fichte or Schelling—cf. *ante* Chapter 17.
[9] *The Beautiful* (Cambridge, 1913), pp. 65–6.
[1] ". . . the experiences we get from successfully riding a bicycle, which presumably cause pleasure and facilitate our vitality, could clearly be recalled by our
projecting similar movements into lines and rhythms, and the resultant state would
be neither more nor less aesthetic than the original one, except in virtue of its new
origin in recall through projection" (*Foundations*, p. 69).

III

ANY experience must involve the arousal and interplay of various impulses, but in the experience of beauty Richards contends that our impulses are organized in a peculiar way. In this peculiar organization which constitutes synaesthesis, the rivalry of conflicting impulses is avoided, not by our suppressing the impulses, but, paradoxically, by our giving them free rein.

> Not all impulses . . . are naturally harmonious, for conflict is possible and common. A complete systematization must take the form of such an adjustment as will preserve free play to every impulse, with entire avoidance of frustration. In any equilibrium of this kind, however momentary, we are experiencing beauty.[2]

Such a conception, indeed, presents its difficulties, for an equilibrium of conflicting impulses is easily confused with the state of "balance" that one finds in irresolution—that is, an oscillation between two sets of opposed impulses in which the mind, like the fabled donkey poised between the equally attractive bales of hay, can only remain suspended in inaction. Richards and his friends warn us that this is not at all what they mean by synaesthesis. Synaesthesis is no such oscillation but a harmonization: the competing impulses sustain not two states of mind but one. They do not split the ego in two, but complete and enrich it. In the experience of synaesthesis, our "interest is not canalised in one direction," [3] and there is a sense of detachment and disinterest. Our lack of commitment to any particular course of action means in reality that we are, like the poised athlete, in readiness for any kind of action.

For this special kind of "disinterest," a technical psychological explanation is offered. Our authors say that whereas two perfectly simple impulses must either oscillate or lock, a "more complex initial conflict" may discharge itself "through its branch connections." Such a complex conflict may "solve" itself "in the arousal of the other impulses of the personality." [4] At any rate, whatever the precise nature of the psychological explanation, Richards and his colleagues are confident that the sense of disinterest in the aesthetic experience means, paradoxically, that the maximum number of interests is actually involved, and that the feeling of "impersonality" that synaesthesis induces means that the "whole of the personality" has been brought into play. By the equilibrium of synaesthesis Richards evidently would suggest, then, not the lifeless balance

[2] *Foundations*, p. 75.
[3] *Foundations*, p. 78.
[4] *Foundations*, p. 77, note.

of deadlock but the vibrant poise of the completely co-ordinated personality.

There is a second state of mind which we are also warned not to confuse with synaesthesis. Our authors remark that the feeling of "lucidity, self-possession and freedom" [5] that characterizes the experience of synaesthesis may also attach to the state of mind that arises when one is possessed by an intense emotion such as anger or joy. In one of his later poems, W. B. Yeats admirably describes this state of "simple resolution":

> Know that when all words are said
> And a man is fighting mad,
> Something drops from eyes long blind,
> He completes his partial mind,
> For an instant stands at ease
> Laughs aloud, his heart at peace. . . . [6]

But since this state of mind gains its "harmony" by having no warring impulses to harmonize, its resemblance to synaesthesis is illusory. Richards and his colleagues offer a test by which it can be distinguished from synaesthesis: synaesthesis "refreshes and never exhausts." [7]

In their theorizing about synaesthesis it is evident that Richards and his colleagues have moved beyond any simple pleasure principle. A few years after the publication of *The Foundations of Aesthetics*, Richards asserted that the pleasure that a competent reader feels is "no more the aim of the activity in the course of which it arises, than, for example, the noise made by a motor-cycle—useful though it is as an indication of the way the machine is running—is the reason in the normal case for its having been started." [8] The main value of literature was to be found in its *after*-effects upon the mind.

One more observation on synaesthesis is pertinent here: though Richards deplored Kant's having created a "phantom problem of the aesthetic mode" through his attempt to define the "judgment of taste" as a judgment "concerning pleasure which is disinterested, universal, unintellectual, and not to be confused with the pleasures of sense or of ordinary emotions," [9] Richards' own doctrine of synaesthesis courts, if it does not actually demand, the same series of adjectives. True, the term synaesthesis has a psychological orientation, not a metaphysical, but synaesthesis is certainly disinterested, and this aspect comes out most plainly when Richards tries to distinguish it from the false equilibrium of irresolution or from that of full emotional commitment.

[5] *Foundations*, p. 77, note.
[6] "Under Ben Bulben," *Collected Poems*, p. 342.
[7] *Foundations*, p. 77, note.
[8] *The Principles of Literary Criticism*, p. 97.
[9] *Principles*, p. 11.

Attitudes, as Richards defines them, are incipient or "imaginal" actions. In synaesthesis, these incipient actions are so ordered and so balanced that the maximum number of them is involved and the minimum number is blocked—but they remain incipient; no action occurs. Synaesthesis is defined as our readiness "to take any direction we choose," but in synaesthesis evidently we do *not* choose. Presumably if we did choose and acted upon that choice, that very fact would indicate that the supposed state of synaesthesis was illusory, not real.

> When works of art produce such action, or conditions which lead to action, they have either not completely fulfilled their function or would in the view of equilibrium here being considered be called not "beautiful" but "stimulative." [1]

Synaesthesis, says Richards, is the ground-plan of all aesthetic experience. Many people obviously have had this experience in the past, but they have confused the experience with a revelation of some sort. The arts, he admits, do seem "to lift away the burden of existence" and we do seem "to be looking into the heart of things," but this state of euphoria, he insists, has actually nothing to do with truth. For truth belongs to science, which represents a "different [principle] upon which impulses may be organized," [2] and which has a very different function from that of the arts.

In his *Principles of Literary Criticism*, Richards never makes use of the key term "synaesthesis." Instead the terms "inclusion" and "synthesis" are used to name the character of the greatest and most valuable poetry. *Synthesis* [3] is, of course, fair coin for synaesthesis, and the key passage in which Richards defines synthesis bears a remarkable resemblance to one of the paragraphs in Santayana's *The Sense of Beauty*. It will be useful to set the two passages side by side.

In a section of his book that he significantly entitled "The Liberation of the Self," Santayana had written:

> Now, it is the essential privilege of beauty to so *synthesize* and bring to a focus the various *impulses of the self*, so to suspend them to a single image, that a great peace falls upon that

---

[1] *Foundations*, p. 77. Stephen Dedalus in *A Portrait of the Artist as a Young Man* (New York, 1916), p. 240, makes a comparable point in denying that "kinesthetic" art (i.e., art that provokes us to a particular action) is truly art at all.

[2] *Principles*, p. 265. Compare with this Santayana's assertion that a great work of art leaves us with the sense that "however tangled the net may be in which we feel ourselves caught, there is liberation beyond, and an ultimate peace" (*The Sense of Beauty*, p. 239).

[3] The term may show the influence of Coleridge's description of the imagination as a "synthetic and magical" power. In any case the adaptation of Coleridge's account of the imagination is frankly acknowledged. See the chapter on "The Imagination," in *Principles*, pp. 239–53.

perturbed kingdom. In the experience of these momentary harmonies we have the basis of the enjoyment of beauty, and of all its mystical meanings. But there are always two methods of securing harmony: one is to unify all the given elements, and another is to reject and expunge all the elements that refuse to be unified. Unity by *inclusion* gives us the beautiful; unity by *exclusion*, opposition, and isolation gives us the sublime. Both are pleasures: but the pleasure of the one is warm, passive, and pervasive; that of the other cold, imperious, and keen. The one identifies us with the world, the other raises us above it.[4]

And now for the passage from Richards:

There are two ways in which *impulses* may be organized; by *exclusion* and by *inclusion*, by *synthesis* and by elimination. Although every coherent state of mind depends upon both, it is permissible to contrast experiences which win stability and order through a narrowing of the response with those which widen it. A very great deal of poetry and art is content with the full, ordered development of comparatively special and limited experiences, with a definite emotion, for example, Sorrow, Joy, Pride, or a definite attitude, Love, Indignation, Admiration, Hope, or with a specific mood, Melancholy, Optimism or Longing. And such art has its own value and its place in human affairs. No one will quarrel with "Break, break, break," or with the *Coronach* or with *Rose Aylmer* or with *Love's Philosophy*, although clearly they are limited and *exclusive*. But they are not the greatest kind of poetry; we do not expect from them what we find in the *Ode to the Nightingale*, in *Proud Maisie*, in *Sir Patrick Spens*, in *The Definition of Love* or in the *Nocturnall upon S. Lucie's Day*.[5]

The two kinds of poetry are not, for Richards as they evidently are for Santayana, on the same level. Richards displays no interest in distinguishing the beautiful from the sublime; his interest is rather to distinguish a richer, deeper, and more tough-minded poetry from a more "limited and exclusive" kind of poetry. Furthermore, Santayana's harmonization of the impulses of the self by rejection and expungement of all "the elements that refuse to be unified" could not, in Richards' terms, qualify as a harmonization at all; instead it rather suggests Richards' state of "simple resolution."[6] But the resemblances between the passages are striking enough.

[4] *The Sense of Beauty*, pp. 235–6. The italics are ours.
[5] *Principles*, pp. 249–50. The italics are ours.
[6] Cf. *ante* p. 617.

Richards proceeds to give a psychological account of the peculiar kind of stability of this second kind of poetry (the poetry of synthesis) and to use the presence of irony as a kind of touchstone for such poetry.

> The difference comes out clearly if we consider how com-
> paratively unstable poems of the first kind are. They will not
> bear an ironical contemplation. We have only to read *The War
> Song of Dinas Vawr* in close conjunction with the *Coronach*,
> or to remember that unfortunate phrase "Those lips, O slippery
> blisses!" from *Endymion*, while reading *Love's Philosophy*, to
> notice this. Irony in this sense consists in the bringing in of the
> opposite, the complementary impulses; that is why poetry which
> is exposed to it is not of the highest order, and why irony itself
> is so constantly a characteristic of poetry which is.
>
> These opposed impulses from the resolution of which such
> experiences spring cannot usually be analysed. When, as is most
> often the case, they are aroused through formal means, it is evi-
> dently impossible to do so.[7]

IV

RICHARDS' confession of the difficulty—not to mention the impossibility —of analyzing the "opposed impulses" throws an interesting light upon the psychological machinery which he has used to account for the effects of this "poetry of inclusion." When we get ready to use the machinery, it evaporates. The poem is before us and is susceptible to analysis, but the psychological goings-on turn out to be below the surface and out of sight. This curious state of affairs is a main object of attack in John Crowe Ransom's criticism of Richards.[8]

Ransom points out that Richards' account of the relevant poetic structure is not only a mere hypothesis, but that this particular hypothesis, if accepted, would destroy criticism. For if the "balanced poise" is, as Richards says it is, in our "response" and not at all "in the structure of the stimulating object," then the labor of criticism in "analysing the po- etic object" is vain. Vain also was the labor of the poet in putting the poem into a particular "shape." On Richards' showing, the

> poem is not needed in that shape; and what the proper shape
> would be we are not likely to know. I for one feel that I cannot
> know even what it is in the poem which constitutes its stimulus.[9]

[7] *Principles*, pp. 250–1.
[8] *The New Criticism* (New York, 1941). Copyright 1941 by New Directions and reprinted by permission of the publisher.
[9] *The New Criticism*, p. 32.

It is indeed questionable whether Richards actually succeeds in cutting his desiderated "balanced poise" cleanly off from all relation to "the structure of the stimulating object." Though Richards is careful to point out that such balanced poise is "not peculiar to Tragedy," significantly it is in tragedy, the form of literature in which conflicts and tensions are obvious structural features, that he finds his clearest illustrations. Nietzsche too had found that in tragedy "contrasts are overcome" and "oppositions" are "conquered," [1] and his insistence that the greatest artists are those "who make harmony ring out of every discord" strengthens the notion that Nietzsche anticipated Richards' conception of a "poetry of inclusion," though Nietzsche gave his "inclusion" a clear structural reference. For the discords are in the composition, and the larger harmony in which these momentary disharmonies are finally resolved is obviously to be referred to the total structure. Not the least important of the "musical" characteristics that Nietzsche attributes to tragedy is this conception of a richer and more intricate harmony, achieved by the resolution of apparent discords, as opposed to the "thinner" harmony of less ambitious works.

Richards himself, when he suggests that one may test the stability of such poetry by exposing it to ironical contemplation, seems to regard the differentia of "inclusive" poetry as structural. For, though the reader supplies the ironical squint, the subsequent collapse in the defective poem is a structural collapse.

Richards' insistence that irony is "so constantly" a characteristic of the highest order of poetry reminds one of Solger's claim that irony is "coextensive with art." [2] It also calls for comparison with T. S. Eliot's notion that the function of wit is to provide an "internal equilibrium" for the poem in which it occurs. If Richards' irony is not made to provide the stability of the experience, it is at least a symptom of the stability. Eliot's notion about wit seems to be the complement of Nietzsche's conception of a "harmony" that is rung "out of every discord." For in saying that witty poetry implies "in the expression of every experience" the recognition of the fact that "other kinds of experience . . . are possible," [3] Eliot is saying that wit calls to our attention the potentially discordant; that is, the unity of the witty poem is not a unity easily won by glossing over the discordant elements of human experience.

Such restatements of Richards' conceptions of "inclusion" and of "tension" would, however, scarcely appease a critic like Ransom. He impartially condemns both Richards and Eliot for talking about the reconciliation of what he insists are in fact irreconcilables:

[1] Cf. *ante* Chapter 25.
[2] Cf. *ante* Chapter 17.
[3] "Andrew Marvell" (1921), *Selected Essays, 1917–32* (New York, 1932), p. 262, by permission of the publishers, Harcourt, Brace and Company, Inc.

My belief is that opposites can never be said to be resolved or reconciled merely because they have been got into the same poem, or got into the same complex of affective experience to create there a kind of "tension"; that if there is a resolution at all it must be a logical resolution; that when there is no resolution we have a poem without a structural unity; and this is precisely the intention of irony, which therefore is something very special, and ought to be occasional.[4]

This statement is of a piece with Ransom's criticism of Eliot's conception of metaphysical poetry: "The aspiration here is for some sort of fusion of two experiences that ordinarily repel one another," and Ransom warns us not to become "the fools of the shining but impractical ideal of 'unity' or of 'fusion.' "[5] Thus, on the special and limited nature of irony, he firmly takes his stand beside Irving Babbitt and the new Humanists.[6] Far from being a "a constant characteristic" of good poetry, irony signifies for Ransom a failure to unify. "In a pointed form of irony," he writes, "the oppositions produce an indecisive effect, just as in tragedy there is an opposition with a negative effect."[7] Richards had been careful to distinguish the poetry of "harmonious equilibrium" (of which irony is "so constantly a characteristic") from mere "irresolution." Ransom's argument is that ironic poetry can represent only irresolution: that is, the oppositions "produce an indecisive effect."

Ransom is no less firm in dismissing Eliot. Though he has called Eliot "The Historical Critic," he says that Eliot's theory of poetry is "equivalent to some version of Richards' psychologistic theory."[8] There is some psychologism in Eliot; and there are certain conceptions that he shares with Richards. One remembers Eliot's statement that for the poet the noise of the typewriter and the smell of cooking, reading Spinoza or falling in love—experiences which for the ordinary man have nothing to do with one another—"are always forming new wholes."[9] And one places beside it this passage from Richards:

> The wheeling of the pigeons in Trafalgar Square may seem to have no relation to the colour of the water in the basins, to the tones of a speaker's voice or to the drift of his remarks. A narrow field of stimulation is all that we can manage, and we overlook the rest. But the artist does not, and when he needs it, he has it at his disposal.[1]

Unless one recognizes the amount of agreement between Richards and Eliot, one will find it difficult to understand the relative ease with

[4] *The New Criticism*, p. 95.
[5] *The New Criticism*, p. 183.
[6] Cf. *ante* Chapter 20.
[7] *The New Criticism*, p. 96.

[8] *The New Criticism*, p. 152.
[9] *Selected Essays*, p. 247.
[1] *Principles*, p. 185.

which Richards' influence upon criticism has merged with that of Eliot, and one will find it difficult to account for some of the later developments in Richards' own criticism—see the next chapter. Nevertheless, the differences between Eliot and Richards are very important, and nowhere more so than in their treatment of thought and feeling. In spite of some waverings and confusions encouraged by an occasional use of affective terminology, Eliot stands by his bold assertion that a poem is a *fusion* of thought and feeling. Richards, on the other hand, from the first has endeavored to maintain a careful distinction between the emotional state produced in the reader (the balance of impulses or state of synaesthesis) and the means used to produce this emotional state.

V

RICHARDS' endeavors to distinguish between the emotional effect produced in the reader and the means by which it is produced give rise in his criticism to a whole series of related separations: between value (content) and communication (as conditioned by form); between the "badness" that results from the communication to the reader of a worthless experience and the "badness" that results from the faulty communication of what was presumably a valuable experience; between technical criticism (which Richards defines as dealing with the make-up of the stimulating object) and evaluative criticism (which deals with the value of the experience communicated). An exploration of some of these topics supplies striking instances of the difficulties with which an affective theory burdens a critic who has genuine literary sensitivity and whose deepest allegiance is evidently to poetry rather than to the psychology of reader response.

In *The Principles of Literary Criticism*, Richards illustrated the two kinds of "badness" by using a tiny Imagist poem by H. D. and a rather glib love sonnet by Ella Wheeler Wilcox. H. D.'s scrap of Imagist verse was said to fail because it did not sufficiently communicate the valuable experience that Richards conceded that the poet might have had. The Wilcox sonnet was said to fail because the experience that it communicated—all too clearly—had no value. The sonnet was dominated by an elaborate analogy between Summer and Love and Friendship and Autumn. And Richards pointed out that those readers "who have adequate impulses as regards *any* of the four main systems [of impulses] involved" in this poem are not "appeased" by the poem. "Only for those who make certain conventional, stereotyped maladjustments instead, does the magic work." [2]

Yet it might have been simpler to deal with adequacy of imagery

[2] *Principles,* p. 202.

rather than with adequacy of "impulses." A critic of the poem could simply have said that any reader who attended to the imagery of the poem would find it absurdly confused. If the reader knew anything about autumn, he would know that an autumn day with a "touch of frost . . . in the air" tends to be crisp and sparkling, not hazy with the mellowness of St. Martin's summer. If he knew anything about love, he would hardly be satisfied with the metamorphosis of Love into "large-eyed Friendship" through a kind of fadeout-dissolve of one obviously trumped up allegorical figure into another.[3]

In spite of a certain superficial plausibility, the distinction between defectiveness of communication and the "worthlessness" of the experience communicated cannot in fact be maintained. We can only speculate about values that are not revealed in the poem itself. That there might have been a valuable experience behind H. D.'s "The Pool" is, and must remain, pure hypothesis. On the other hand, one *could* argue that the alleged clarity of the Wilcox sonnet is actually an illusion since what is inextricably confused cannot have "clarity." The "badness" of this poem consists in a pretension to coherence that is not made good; the analogy between Summer-Autumn and Love-Friendship is asserted but never realized dramatically. The essential act in condemning the poem consists therefore in exposing the basic *incoherence*.[4]

The motive for Richards' various "separations" is, of course, rooted in his desire to discuss poetry in terms of stimulus and response. This fact comes out most clearly in his attempt to distinguish "technical" remarks from "critical" (i.e., evaluative) remarks. He regards the distinction as important because, as he writes, the trick of mistaking "the means for the end, the technique for the value, is in fact the most successful of the snares which waylay the critic."[5] Yet on the same page Richards indi-

---

[3] As a measure of the coherence proper to a genuine poem, one might contrast with the Wilcox sonnet, Keats's "To Autumn," in which the "completeness" of an autumn day is made to subsist *with* a note of melancholy, or with Shakespeare's "How Like a Winter hath mine Absence Been," where there is a responsible alignment of the vicissitudes of love with seasonal change, or with Edna St. Vincent Millay's "The Cameo," which gives a *coherent* rendering of something like the specific theme of the Wilcox poem.

[4] Richards' very proper concern for the pernicious social effects of bad art seems to be as well served by this account as by his own: the reader who asks only that certain of his stock responses be titillated, who is content with certain "conventional, stereotyped maladjustments," is a reader who is oblivious to the kind of incoherence that characterizes the Wilcox sonnet. Such a reader will be baffled by the incoherence of H. D.'s "The Pool," but the incoherence of the Wilcox sonnet, because it mirrors his own distortions and oversimplifications, will probably be seen in quite other terms: as a clear and exalted vision of life. His inability to make sense of a poem—any poem—may well be coterminous with his inability to make sense of his own experiences; but with this latter problem we move from the field of criticism proper into a consideration of education, ethics, and the analysis of popular culture.

[5] *Principles*, p. 24.

cates his belief in an *organic* theory of poetry. There are problems: in what sense can a part of a poem be regarded as the means to an end? There is a sense, to be sure, in which all the parts of an organic whole may be regarded as reciprocally means and ends. The head is a "means" to the functioning of the heart and the heart is a "means" to the functioning of the head. But within the poem, it is not clear how there can be ends and means; the correct relation would seem to be that of parts to a whole.

By 1934 Richards himself had become suspicious of this distinction. In *Coleridge on Imagination* he wrote:

> It is with deceptive ease . . . that the inquiry [into poetic mean-
> ing] divides into questions about the *what* and the *how*. Or into
> questions about the *methods* a poet uses and the *feats* he thereby
> achieves. Or into questions about his *means* and his *ends*. Or
> about the *way* of his work and the *whither*.[6]

Though he regards the division as for some purposes "necessary" and for other purposes "convenient," he warns that it tends to distort the whole meaning of the work by abstracting "some component to be treated as its *whither* and to be set over against the rest as its *way*." [7]

VI

THE best-known and the most radical of Richards' separations is, of course, that which he made between the emotive and the referential "uses of language." [8] Richards denied to poetry any truth of reference and argued that the "truth" as applied to a work of art could mean only the "internal necessity" or "rightness" of the work of art: that is, whereas scientific truth has to do with correspondence to the nature of reality, artistic "truth" is a matter of inner coherence.

> The "Truth" of *Robinson Crusoe* is the acceptability of the
> things we are told, their acceptability in the interests of the ef-
> fects of the narrative, not their correspondence with any actual
> facts involving Alexander Selkirk or another. Similarly the falsity
> of happy endings to *Lear* or to *Don Quixote*, is their failure to be
> acceptable to those who have fully responded to the rest of the
> work. It is in this sense that "Truth" is equivalent to "internal
> necessity" or rightness. That is "true" or "internally necessary"
> which completes or accords with the rest of the experience. . . .[9]

[6] *Coleridge on Imagination* (New York, 1934), p. 198.
[7] *Coleridge on Imagination*, p. 199.
[8] *Principles*, pp. 261 ff.
[9] *Principles*, p. 269.

The "truth" of *Robinson Crusoe* or of *King Lear*, in short, has nothing to do with objective truth. The "effects of the narrative" which determine the "acceptability" of the "things we are told" are psychological effects. The happy ending supplied by Nahum Tate for *Lear* is "false" because it is at odds with the rest of the play; the play as a whole is "true" only in virtue of giving rise to the proper psychological effects, in helping us, that is, to "order our attitudes to one another and to the world." That is why "we need no beliefs" in order to read *King Lear*. Indeed, Richards goes much further and writes that "we must have [no beliefs], if we are to read *King Lear*";[1] for beliefs, with their claims to objective truth, would disturb the self-contained coherence, the "internal necessity" which is the only "truth" that Richards will allow to the play.

Such was Richards' solution to the conflict of science and poetry: it is as drastic as it is neat. There could be no conflict for the good reason that there was no common ground upon which science and poetry (properly understood) could meet. They were held to utilize radically different aspects of language.

There are, to be sure, certain things that Robinson Crusoe cannot do because they would violate our sense of his character as built up in the earlier pages. The happy ending that Nahum Tate clapped onto *King Lear* simply does not accord with the earlier parts of the play. And yet more would seem to be operative in forming our rejections than what is contained in previous chapters or previous scenes of a specific novel or play: we appeal to, and are influenced by, our whole previous acquaintance with human beings. When we decide that Crusoe cannot do this or that, we are relying upon our notions of human psychology—very general notions perhaps—but notions that refer to a world outside the formmal limits of the art work itself. Even the world of Aesop's fables or of the fairy tale or of "science fiction" has not cut all connections with a world of our experience.

There would have been little debate if Richards' severance of poetry from all "reference" had amounted to no more than saying that the reader of Shakespeare did not need to worry about the inaccurate Scottish history in *Macbeth*, or that the reader of Coleridge had no cause to be disturbed by such scientifically impossible descriptions as that which places a star within the nether tip of the moon. On this level, the severance between poetry and history and poetry and science had been made by the ancients. But Richards, going further, seemed to be arguing that poetry was literally nonsense, though, for reasons bound up with his psychologistic theory, a peculiarly valuable kind of nonsense. It was difficult for critics like Allen Tate and John Crowe Ransom to see how one

[1] *Science and Poetry* (London, 1925; 2nd ed. 1926), p. 67.

could deny all truth to poetry, and yet at the same time argue in the fashion of Matthew Arnold that "poetry could save us."

VII

YET the temptation to make such severances and separations as Richards makes is stubbornly persistent in modern criticism. A striking instance occurs in the work of Ransom himself. Earlier in this chapter we have referred to Ransom's denial that there can be any "fusion" of "experiences that ordinarily repel one another" [2]—as that notion is held either by Richards or by Eliot.

Ransom drew a crucial distinction between the *texture* and the *structure* of a poem. The texture of a poem is constituted of its rich local values, the quality of things in their "thinginess." The structure is the "argument" of the poem. It gives the poem such shape as it has; it regulates the assemblage of sensory data, providing order and direction. Science has, properly speaking, no texture; it is content with pure structure and exhibits no rich particularity. A poem, on the other hand, has a texture *and* a structure. Though the texture is strictly irrelevant to the logic of the poem, yet it does after all affect the shape of the poem; it does so by *impeding* the argument. The very irrelevance of the texture is thus important. Because of its presence we get, not a streamlined argument, but an argument that has been complicated through having been hindered, and diverted, and having thus had its very success threatened. In the end we have our logic, but only after a lively reminder of the aspects of reality with which logic cannot cope.

A main source of Ransom's dissatisfaction with Richards' theory was its affectivity, and Ransom stressed the cognitive element in his own theory. But his would have to be described as a kind of "bifocal" cognitive theory: poetry gives us through its structure and texture, respectively, knowledge of universals and knowledge of particulars. Poetry is the complement of science which, restricting itself to universals, can mirror only a world of abstractions. Ransom hands over the realm of the universals to science, and in effect retains for poetry no more than an apprehension of particulars.

There are some problems here: are the two knowledges on the same level? Can they be kept from fusing? Or do they function intermittently, and if they do, is there any reason why they should occur in connection with each other? Ransom has rejected any notion of the union of the levels as an impossible oil-and-water mixture: neither component will dissolve into the other. What he proposes would have to be described as

---

[2] See *ante* p. 622.

a sort of emulsion—the little droplets of local "knowledge" suspended in, and diffused through, the other "knowledge" of universals.

> [The imagination] presents to the reflective mind the particu-
> larity of nature; whereas there is quite another organ, working
> by a technique of universals, which gives us science.[3]

On a strict interpretation, Ransom would seem to confine the imagination to such matters as the reflection of odors, tactile impressions, tone, colors, and other sensations, leaving out larger patterns such as those woven by the "moral" imagination.

The doctrine of the irrelevance of the texture poses another formidable problem. Yvor Winters has asked why, in view of the irrelevance of all texture, one "irrelevant" detail should be preferred to another.[4] Would not one texture do for any given poem as well as another? Marvell's "To his Coy Mistress" is, in terms of Ransom's thesis, the fine poem that it is because the lover's argument runs such an obstacle race before it can come to its conclusion. But Winters conjectures that in terms of such a theory as this, Crashaw's poem "The Weeper" would prove to be a finer poem still, its argument being even more besettingly impeded by the irrelevance of its texture.[5] Irrelevance, he urges, is irrelevance. To argue that some forms of irrelevant detail are more suitable to the poem than other forms of irrelevant detail would be to admit that *irrelevant* was not, after all, the proper term.

Ransom's theory that "impeding" the argument gives poetry's special knowledge of particularity finds a parallel in Eastman's notion that the hyperconsciousness achieved in poetry comes through "obstruction." As was noted earlier in this chapter, Eastman assumes that the function of art is to heighten consciousness. The artist does this by stimulating a response and yet obstructing it. To invoke an analogy: putting on a coat is a largely automatic action; we need not be conscious, and usually are not fully conscious, of what we are doing. But if the lining of the sleeve is torn and the action of thrusting the arm through it proves unexpectedly difficult, we become intensely aware of what we are doing. And so:

> [Art] must arouse a reaction and yet impede it, creating a ten-
> sion in our nervous systems sufficient and rightly calculated to
> make us completely aware that we are living something—and
> no matter what.[6]

[3] *The World's Body* (New York, 1938), p. 156.
[4] *The Anatomy of Nonsense* (1943), included in and reprinted from *In Defense of Reason* by Yvor Winters by permission of the publisher, Alan Swallow. Copyright 1937 and 1947 by Yvor Winters, pp. 537-9.
[5] *In Defense of Reason*, pp. 538-9.
[6] *The Literary Mind*, p. 205. Richards has made considerable play with the careless abandon of Eastman's "and no matter what." He points out that if one ties a man down and then approaches him brandishing a red-hot poker—stimulating and yet

To pursue this parallelism between Ransom and Eastman: Eastman asserts that the "impractical identifications" made by metaphor and the "luxury of surprising and rich adjectives and figurative expressions . . . do not help to explain like maps or illustrations, but rather obscure the meaning of the sentence in which they occur." [7] Ransom has been careful to make his details of texture "impractical," and to show that, from the point of view of prose discourse, they are a "luxury"; yet he insists that it is just because they are impractical, that they force us to take in the rich particularity of experience. But Eastman's theory of poetry is frankly affective and psychologistic. [8]

On closer examination, the function that Ransom accords to "statement" or "structure" in poetry resembles very closely that accorded to statement in poetry by Richards. Richards makes it plain that referential statements in poetry are not important in themselves, though they frequently occur and indeed usually must occur *"as conditions for, or stages in,* the ensuing development of attitudes"—the elements that *are* important. [9] Likewise Ransom stresses the fact that a poem cannot do without structure (i.e., a determining argument): the human mind is so constituted that it has to have an argument to follow. But the arguments of most poems, Ransom concedes to be, in themselves, usually dull affairs; [1] we follow the pathway of the argument really for the sake of the details that border the path. We are tempted to pick a daisy or to investigate an oddly shaped bush (the elements of "texture"). We keep returning to the path and eventually arrive at our elected destination, but we arrive having seen the country—as we would not have had we kept to the strait and narrow path of science. The incidental details give the journey its value. [2] For Ransom as well as for Richards, the statements made in the poem are important only in so far as they are a means to something else.

---

impeding a response—one will produce a spectacularly heightened consciousness but scarcely anything that can be called art. See *The Philosophy of Rhetoric* (New York, 1936), p. 124.

[7] *The Literary Mind,* p. 183.

[8] Eastman's praise for Richards amounts to commendation for his serious effort to apply psychology to criticism. Eastman has little patience with the actual results. He finds in Richards' "harmonious equilibrium of impulses" no "foundation of aesthetics." If perchance we do find in a work of art a "reconciliation of our conflicting impulses," then that particular art "besides being art . . . is for us a kind of medicine" (*The Literary Mind,* p. 205). But most art is not, and no art need be, medicinal. In general Eastman deplores Richards' attempt to regard the scientific (the referential) apart from the emotive. A scientific interpretation of an event (e.g., that the snake in the path is not a garter snake but a copperhead) can evoke as much emotion and make the percipient jump as quickly as a merely "emotive" interpretation—besides being a better basis for proper action (*The Literary Mind,* p. 302).

[9] *Principles of Literary Criticism,* p. 267.

[1] The paraphrase of a poem, Ransom writes, "is a fair version of the logical structure," and since the paraphrase of even a fine poem usually reveals an undistinguished and commonplace argument, he concludes that the structure is not the valuable element of the poem.

[2] *The New Criticism,* p. 73, and pp. 184-5.

Ransom's justification of poetic structure, no less than Richards', rests upon an appeal to psychology: that is, human beings demand at least an apparent argument; we will not swallow our local detail neat. Ransom remarks that "it is hard to say what poetry intends by its odd structure," and the makeup of poetry, as he has described it, *is* odd— so odd that one must despair of accounting for it in terms of any entelechy of its own. Only the cravings of the human psyche can account for it, and Ransom, in a later phase of his theory,[3] came to seek for the explanation in Freudian psychology. The conscious and reasonable *ego* flourishes upon neat and tidy orderliness, but the unconscious *id* requires the concrete and unpredictable particulars for its sustenance. Poetry thus ministers to the health of the mind, and Ransom's later position tends to approximate in some features the earlier position of Richards. This fact, taken together with the counter-fact that Richards, in *his* own later criticism, has moved toward a cognitive position, is eloquent testimony to the difficulties inherent in any critical theory which begins by slicing apart value and knowledge—whether it be Richards' cutting the emotive use of language free from the referential or Ransom's cutting the valuable illogical "texture" free from logical "structure." The critic may indeed make refinements that push his theory nearer to a cognitive view, but in so far as the value of the poem is something that cannot be figured forth in the poetic meaning before us, psychology will have to be called in, either at the beginning or at the end, to justify the irrational elements in which the value has been made to reside.

Ransom's appeal to Freud is, however, somewhat startling in view of the embarrassing simplicity of Freud's own theory of literature as offering a kind of surrogate gratification, a theory touched upon briefly earlier in this chapter.[4] But it ought to be observed that Freud's concept of the mind and of its workings has exerted a profound influence, even upon critics who are quite willing to dismiss Freud's specific literary theory as inadequate. Lionel Trilling, for example, who admits that Freud has said "many clumsy and misleading things about art," and remarks that Freud "eventually . . . speaks of art" with "what we must indeed call contempt,"[5] nevertheless has urged us not to underestimate the value of Freud's contribution to literary criticism.

VIII

THERE is a certain propriety in ending this chapter as we began it with some observations upon Freud, the more so since those made in the open-

---

[3] See in particular two articles in *The Kenyon Review*, IX (Summer and Autumn, 1947), Nos. 3 and 4.

[4] See *ante* p. 611.

[5] *The Liberal Imagination*, p. 42.

ing pages could scarcely do justice to his influence. We owe to Freud a whole new psychological vocabulary—the *Id*, the *Ego*, the *Super-ego*, *transference*, and *repression* are only a few of its terms—a vocabulary which reflects a new conception of the psyche and its functioning. In elucidating the symbolic content of dreams and the way in which the "dream-work" is performed—through *condensation, substitution*, and *displacement*—and in calling attention to typical *motifs* (like the Oedipus Complex) which recur in literature, Freud has enlarged our notions of the richness and complexity to which a literary symbol may attain. In his concept of the *overdetermination* or multiple relevance of accurately used language, Freud has paralleled such more specifically literary concepts of ambiguous verbal riches as those which we shall consider in succeeding chapters. Trilling's summary of Freud's accomplishment on this level is probably not overstated:

> In the eighteenth century Vico spoke of the metaphorical, imagistic language of the early stages of culture; it was left to Freud to discover how, in a scientific age, we still feel and think in figurative formations, and to create, what psychoanalysis is, a science of tropes, of metaphor and its variants, synechdoche and metonymy.[6]

The value of the tools with which Freud has supplied the literary critic ought indeed to be acknowledged, even though the tools are at the mercy of the tool-users, and they in turn are at the mercy of whatever literary theory they may hold. A new "science of tropes" does not necessarily provide a new theory of literature. Suffice it to say that up to this time most Freudian critical studies have devoted themselves to psychoanalyses of the artist[7] while making very questionable assumptions about the nature of his accomplished work, or else they have occupied themselves with the effect of the work upon the reader and have thus tended to move off into studies in reader psychology.

The most fruitful and intensive application to literature of something like a new "science of tropes" has in fact come out of the influence of Richards rather than that of Freud, and this fact itself serves to point a difference between Richards' affectivism and Freud's. (That some of the most brilliant "Freudian" critical studies have been written by critics like William Empson, who are even more deeply indebted to Richards,

---

[6] *The Liberal Imagination*, p. 53.

[7] See, for example, Ernest Jones, *Hamlet and Oedipus* (London, 1911), in which he attempts to probe into "the deeper working of Shakespeare's mind." Trilling's criticism of Jones's assumption is to be found in *The Liberal Imagination*, pp. 48–51. See also Daniel E. Schneider, *The Psycho-Analyst and the Artist*, (New York, 1950); and Ernst Kris, *Psychoanalytic Exploration in Art*, (New York, 1952). Dr. Kris makes the comment (p. 286) that "Literary critics seem of late weary of the intrusion of psychoanalysis. However politely, they assert—and rightly so—their independence."

tends to confirm this point.) As Susanne Langer has put it: to make all art a natural self-expressive function like dream and "make-believe" tends to put good art and bad art on a par. "One does not say of a sleeper that he dreams clumsily, nor of a neurotic that his symptoms are carelessly strung together; but a poem may certainly be charged with ineptitude or carelessness." [8] Richards, on the other hand, has from the beginning focused attention upon the problem of discriminating good art from bad and he has to a remarkable degree, sometimes one feels in spite of his own more extravagant theories, stressed the organic structure of the work itself.

SUPPLEMENT

Selection will be sure to take care of itself, for it has a constant motive behind it. That motive is simply experience. As people feel life, so they will feel the art that is most closely related to it. This closeness of relation is what we should never forget in talking of the effort of the novel. Many people speak of it as a factitious, artificial form, a product of ingenuity, the business of which is to alter and arrange the things that surround us, to translate them into conventional, traditional moulds. This, however, is a view of the matter which carries us but a very short way, condemns the art to an eternal repetition of a few familiar *clichés*, cuts short its development, and leads us straight up to a dead wall. Catching the very note and trick, the strange irregular rhythm of life, that is the attempt whose strenuous force keeps Fiction upon her feet. In proportion as in what she offers us we see life *without* rearrangement do we feel that we are touching the truth; in proportion as we see it *with* rearrangement do we feel that we are being put off with a substitute, a compromise and convention. It is not uncommon to hear an extraordinary assurance of remark in regard to this matter of rearranging, which is often spoken of as if it were the last word of art. Mr. Besant seems to me in danger of falling into the great error with his rather unguarded talk about "selection." Art is essentially selection, but it is a selection whose main care is to be typical, to be inclusive. For many people art means rose-coloured window-panes, and selection means picking a bouquet for Mrs. Grundy.

—Henry James, *The Art of Fiction* (New York, 1948), pp. 16–17

Irony arises when one tries, by the interaction of terms upon one another, to produce a *development* which uses all the terms. Hence, from the standpoint of this total form (this "perspective of perspectives"), none of the participating "sub-perspectives" can be treated as either precisely right or precisely wrong. They are all voices, or personalities, or positions, integrally affecting

[8] *Feeling and Form* (New York, 1953), p. 245.

one another. When the dialectic is properly formed, they are the number of characters needed to produce the total development. Hence, reverting to our suggestion that we might extend the synecdochic pattern to include such reversible pairs as disease-cure, hero-villain, active-passive, we should "ironically" note the function of the disease in "perfecting" the cure, or the function of the cure in "perpetuating" the influences of the disease. Or we should note that only through an internal and external experiencing of folly could we possess (in our intelligence or imagination) sufficient "characters" for some measure of development beyond folly.

People usually confuse the dialectic with the relativistic. Noting that the dialectic (or dramatic) explicitly attempts to establish a distinct set of characters, all of which protest variously at odds or on the bias with one another, they think no further. It is certainly relativistic, for instance, to state that any term (as per metaphor-perspective) can be seen from the point of view of any other term. But insofar as terms are thus encouraged to participate in an orderly parliamentary development, the dialectic of this participation produces (in the observer who considers the whole from the participation of all the terms rather than from the standpoint of any one participant) a "resultant certainty" of a different quality, necessarily ironic, since it requires that all the sub-certainties be considered as neither true nor false, but *contributory* (as were we to think of the resultant certainty or "perspective of perspectives" as a noun, and to think of all the contributory voices as necessary modifiers of that noun).

—Reprinted with permission of publishers from *A Grammar of Motives* by Kenneth Burke. Copyright, 1945, by Prentice-Hall, Inc.

It is possible to interpret aesthetic response in a purely subjectivistic manner by denying that aesthetic quality actually characterizes the object of awareness. The subjectivist admits that aesthetic response has psychological characteristics which distinguish it from other types of response. But he denies that some objects of awareness actually possess in greater or less degree an objective aesthetic character of their own. He explains the *apparent* objectivity of aesthetic quality by saying that we unconsciously project our aesthetic feelings into the object of our awareness, and thus ascribe to it a quality which the object itself completely lacks. The subjectivist may admit that some objects occasion this projection more readily than other objects, and that some aesthetic preferences are idiosyncratic, some more general, and some very widespread. But this fact is explained solely in terms of temperamental variations, social habits, and cultural traditions, and not at all in terms of the presence or absence of an aesthetic quality in different objects of awareness. Aesthetic quality is thus asserted to be merely a function of aesthetic evaluation, and evaluation, in turn, is not conceived to be the discovery of an objective quality in things. . . .

Aesthetic quality is, I believe, *as* objective as the secondary qualities of color and sound, and may (following G. E. Moore) be entitled a tertiary quality. It is "objective" in the sense of actually characterizing certain objects of awareness and not others, and therefore as awaiting discovery by the aesthetically sensitive observer. It is correctly described as "objective" because it satisfies the generic criterion of objectivity, namely, coercive order. Aesthetic quality is apprehended by the aesthetically-minded observer as a quality which presents itself to him with compelling power; which characterizes different objects in different degrees and in conformity to certain basic principles; which he can rediscover on different occasions and explore as he explores other objective qualities; and which other aesthetically sensitive observers can also discover and investigate.

I have adopted this position because it seems to me to do full justice to the sensitive layman's and the thoughtful critic's normal interpretation of the aesthetic experience, whereas the subjectivistic interpretation does unnecessary violence to this experience. . . . the burden of proof must rest with the iconoclastic philosopher. And no defense of subjectivism yet formulated seems to me to be compelling or even plausible. I shall therefore presume the objectivity of aesthetic quality in the following analysis.

—Theodore Meyer Greene, *The Arts and the Art of Criticism* (Princeton, 1947), p. 4, by permission of Princeton University Press, Publishers.

CHAPTER 28

THE SEMANTIC PRINCIPLE

§ *Coleridge as a "semasiologist": his verbal analyses of imaginative syntheses—Richards' practical criticism and its cognitive implications—II. Empson's concern for multiplicity of meaning: his concept of ambiguity, his analyses of verbal structures, his psychologism, his ultimate repudiation of Richards' "two uses of language"—III. Richards' contextual theory of meaning—IV. the consequences of the contextual theory for rhythm and for the general interaction of words within a given context—Richards' definition of metaphor as a "transaction between contexts"—W. B. Stanford's account of metaphor as a "stereoscope of ideas"—V. Richards' "poetry of inclusion" related to his contextual theory of meaning: the significance of irony in this connection, as interpreted by Richards, and by R. P. Warren—VI. the problem of the width of context properly relevant to the discussion of a poem, and the related problem of "simplicity"—E. B. Burgum's method of rendering all poetry "complex" by viewing it in "sociological perspectives"—VII. Empsonian-Ricardian complexity and the protests it has evoked—VIII. its bearing upon lyric simplicity: its connection with the problem of simplicity as envisaged by Plotinus* §

RICHARDS' INTEREST IN SEMANTICS [1] HAS BEEN MENTIONED IN THE preceding chapter. In *The Meaning of Meaning*, written in collaboration with C. K. Ogden, the preferred term is "science of Symbolism." Such a science, the authors believed, had now become pos-

[1] In Charles W. Morris' terminology (see *Foundations of the Theory of Signs*, Vol. I, no. 2 of *The Encyclopaedia of Unified Science*, Chicago, 1938) *semantics* proper involves the reference of a sign to its object. It is a subdivision of the general

sible largely through developments in psychology.[2] The function of such a science would be to purify thinking of the errors and distortions forced upon it by the "Power of Words."

> . . . words may come between us and our objects in countless subtle ways, if we do not realize the nature of their power. In logic . . . they lead to the creation of bogus entities, the universals, properties and so forth. . . . By concentrating attention on themselves, words encourage the futile study of forms which has done so much to discredit Grammar; by the excitement which they provoke through their emotive force, discussion is for the most part rendered sterile; by the various types of Verbomania and Graphomania, the satisfaction of naming is realized, and the sense of personal power factitiously enhanced.[3]

But the power of words need not be merely negative; it can be positive and beneficent, and to this positive power Richards turns in his *Principles of Literary Criticism*. That book "endeavours to provide for the emotive function of language the same critical foundation" as *The Meaning of Meaning* attempted to provide "for the symbolic [i.e., referential]." [4]

Even in Richards' earliest work his concern for semantic analysis—the subtle and elaborate examination of verbal complexities—is evident. His discussion of Coleridge will show how closely synaesthesis and semantics are in practice associated in Richards' mind. Richards finds in Coleridge's celebrated description of the imagination as a "synthetic and magical" power an early hint of the doctrine of synaesthesis.[5] Coleridge's discussion of concrete instances of the "synthetic and magical power" reveals him to be a *semasiologist*, that is, a man centrally concerned with "the meanings of words," and as part of this concern, anxious to inquire into "the behaviour of words in poetry." [6] Moreover, Coleridge's account of the behavior of words in certain passages of Shakespeare's *Venus and Adonis* provides admirable instances of poetic analysis. For example, Richards quotes Coleridge's commentary upon the lines:

> Look! how a bright star shooteth from the sky,
> So glides he in the night from Venus' eye.

study of linguistics signs, which is *semiotic*. (The other subdivisions of semiotic are the *syntactical*, having to do with the relations of linguistic signs to one another, and the *pragmatic*, having to do with the practical effects of such signs.) Richards occasionally makes use of the term *semiology*, and, as we shall see, he refers to Coleridge as a *semasiologist*.

[2] *The Meaning of Meaning* (New York, 1923), p. 8.

[3] *Meaning of Meaning*, p. 45, by permission of the publisher, Harcourt, Brace and Company, Inc.

[4] See the Preface to the second edition of *The Meaning of Meaning* (1926).

[5] *Principles of Literary Criticism*, pp. 242 ff.

[6] *Coleridge on Imagination*, pp. xi–xii.

Coleridge emphasizes the number of "images and feelings" that

> are here brought together without effort and without discord—
> the beauty of Adonis—the rapidity of his flight—the yearning
> yet helplessness of the enamoured gazer. . . .

And Richards, picking up the theme, enlarges further upon the intercon-
nections among the various images.[7]

A great deal of Richards' practical criticism, much of it incidental
to the stated topic of discussion and scattered through his various books,
is criticism of this kind. For an impressive body of such criticism, however, it is convenient at this point to turn to the work of Richards' pupil,
William Empson. Empson's contributions to this kind of criticism are
more extensive than those of Richards and they are on the whole more
daringly ingenious. They illustrate the substantial achievement of semantic analysis; they also reveal some of the problems that it raises.

II

EMPSON, impressed by the multiplicity of meanings revealed in an analysis by Robert Graves and Laura Riding of Shakespeare's sonnet "The
Expense of Spirit in a Waste of Shame," [8] set out to explore the applica-
bility of this kind of analysis to English poetry in general. The result
was the publication in 1930 of his brilliant study *Seven Types of Ambiguity*. The choice of the term "ambiguity" was perhaps not altogether
happy, for this term reflects the point of view of expository prose, where
one meaning, and only one meaning, is wanted. The presence of a second or third meaning creates a puzzle. The man habituated to expository
prose asks: which is *the* meaning? [9] Because the term "ambiguity" con-
notes doubt and puzzlement, Philip Wheelwright has argued that we need
a more positive term, and one that will suggest richness of meaning. He
proposes *plurisignation*.[1]

---

[7] *Coleridge on Imagination*, pp. 82-3. M. H. Abrams in *The Mirror and the
Lamp* (New York, 1953), p. 182, criticizes Richards for translating "the difference
between the products of the faculties [of fancy and imagination as distinguished by
Coleridge] into that of the number of 'links' or cross-connections' between their
'units of meaning.' " Cf. *ante* Chapter 18.

[8] Robert Graves and Laura Riding, *A Survey of Modernist Poetry* (New York,
1929).

[9] So also with the literary theorists of the past, including Aristotle. As W. B.
Stanford points out in his *Ambiguity in Greek Literature* (Oxford, 1939), p. 1,
Aristotle was "inclined to consider all ambiguity as a perversion or failing of language instead of its natural and valuable quality. . . . he allowed the danger of dialectical dishonesty in ambiguities to obscure their poetic value—and this even in his
literary criticism." Yet ambiguity is, in Stanford's words, "a natural, subtle and effective instrument for poetry and dramatic purposes," and for that reason it occurs very
frequently in Greek literature.

[1] *The Burning Fountain* (Bloomington, 1954), p. 61.

Whatever the proper term, the phenomenon in question is one of multiple implication, as a typical passage of Empsonian analysis will reveal:

When a word is selected as a "vivid detail," as particular for general, a reader may suspect alternative reasons why it has been selected; indeed the author might find it hard to say. When there are several such words there may be alternative ways of viewing them in order of importance.

> Pan is our All, by him we breathe, we live,
> We move, we are; . . .
> But when he frowns, the sheep, alas,
> The shepherds wither, and the grass.
> (Ben Jonson, *Pan's Anniversary*)

Alas, the word explaining which of the items in this list we are to take most seriously, belongs to the *sheep* by proximity and the break in the line, to the *grass* by rhyming with it, and to the *shepherds*, humble though they may be, by the processes of human judgment; so that all three are given due attention, and the balance of the verse is maintained. The Biblical suggestions of *grass* as symbolic of the life of man ("in the mornings it is green and groweth up; in the evening it is cut down, dried up, and withered") add to the solemnity; or from another point of view make the passage absurdly blasphemous, because Pan here is James I. The grace, the pathos, the "sheer song" of the couplet is given by an enforced subtlety of intonation, from the difficulty of saying it so as to bring out all the implications.[2]

Empson's classification of ambiguities into *seven* types is not, as he himself makes clear, to be pressed too hard. The types overlap and at points the definitions are highly arbitrary. Some such classification was apparently necessary to allow him to lay out his material and to provide him with a framework for the many acute analyses of particular poems —analyses which brought home to a whole generation of readers the fact of the manysidedness of language. That would be our perhaps biased way of disposing of the scheme itself, and of acknowledging the qualifications of his scheme that Empson himself has made.

Empson has a general psychologistic bias which comes out clearly in such a passage as the following:

Ambiguities of this sort [he has been discussing Shakespeare's sonnet XVI] may be divided into those which, once understood,

[2] Quoted from the second edition of *Seven Types of Ambiguity* (New York, 1947), p. 27. Reprinted by permission of the publishers, New Directions.

remain an intelligible unit in the mind; those in which the pleasure belongs to the act of working out and understanding, which must at each reading, though with less labour, be repeated; and those in which the ambiguity works best if it is never discovered. Which class any particular poem belongs to depends in part *on your own mental habits and critical opinions.*[3]

This is to classify in terms of the reader rather than the poem. The second kind of ambiguity (in which the "act of working out and understanding . . . must . . . be repeated") would seem to be in fact merely an imperfectly apprehended version of the first kind. That is, if the labor of working out the meaning becomes, on further readings, progressively less, one might plausibly expect that it would eventually disappear. But it is for the third kind of ambiguity that Empson provides a completely baffling definition. Here the reader is required to be *unaware* that he is confronted with an ambiguity, for this third kind is said to work "best if it is never discovered." What Empson has done is to classify three kinds of response—not three kinds of poems, but three grades of reading.

Empson's general psychologistic emphasis has an important negative bearing on the problem of evaluation. His "method" can obviously be applied to a poor poem just as easily as to a good one—a fact of which he himself is well aware. For example, in discussing Eliot's criticism of the first stanzas of Shelley's "Sky Lark," he proceeds to show how the various images which Eliot believed to be unrelated could actually be related; but he goes on to remark of his own analysis:

> At the same time the thought [in Shelley's poem] seems excessively confused; this muddle of ideas clogging an apparently simple lyrical flow may be explained, but it is not therefore justified; and it is evident that a hearty appetite for this . . . type of ambiguity would apologise for, would be able to extract pleasure from, very bad poetry indeed.[4]

In at least one passage in *Seven Types* Empson does attempt to deal explicitly with the problem of value. An ambiguity is valuable, he says, and not merely a bothersome muddle "in so far as [it] . . . sustains intricacy, delicacy, or compression of thought, or is an opportunism devoted to saying quickly what the reader already understands." But ambiguity is a nuisance—Empson's precise phrase is "not to be respected"—in so far as "it is due to weakness or thinness of thought," when it "obscures the matter in hand unnecessarily," or when, because it is so removed from the focus of interest, its presence gives the reader "a general impression of incoherence." A valuable ambiguity is indeed a "plurisignation," add-

---

[3] *Seven Types* (1947), p. 57. The italics are ours.
[4] *Seven Types* (1947), p. 160.

ing richness and complexity to, but not obscuring, the structure of meaning.

The foregoing justification of ambiguity reflects the strong cognitive tendency that runs throughout Empson's criticism. But he has other passages in which the cognitive element is overshadowed or is suppressed in favor of other interests. Empson's inveterate psychologism constantly makes him put such questions as these: Why would a reader of such and such a kind find this ambiguous? What historical circumstances make the 18th-century reader, say, prone to take this rather than that as the primary meaning? Did the poet put this in by design or by inadvertence? Indeed, Empson's interest sometimes seems to be merely a curiosity as to what could be made of a particular passage if he simply gave his mind to the search for puzzles. His raccoon-like curiosity [5] perhaps goes a long way to account for the hostility toward Empson felt by many scholars and critics who have been able to see in his work only the naughtiness of the little boy who dismembers the clock in order to see what makes it go.

In his latest book,[6] the psychologism continues as a dominant element. In the literary analyses that occupy him here, Empson sometimes works overtly in terms of author psychology, speculating upon the author's unconscious motivations, his private beliefs, his sense of what kind of rhetorical tricks he could play upon his audience; sometimes, in terms of audience response, examining the ideas that the particular audience had inherited, the literary conventions to which it had been conditioned, its sensitivity or its stupidity. In one very important regard, however, *Complex Words* makes a signal advance toward a cognitive position. In his very first chapter, Empson finds it necessary to reject Richards' doctrine that the "Emotions of the words in poetry are independent of the Sense." In fact, Empson argues, whenever you find

> a case where there are alternative ways of interpreting a word's action, of which one can plausibly be called Cognitive and the other Emotive, it is the Cognitive one which is likely to have important effects on sentiment or character, and in general it does not depend on accepting false beliefs. But in general it does involve a belief of some kind . . . so that it is no use trying to chase belief-feelings out of the poetry altogether.[7]

[5] Compare Marianne Moore's lines on Kenneth Burke:

> and Burke is a
> psychologist—of acute, racoon-
> like curiosity.

From "Picking and Choosing," *Selected Poems* (London, 1935). A reviewer of Empson's book complained that: "Quite a number of Mr. Empson's analyses do not seem to have any properly critical conclusion; they are interesting only as a revelation of the poet's, or Mr. Empson's, ingenious mind."—*Criterion*, July, 1931.

[6] *The Structure of Complex Words* (New York, 1951).

[7] *Complex Words*, p. 10. All rights reserved. Reprinted by permission of the publisher, New Directions.

Empson makes the further observation that by the time Richards had come to write *The Philosophy of Rhetoric*, Richards himself "seems to have dropped the idea that a writer of poetry had better not worry about the Sense"; indeed, in this book he finds Richards arguing "that the only tolerable way to read poetry is to give the full Sense a very sharp control over the Emotion." [8]

III

THE comment upon the shift in Richards' emphasis is just. In his *Philosophy of Rhetoric* (1936), Richards seems to have quietly laid aside the distinction between the referential and the emotive aspects of language and to have devoted himself to an account of a new rhetoric founded upon semantic analysis.

> . . . the old Rhetoric treated ambiguity as a fault in language, and hoped to confine or eliminate it[;] the new Rhetoric sees it as an inevitable consequence of the power of language and as an indispensable means of most of our important utterances— especially in Poetry and Religion. [9]

Richards admits that the ambiguity of words is not absolute; a condition of general conformity among users is a condition of communication. "*That*," he writes, "no one would dream of disputing"; for language is a social fact as well as a part of personal experience. [1] Stable meanings derive from stable contexts. The meaning of a word like *knife* is rather stable, because the situations in which *knife* occurs are much the same. Stability may be imposed artificially. The stability of the meaning of *mass* as a technical term in physics has been established by limiting and specializing the contexts which we will take into account in using the word technically. Scientific terms are thus limited by convention to one "right or good use"—one proper meaning that the term always and invariably bears.

But this tidy arrangement, Richards goes on to say, is impossible outside of the technical language of the sciences, and most of our discourse, including some of our most important discourse, is not technically scientific. In nontechnical discourse, words "must shift their meanings." If they did not, "language, losing its subtlety with its suppleness, would lose also its power to serve us." [2] The last sentence is worth careful inspection. Not only does Richards see ambiguity as normal; he

[8] *Complex Words*, p. 14.
[9] *Philosophy of Rhetoric*, p. 40, by permission of the publishers, Oxford University Press, Inc.
[1] *Philosophy of Rhetoric*, p. 54.
[2] *Philosophy of Rhetoric*, p. 73.

couples "suppleness" of language with "subtlety." Terms that have lost their pliability, their capacity for being stretched or wrenched a little so as to apply to a new context, are no longer subtle terms. As terms become incapable of ambiguous use they become incapable of precise use.

This view runs quite counter to our conventional notions of precision of meaning, which are founded for the most part on the nature of scientific terminology. Richards had written much earlier in the *Principles* that "Words, when used . . . scientifically, not figuratively . . . , are capable of directing thought to a comparatively few features of the more common situations," [3] and he is making the same point here. Scientific language has its own kind of precision; but another kind of precision, or if not precision, then "subtlety," is required for "the topics with which all generally interesting discussion is concerned." [4]

Richards extends this view of meaning to include rhythm. Poetic rhythm, he had already argued in *Practical Criticism* (1929), influences and is influenced by meaning: ". . . the difference between good rhythm and bad is not simply a difference between certain sequences of sounds; it goes deeper, and to understand it we have to take note of the meanings of the words as well." [5]

We commonly think of rhythm as making a direct appeal to the emotions: a vigorous march is stirring, certain minor airs are plaintive. And, it should be pointed out, Richards does not take the extreme position of denying that the rhythm of a poem *as such* may have emotional efficacy. The actual sounds are important. They are the stuff with which the poet works—comparable, one supposes Richards would say, to the "dictionary" meanings of the words that the poet uses. But the "actual sounds . . . do not carry the whole responsibility for the rhythm." And if we want to praise or condemn the rhythm of a particular poem, we shall not be able, except in the loosest sort of way, to deal with rhythm apart from meaning. [6]

Richards exhibits a phonetic dummy in nonsense syllables of Stanza XV of Milton's "On the Morning of Christ's Nativity." He challenges the reader to find in the dummy the aesthetic virtues which are sometimes ascribed to the "mere sound" of Milton's stanza, including its "expressiveness" as mere sound. If the reader of the dummy finds in it as a

[3] *Principles*, p. 131.
[4] *Philosophy of Rhetoric*, pp. 72–3.
[5] *Practical Criticism* (New York, 1929), p. 227.
[6] In *Practical Criticism*, p. 229, Richards says that the rhythm that we admire and feel that we detect in the sounds themselves is something that we "ascribe" to them. Later, in *Coleridge on Imagination*, p. 119, he puts the matter in terms nearer those of Coleridge: "The movement of the verse becomes the movement of the meaning; and prosody, as a study of verse-form apart from meaning, is seen to be a product of unwary abstraction. In saying that 'the sense of musical delight . . . is a gift of the imagination,' Coleridge set aside the conventional conception to restore a wholeness to our view of the act of speech. . . ."

mere series of sounds the phonetic virtue characterizing Milton's stanza, then successful verse must be amenable to a formula, for one can make up such dummies *ad infinitum*. If, on the other hand, the reader protests that the dummy is not a phonetic replica of Milton's sonnet, he is in reality arguing that the difference *in sound* between the dummy and original is what deprives the dummy of all merit. "In which case," Richards points out, the reader "will have to account for the curious fact that just those transformations which redeem it as sound, should also give it the sense and feeling we find in Milton. A staggering coincidence, unless the meaning were highly relevant to the effect of the form." [7]

IV

AT THIS point it may be well to summarize some of the consequences of what Richards calls broadly a "context" theory of meaning.

First, words interanimate one another. They are qualified by the whole context in which they figure, and they bring to that context powers derived from other contexts in which they have figured in the past. Much of modern criticism devoted to the "close reading of texts," including that of Empson, illustrates the subtle and rich complex of meaning which a finely wrought poetic context can yield.

Second, the problem of meaning—especially *the* meaning of a poem or drama or piece of fiction—is seen to be a matter not easily and summarily determined. It is not enough to seize upon one or two "statements" as indicating the thesis and to relegate everything else to the role of ornament or detailed illustration. "Statements" (such as "Beauty is truth" or "Ripeness is all") may indeed bear importantly upon the meaning of the whole work and may in some instance summarize that meaning, but not necessarily: they are subject to all the pulls and attractions of the other elements of the work.

Third, the poet necessarily tailor-makes his language as he explores his meaning. He does not (and cannot) "build up the meaning of his sentences as a mosaic is put together of discrete independent tesserae." The senses of the author's words are not such "fixed factors" as these. Instead, what we call the "meanings" of his words "are resultants which we arrive at only through the interplay of the interpretative possibilities of the whole utterance." [8]

---

[7] *Practical Criticism*, pp. 232-3. T. S. Eliot, following the main line of French symbolist doctrine, affirms the interconnection between rhythm and meaning quite as emphatically. In *The Music of Poetry* (Glasgow, 1942), he writes (p. 13): "the music of poetry is not something which exists apart from the meaning. Otherwise, we could have poetry of great musical beauty which made no sense, and I have never come across such poetry."

[8] *Philosophy of Rhetoric*, p. 55.

Fourth, the reader, like the writer, finds the meaning through a process of exploration. "Inference and guesswork!" Richards exclaims. "What else is interpretation? How, apart from inference and skilled guesswork, can we be supposed ever to understand a writer's or speaker's thought?" [9]

Fifth, in the light of the context theory, metaphor is seen to be a typical instance of the merging of contexts. A metaphor is more than a mere "comparison" that illustrates a point, or recommends a doctrine by lending it an attractive coloring. A metaphor is the linchpin joining two contexts, contexts which may be quite far apart and, in conventional discourse at least, utterly unrelated. The meaning achieved by a metaphor —and certainly by the most vigorous and powerful metaphor—is not simply a prettified version of an already stated meaning, but a new meaning in which imagination pushes itself forward and occupies new ground.

Mere vividness has never been the aspect of imagery that has interested Richards. He has countenanced neither Max Eastman's quest for intense realization, nor even T. E. Hulme's insistence that poetic language should "hand over sensations bodily." Poetry's inveterate concern for concrete particulars has for Richards a very different importance: concrete particularity means heterogeneity; it means difference; and it insures the sort of confrontation of unlike elements that is necessary to prevent discourse from collapsing into literal statement.

In fact, what determines that a given usage is metaphorical rather than literal is this linkage with a second context. As a test case, Richards instances Hamlet's question: "What should such fellows as I do crawling between earth and heaven?" Is *crawling* to be taken literally or metaphorically? Metaphorically, Richards answers. A baby literally crawls, and, on occasion, a man may literally crawl, but here "there is an unmistakable reference to other things that crawl," such things as cockroaches or snakes. If we substitute for *crawling, walking,* or more decisively still, the more general word *moving*, we shut out the context of *crawling* creatures and the use becomes literal. Metaphors die into fixed and literal terms when habitual usage confines them to one context: the *eye* of a needle or the *leg* of a table have lost all metaphoric force. They are no longer what Richards calls metaphor, "a transaction between contexts."

This last definition has a bearing on the problem of triteness, a topic we have touched upon in an earlier chapter.[1] It would be oversimple to conclude that every trite expression has become so through simple repetition. The attrition by repetition is only one, and perhaps not an essential, factor. Some expressions may attain triteness, and some have undoubtedly had triteness forced upon them, but some again are born trite. Even at a first hearing some phrases seem "shopworn." On the other hand, many

[9] *Philosophy of Rhetoric*, p. 53.
[1] Cf. *ante* Chapter 16, pp. 354–60.

readings do not impoverish Shakespeare's *King Lear*. Even passages like Hamlet's "Something is rotten in the state of Denmark," which may be said to have had triteness forced upon them, slough off their triteness at once when set back into the context of the whole play.

W. B. Stanford (whose *Ambiguity in Greek Literature* has been mentioned earlier in this chapter) calls metaphor a "stereoscope of ideas."[2] Stanford offers this definition:

> The term metaphor is fully valid only when applied to a very definite and a rather complicated concept, *viz.* the process and result of using a term (X) normally signifying an object or concept (A) in such a context that it must refer to another object or concept (B) which is distinct enough in characteristics from A to ensure that in the composite idea formed by the synthesis of the concepts A and B and now symbolized in the word X, the factors A and B retain their conceptual independence even while they merge in the unity symbolized by X. . . .[3]

Stanford says that the objects or concepts related by the metaphor must be sufficiently "distinct" to retain conceptual independence. Consider such an example as the following: "The dog raged like a wild beast." This sentence has almost no metaphoric force, for the dog, a tamed beast, is not sufficiently distinct from a wild beast. "The man raged like a wild beast" or "The sea raged like a wild beast" are poor enough as metaphor, but with the substitution of *man* or *sea*, a trace of metaphoric power begins to be perceptible.

Stanford's own metaphor of a stereoscope insists upon this necessary maintenance of difference: only by keeping the two pictures distinct can the stereoscope use them to create a third thing, the depth picture, which is a "synthesis" of the two flat pictures, a picture in which the flat pictures may be said to "merge" but which is in fact a third thing, quite different from either.

Metaphor "means" a third thing, different from the meaning of either of its terms taken in isolation. "The traditional theory," notes Richards, made metaphor seem to be only "a shifting and displacement of words," whereas "fundamentally it is a borrowing between and intercourse of *thoughts*, a transaction between contexts."[4] Metaphor is not merely "a grace or ornament or *added* power of language"; it is "its constitutive form."[5] And again, "*Thought* is metaphoric, and proceeds by comparison, and the metaphors of language derive therefrom."

---

[2] See his *Greek Metaphor* (Oxford, 1936), p. 105, by permission of the publishers, Oxford University Press, Inc.
[3] *Greek Metaphor*, p. 101.
[4] *Philosophy of Rhetoric*, p. 94.
[5] *Philosophy of Rhetoric*, p. 90.

V

WE ARE invited to apply the contextual theory of meaning as elaborated by Richards in his *Philosophy of Rhetoric* to his earlier distinction between a poetry of "exclusion" and a poetry of "inclusion." [6] That which is "excluded" for the sake of unity, one might argue, is a different "context." A sentimental love poem, to take an easy and obvious example, systematically excludes from its context such matters as doctors' bills, squalling babies, and the odors of the kitchen. Its unity depends upon the reader's viewing it from a certain perspective and in a certain light. When the reader, because of the enlargement of the relevant context, is forced to view such a poem from a different perspective, the essential flimsiness of the poem is revealed. The altered perspective reveals that the recalcitrant and contradictory elements of the experience in question have not been taken into account—they have simply been ignored. The poetry of "inclusion," on the other hand, systematically draws upon other and larger contexts. It has already made its peace with the recalcitrant and the contradictory. That is why it is, as Richards says, "invulnerable" to "ironic contemplation."

Thus might a sympathetic critic be expected to relate certain key terms of Richards' earlier critical theory to the "context" theory elaborated in his *Philosophy of Rhetoric*. Such an interpretation of Richards' views has the merit of implying a conception of irony congenial to that held by many critics of the present and of the recent past. For example, Henry James, in his Preface to *The Lesson of the Master*, declared that "operative" irony "implies and projects the possible other case" [7]—an observation possibly echoed by T. S. Eliot in his definition of wit as involving "a recognition, implicit in the expression of every experience, of other kinds of experience which are possible." [8] Such also is the function of irony described in R. P. Warren's "Pure and Impure Poetry" (1943). The unwillingness to face up to the "other possible case" constitutes for Warren the characteristic weakness of the "pure" poetry that avoids on principle any manifestation of irony and witty intellection.

Why, Warren asks, should a love poem, for instance, include in its make-up "self-contradictions, cleverness, irony, realism—all things which call us back to the world of prose and imperfection"? [9] He answers his

[6] Cf. I. A. Richards, *Principles of Literary Criticism* (New York, 1929), p. 240, the discussion of metaphor as "the supreme agent by which disparate and hitherto unconnected things are brought together in poetry."

[7] *The Art of the Novel*, introduction by R. P. Blackmur (New York, 1953), p. 222.

[8] "Andrew Marvell," *Selected Essays*, p. 262.

[9] "Pure and Impure Poetry," *The Kenyon Review*, V (Spring, 1943); reprinted in R. W. Stallman, *Critiques and Essays in Criticism, 1920-1948* (New York, 1949), p. 86, by permission of the author.

question by making a comparison of three love poems: Tennyson's "Now sleeps the crimson petal, now the white," Shelley's "Indian Serenade," and *Romeo and Juliet*. The first two poems aspire to purity of effect: they "exclude" the sordid and the realistic. *Romeo and Juliet* does not: it "includes" the bawdy jests of Mercutio, just outside the wall of Juliet's garden, and it includes the earthy and common-sense nurse who also has her bawdy jests and who will offer her counsel of half-measures and compromises. It is, as Warren puts it, as if the

> poet seems to say: "I know the worst that can be said on this subject, and I am giving fair warning. Read at your own risk."
>
> Let us return to one of the other gardens, in which there is no Mercutio or nurse, and in which the lady is more sympathetic. Let us mar its purity by installing Mercutio in the shrubbery, from which the poet was so careful to banish him. You can hear his comment when the lover says:
>
> > And a spirit in my feet
> > Hath led me—who knows how?
> > To thy chamber window, Sweet!
>
> And we can guess what the wicked tongue would have to say in response to the last stanza.
>
> It may be that the poet should have made his peace early with Mercutio, and have appealed to his better nature. For Mercutio seems to be glad to cooperate with a poet. But he must be invited; otherwise, he is apt to show a streak of merry vindictiveness about the finished product.[1]

Warren, for the sake of making his point, has proposed to "install" Mercutio "in the shrubbery." But in suggesting that poets should always make their peace with Mercutio, he implies that Mercutio is actually lurking in Shelley's poem all the time—and that he lurks in all poems. Mercutio, the implied argument runs, had best be invited for the simple reason that it does not lie in the poet's power to keep him away. The many-sided complexity of reality and the nature of language are facts that have to be reckoned with: only technical language—that is, language that allows a systematically literal reading—would seem to offer a setting quite bare of any cover in which a Mercutio might lurk. Looked at in this fashion, the exclusions made by a poetry that strains after purity reveal themselves as failures to develop and exploit latent meanings, meanings which, since they are in the words, must be brought to bear positively or else must be neglected in the hope that the neglect will not be noticed. In a poetry of "inclusion," the metaphoric potentialities have been taken into account. They have been harnessed to support each other and to sustain

[1] Stallman, p. 88.

the meaning of the whole. In a poetry of exclusion, the unrecognized and unused potentialities are a threat to any superficial unity that the poet has established: a vigorous and imaginative reading brings these elements to life—to the distraction of the poem.[2]

VI

Though Warren's essay seems to invite even a further development along the lines we have just indicated, it is only fair to observe that an exploration in this direction would uncover a series of problems not fully solved in Warren's essay, nor—for they are substantially the same problems—solved in the work of Empson and Richards.

A poetry capable of surviving an ironic contemplation must not, Warren would say, be purged of all "impurities" or, as Richards might put it, draw upon too narrow a context. Thus, these critics would seem to demand a certain complexity as the desideratum of any "good" poem. But, by insisting that poetry is a complex structure capable of richness (ambiguity) and toughness (irony), they have alarmed some readers by seeming to deny any value to simplicity. Their attack—or at least what those readers took to be an attack—upon a virtue so long honored by critics of all schools prompted sharp protests. But before looking directly at such protests, it may be well to notice at this juncture a second, closely related problem. It may be called the problem of relevant context.

This problem may be put as a question: against how wide a context should a given poem be read? A play like *Romeo and Juliet* obviously can appeal to, and make use of, much wider and richer contexts than any lyric can. What, in this connection, is the proper "magnitude" (if we may use Aristotle's term) of an art work? How many competing contexts must be active in a lyric in order for it to be properly and sufficiently complex?

Socially minded critics of our time sometimes dispose of the problem by disposing of simplicity. The Marxist E. B. Burgum, for example, argues[3] that there is no lyric so humble that it need be ashamed of its simplicity. There was nothing wrong with "Empson's method," but only with Empson's "non-social use of it." Burgum's use of the method applies "sociological perspectives" to poetry. Even though the closing choral

---

[2] What happens in such a case is analogous to what happens sometimes in bad prose when dead or benumbed metaphors, unwanted by the author who has failed to take their potentialities into account, waken into life, to the embarrassment of the whole passage. Such prose fares better under a superficial reading: it dare not invite, and may seriously suffer under, a vigorously imaginative reading.

[3] "The Cult of the Complex in Poetry," *Science and Society*, XV (Winter, 1951), 31–48.

lines of Aeschylus' *Prometheus Bound* [4] present no evident ambiguity, a more careful consideration manages to reveal that they imply two Greek philosophical systems, the religious and the materialistic, in conflict. Complexity enters "when it is recognized that the play is ending with this contradiction . . . unresolved." Burgum urges "the fact that the simplest idea becomes complex when related to human experience." [5]

The show-piece of the essay is Wordsworth's lyric "She dwelt among the untrodden ways." Though this poem, according to Burgum, would have to be regarded "in Empsonian terms" as simple and straightforward, it actually involves all sorts of complexity: the speaker is revealed to be conscious of his moral isolation; Lucy herself turns out to be a neurotic personality; [6] the value system as implied in the poem reveals itself as that of an era of rapid social change, and so forth. But in distinguishing the complexity that he finds in this poem from any complexity "in the phrasing (as Empson would put it)," Burgum, of course, has given over any specific literary problem, or rather he has denied that any specific literary problem exists. He treats Wordsworth's poem about Lucy as merely a document of the manners, morals, and value judgments of its age. The "problem of poetic meaning, like all problems of meaning, is fundamentally sociological." [7]

Burgum, in his exploration of complexity, does not stop with the poem conceived as a unit. By relating it to that grand manifold "human experience," he is able to propose that even a single line of poetry—his example is the Arnoldian touchstone "In his will is our peace"—is "complex." He obviously might have gone further still, for it is evident that by this sort of method one will be able to show just as convincingly that a single word possesses "complexity." For if Dante's line about God's will and our peace is "complex," the word "God," or the word "peace," with its varying and manifold implications, is "complex" also.

VII

MOST protests against Empsonian-Ricardian complexity have, however, stopped short of merging all poetic meaning into general psycho-socio-

---

[4] 'Tis Zeus who driveth his furies
  To smite me with terror and madness.
  O Mother Earth all-honored,
  O Air revolving thy light
  A common boon to all,
  Behold what wrongs I endure.
[5] *Science and Society*, XV, 43.
[6] Burgum's treatment of this poem makes the examples of the application of the historical method that we observed earlier in Chapter 24 seem very conservative indeed.
[7] *Science and Society*, XV, 37.

logical meaning. The protestants, indeed, have tended, when it came to a matter of the relevant context, to be strict constructionists. They have deplored Empson's method, not because it is "non-social" but because they think it implies a license to read "anything one likes" into the text. Such was the nature of the protest made by F. L. Lucas in his *Decline and Fall of the Romantic Ideal* (1937).[8] Another typical protest was that voiced by Donald Stauffer: critics who insisted upon the complexity of poetry were guilty of partial sympathies: they demanded that all poems be "original, spare, and strange" and thus disparaged verses written "with simplicity and sentiment." [9] What, he asked, would such critics do with the simple lyrics of a Wordsworth or a Blake? Or with the simple eloquence of the Psalms?

There is often latent in such protests the misconception that a complex structure must necessarily reflect an equally complex intention on the writer's part. The poem could not be so complex as Empsonian analysis would make it, for that would argue that the writer was intolerably self-conscious. To this criticism, Richards and Empson would no doubt answer that it is naive to equate a theory of structure with a theory of composition.

A second misconception reveals itself when someone offers a great line or a memorable passage of poetry as an example of how truly *simple* great poetry can be, *forgetting* that it depends for its power upon the great literary context from which it has been taken. Thus Herbert Muller, echoing the method of Matthew Arnold,[1] has quoted brief memorable passages from Shakespeare and Dante as proof of the poetic power to be found in the simple statement of a great master.[2] It may be hard for us to realize how powerfully the context of a great literary work may qualify our reading of a passage that we *believe* we are dealing with in isolation. Shakespeare's "Ripeness is all," for example, may seem movingly eloquent because of its very naked simplicity, but if we repeat "Ripeness is all" to someone who *really* knows nothing of its context, especially if we divorce it from all literary contexts by speaking it casually at a fruit-stand, we shall find that its eloquence has been lost upon our auditor. For him it will not be poetry at all.[3]

[8] "In a recent work with the apocalyptic title, *Seven Types of Ambiguity*, it has been revealed to an admiring public that the more ways a poem can be misunderstood, the better it is" (p. 228).

[9] "The *Mesures* Lectures," *Kenyon Review*, IV (Autumn, 1942), pp. 412–13.

[1] Cf. *ante* Chapter 20.

[2] "The New Criticism in Poetry," *The Southern Review*, VI (Spring, 1941), 823.

[3] The whole matter of context is rightly seen by historical critics to be very important. How much can one poem be isolated from the context of the author's work in general? (Blake's "Lamb" taken in isolation is not quite the same poem as when viewed as a part of a whole which is the *Songs of Innocence*; it becomes a third thing when paired with "The Tiger" and viewed as one half of a double poem.)

The problem of "simplicity" has its complications. They begin to emerge as soon as we notice how little a "simple" lyric differs in its general structure from a "complex" poem. Warren urges this consideration in the essay we have previously cited. He argues there very persuasively for a considerable complexity in "Western wind, when wilt thou blow," a tiny four-line lyric usually celebrated as a pure cry of the heart.[4]

VIII

AN AMUSING illustration of the amount of complexity that may lurk beneath a commonly accepted simplicity is provided by Laura Riding and Robert Graves. In their *Pamphlet Against Anthologies*,[5] published one year before their *Survey of Modernist Poetry* which was to send William Empson out upon his career of semantic analysis,[6] they set forth a detailed discussion of the complications of meaning to be found in Wordsworth's "A Slumber Did My Spirit Seal."

Convinced that William Wordsworth was too "simple" and straightforward to have "meant" the logical contradictions that they found in his little poem, they experimented with a rewriting to correct Wordsworth's mistakes.

> The details [of the poem] are even more illogical than the main argument. Apparently what Wordsworth has in his mind is that "I thought once she was non-human in a spiritual sense, but now she is dead I find her non-human in the very opposite sense." But all the words have got misplaced. "Spirit" has got attached to Wordsworth [A slumber did *my* spirit seal] when it should go with Lucy; "no human" [*I* had no human fears] likewise. There is a false comparison made between "A slumber did my spirit seal" and "She neither hears nor sees." "Trees" is an irrelevant climax to "rocks and stones." "Thing" should not qualify the first Lucy [She seemed a thing that could not feel] but should be with the second Lucy among the rocks and stones. . . . [The poem] would run more logically, something like this:

> A slumber sealed my *human fears*
>   For her mortality:
> Methought *her spirit* could withstand
>   The touch of earthly years.

[4] "Pure and Impure Poetry," Stallman, pp. 88–9.
[5] *A Pamphlet Against Anthologies* (London, 1928), by permission of the authors.
[6] See *ante* p. 637.

> Yet now her spirit fails, she is
> Less sentient than a *tree*,
> Rolled round in earth's diurnal course
> With rocks and stones and things.[7]

But the revision reduces the poem to a tidy emptiness: the loss of the rhymes is the very least of the losses incurred. Riding and Graves themselves prefer Wordsworth's own version of the poem, arguing that in spite of its illogical details, it has not a "sublogical" incoherence but a "supra-logical harmony." They justify the form that he has given to his poem by a kind of Longinian argument to the effect that the "inability of the mind to face the actual reality of death" mirrors itself here in the speaker's "inability to get the right words to pair off in a logical prose manner";[8] i.e., the speaker's very incoherence points to the depth of the emotional shock that he has suffered.

But this would seem to be an unnecessarily desperate line of defense. For it can be argued that Wordsworth's "misplacing" of words is the best placing of them. The apparent contradictions and violations of logic turn out to be in fact refinements of meaning and subtleties of statement. The lover, for example, is saying that Lucy's present strange slumber has waked him out of his—out of that strange slumber in which he, unable to conceive that *she* could ever feel the "touch of earthly years," had been indifferent to the possibility of her death. But now Lucy "feels" the touch of earthly years indeed in her very lack of feeling—in the numbing of hearing, sight, and her other senses at the touch of mortality. "No motion has she now," and yet her inert body is hurled in violent motion, along with the stones and the trees, as the planet spins them all in the empty whirl that measures out each earthly day and each of the "earthly years."[9] Be the proper justification of the poem what it may, Riding and Graves by their proposed revisions, clearly showed how far this "simple" poem departs from straightforward statement and how much it partakes of the ambiguous and the paradoxical.

Semantic analysis such as that associated with Richards and Empson does seem to imply a value in complexity itself. The great poems reveal an organic structure of parts intricately related to each other, and the totality of meaning in such a poem is rich and perhaps operative on several levels. In terms of this view of poetic excellence, a principal task of criticism—perhaps *the* task of criticism—is to make explicit to the reader the implicit manifold of meanings. That this view implies a rejection of any *simpliste* notion of art is quite clear; yet it is only

[7] *Pamphlet Against Anthologies*, pp. 128–9.
[8] *Pamphlet Against Anthologies*, p. 129.
[9] For the detail of such an interpretation, see Cleanth Brooks, "Irony as a Principle of Structure," *Literary Opinion in America* (New York, 1951), pp. 735–7.

fair to observe that there are senses of the term simplicity which the semantic critic does not need, and presumably does not want, to reject. In any case, the problem is not new. It goes back at least to Plotinus and the third century of our era. In an earlier chapter we noted that the term used for "simple" by Plotinus (*haplous*)

> may describe either *absence* of *internal differentiation* (as with the simplicity or unity of a pebble) or precisely the opposite, a high degree of *internal differentiation*—in other words, organic unity (as with the unity of a living body).[1]

For the semanticist, it is no praise to say that poetry is simple in the first sense. The sheer simplicity of the pebble is to be despised; a high degree of "internal differentiation" is praiseworthy. Our modern semantic criticism has insisted upon its debt (as through Richards) to Coleridge, remembering his emphasis upon organic form. But it might properly also pay its respects to one of Coleridge's masters, Plotinus. It might claim still another ancestor in the person of St. Augustine who wrote:

> Any beautiful object whatsoever is more worthy of praise in its totality as a whole than in any one of its parts. So great is the power of integrity and unity that what pleases as a part pleases much more in a unified whole.—*Contra Manichaeos*, I, xxi [2]

SUPPLEMENT

> We, too, had known golden hours
> When body and soul were in tune. . . .
> And would in the old grand manner
> Have sung from a resonant heart.
> But, pawed-at and gossipped-over
> By the promiscuous crowd,
> Concocted by editors
> Into spells to befuddle the crowd,
> All words like peace and love,
> All sane affirmative speech,
> Had been soiled, profaned, debased
> To a horrid mechanical screech:

[1] Cf. *ante* Chapter 7, p. 118.
[2] Cf. *ante* Chapter 7, p. 123.

No civil style survived
That pandaemonium
But the wry, the sotto-voce,
Ironic and monochrome:
And where should we find shelter
For joy or mere content
When little was left standing
But the suburb of dissent.

—"To Reinhold and Ursula Niebuhr," from *Nones* by W. H. Auden, copyright 1951 by W. H. Auden. Reprinted by permission of Random House, Inc.

In the celebrated description of cold weather in the beginning of *The Eve of St. Agnes* [ll. 14–16], the poet intensifies the cold with the added suggestion of silence and immobility. It is not a blustery north-wind that he has described, but the penetrating cold of a still, dead air. In the second stanza of the poem, Keats makes use of three puns, which, *though often unnoticed*, assist in the poetic fusion of ideas.

In the first stanza he begins with the outside world. The sheep are silent; and when the hare moves, it is in a limp, a cataleptic movement from one rigid posture to another. The poet then moves inside to the monk, in the attitude of prayer, or moving down the chapel aisle with the slow shuffle of age, a muffled noise which in the deserted chapel accentuates the stillness and the cold.

Following the first quatrain of the second stanza, however, Keats moves away from all forms of life to the complete immobility of art, "the foster child of silence and slow time." Each of three successive lines contains a pun, but so fused in the imagination are the various suggestions of the three words that *the reader is unaware of the poetic alchemy*. The most obvious perhaps is "freeze" in line 14, which, while establishing the relationship of coldness with the stone figures, at the same time reemphasizes the immobility and imprisonment of the "sculptured dead" by fixing them in a frieze along the chapel walls.

In line 15, in "rails," Keats undoubtedly has in mind a word derived from OE *hrægl*, "garment, dress, cloak," which according to the NED was *last used in this sense in the thirteenth century* in "The Owl and the Nightingale." The more obvious meaning of "rails" as bars strengthens the word "emprison'd" and indeed has a suggestion of coldness; but "purgatorial rails," or the bars which enclose purgatory, a place of punishment and unrest, suggest just the opposite of coldness and immobility, with which Keats is primarily concerned here. The other meaning of "rail" as a garment or a cloak has a subtle influence on the word "purgatory," quieting any suggestion of restlessness and torment, and presenting merely a picture of death and grave clothes.

In line 16, the word "orat'ries" likewise carries a double meaning. In such a poem so particularly concerned with the terminology as well as the atmosphere of the mediaeval church, "orat'ries" suggests other places of devotion, like the cold, deserted chapel Keats has just described, in which the knights and ladies prayed in a dimmer and more distant time. However, with its qualifying adjective "dumb" the word takes on its more obvious meaning in the secular world. The "orat'ries" are the words that might have been spoken in the articulated prayers of the dead figures, but which, frozen in stone, remain "dumb."

In the last two lines of the stanza, Keats returns to the monk to show the effect of the "sculptured dead" on his thin, meagre life. More than before, his weak spirit fails before the idea of death so subtly suggested in the cold silence of the chapel air. The three puns are not only inoffensive *to the point of being unnoticed:* they amplify beyond analysis the fused idea of stillness and cold culminating in death, which Keats wished to establish in the beginning of the poem, as a counterpoint to the happier idea of mobility and warmth leading to life, which in the climax of the poem is expressed in the consummated love of Madeline and Porphyro.

—Elmo Howell, "Keats' The Eve of St. Agnes, 14–16," *The Explicator,* XIV (February, 1956), No. 5, by permission of the editors. The italics are ours—with no real misgivings about the interpretation of them.

Words can be effective only if they have a definite meaning. And what defines the meaning of a word is its undeniable correspondence with certain things, certain feelings, the fact that it necessarily pledges acts. Now this correspondence ceases to be arbitrary only by virtue of a unanimous agreement, which is to say that it can be brought about only in the midst of a living group or community. A common tradition, law, faith and authority alone are capable of defining the meaning of what we call current words. But all these things have disappeared in our century. Then the words that circulate everywhere lead nowhere. Our language is *out of gear.* The more we speak the less we understand one another. Death alone can put everyone into agreement.

The twentieth century will appear in the future as a kind of verbal nightmare, of delirious cacophony: people spoke more often than they had ever spoken (imagine those radio stations which *can* no longer be silent day or night, where words are delivered at so much per minute, whether or not there are listeners, whether or not there are things to say), a time when words wore out faster than in any century of History, a time of prostitution of language, which was to be the measure of the true, and of which the Gospel says that at its source it is "the life and the light of men!"

Alas, what have we done with language! No longer able even to lie in certain mouths, language has fallen lower than the lie, I mean into insignificance. How the Devil rejoices over the pleasant or excited chatter of the radio-speakers! He, the great confusionist, who likes nothing better than flattering equivocation, the drone of official style, the senile incontinence of after-dinner verbiage. He, the romantic, who, when we are stupefied by speeches, suggests to us that the *inexpressible* is perhaps truer than clear, sharp speech! . . . He knows that . . . by . . . debasing the meaning of words he destroys the very basis of our loyalties. He knows that wherever a spade is called a spade, evil recedes and loses something of its prestige; this is why he has invented the language of diplomats and its insane coyness. He knows that nothing in the world can make us be silent, now that we have the radio, and he takes up his post in all the microphones. He finally organizes that verbal inflation, words no longer being "covered" by acts, which he hopes, not without reason, will complete, more effectively than the worst tyrannies, the utter confusion of our moral sense. . . .

I was about to write that the only remedy would be to combat him with *semantics*, which is the science of meanings, of precise and shaded language, guaranteed by a long tradition and by etymologies. A *Ministry of the Meaning of Words*, endowed with discretionary powers—this is what a Democracy needs—since after all it is a regime entirely founded on words.[3] (This ministry was formerly the Church. An analysis of our vocabularies would show that the little common sense which they preserve comes from biblical and liturgical reminiscences.)

> —Denis de Rougemont, *The Devil's Share*, trans. Haakon Chevalier (Pantheon Books, 1944), Chapter 64, "The Meaning of Words," pp. 211–13, by permission of the publishers, Pantheon Books, Inc.

---

[3] The parliamentary regime, social contracts, laws, public opinion, free press, meetings, conferences. The monarchy was founded on ritual, consecrated formulae, plastic ceremony. Dictatorship is the regime of blows where speech has ceased to be anything but planned and directed lying.

CHAPTER 29

ELIOT AND POUND: AN IMPERSONAL ART

§ *Eliot's classicism: discriminated from that of Matthew Arnold and Irving Babbitt, its relation to the French symbolists and particularly to Remy de Gourmont—II. T. E. Hulme's classicism: his association of the classic view of man with the religious view, his indifference towards kinds of subject matter, his exaltation of craftsmanship, his stress upon metaphor and on the organic character of the poem—III. Pound's insistence that poetry should possess the virtues of good prose, his interest in the Chinese ideograph as a paradigm of the poetic method, and his stress upon poetry as a kind of "inspired mathematics"—IV Eliot's doctrine of the impersonality of poetry, his association of the method of the 17th century "metaphysical" poets with that of the 19th century French symbolist poets—Eliot's theory of a "dissociation of sensibility" with its implications for a poetics of tension—V. his doctrine of the objective correlative—the attack upon that doctrine by Eliseo Vivas, and by Yvor Winters—VI. Winters' classicism: his indictment of the "fallacy of imitative form," his insistence upon the need for a rational structure, and his attack upon "qualitative progression" as a method for organizing a poem—VII. Winters' reprehension of irony as reflecting either the poet's carelessness or his irresponsibility: this view of irony contrasted with that held by Eliot and by Warren—VIII. Winters' criticism of modern poetry interpreted as a reassertion of the importance of "plot" and of dramatic organization—the implications of this view: the lyric as drama, metaphor as drama—IX. Eliot's doctrine of the impersonality of poetry reconsidered: the view that the poem has a "life" of its own, as interpreted by Eliot, and by Allen Tate* §

WHEN T. S. ELIOT ANNOUNCED IN 1928 THAT HE WAS A ROYALIST in politics, an Anglo-Catholic in religion, and a classicist in literature, the reaction was immediate and noisy. The revelation of his political and religious position elicited most of the cat-calls and solemn protests, but his profession of classicism drew its share too, mingled with expressions of honest bewilderment. For Eliot's own poetry was surely "romantic," was it not? And how could a poet who had obviously derived so much from the French symbolist poets of the 19th century maintain with a straight face that he honored "classicism"?

The line of descent from the classicism of Matthew Arnold to that of Eliot is certainly neither an evident nor an unbroken one. Of Arnold, Eliot has remarked that he "might have become a critic," [1] but had in fact devoted his energies to "attacking the uncritical." Though Irving Babbitt had been one of his teachers at Harvard, Eliot felt that Babbitt, like Arnold, had confused literary criticism with something else. Neither Babbitt nor his fellow neo-Humanist, Paul Elmer More, Eliot had been forced to conclude, was "primarily interested in art." Primarily they were moralists, and whereas he acknowledged that it was a "worthy and serious thing to be" a moralist, Eliot had had to write down Babbitt and More among his "Imperfect Critics." [2]

Yet Eliot made it plain in his essay entitled "The Perfect Critic" (1920) that he did not consider that the proper alternative to moralization was impressionism. A critic like Arthur Symons, for example, undertook to give us his impressions of the work in hand; but Eliot points out that it is impossible for the critic to rest there; for "the moment you try to put the impressions into words, you either begin to analyse and construct, to 'ériger en lois,' or you begin to create something else." [3] By taking the second alternative, Symons produced, instead of a work of criticism, a prose poem about his own responses.

Eliot had borrowed the phrase "*ériger en lois*" [4] from the French critic, Remy de Gourmont. The sentence from which it is taken serves as an epigraph for Eliot's whole essay, and strikes its keynote: the true critic will strive to build his impressions up into laws. His impressions will be subjective and personal—how could they be otherwise?—but because he will try to refer them to principles he will move away from mere impressionism toward objectivity. Aristotle is for Eliot the classic instance of such critical power, and of "all modern critics," he

---

[1] "Introduction," *The Sacred Wood* (1920), 2nd ed. (London, 1928), p. xiii, by permission of the author and of the publishers, Methuen and Co., Ltd.
[2] See "Imperfect Critics" (1920), *The Sacred Wood*, pp. 41-4.
[3] *The Sacred Wood*, p. 5.
[4] "*Ériger en lois ses impressions personelles, c'est le grand effort d'un homme s'il est sincère*" occurs in *Lettres à l'Amazone* (1914).

writes, "perhaps Remy de Gourmont [has] had most of the general intelligence of Aristotle." [5]

Eliot's emphasis upon the "generalizing power" and upon the critic's need to objectify gives the clue to his special kind of classicism. Of that we shall have more to say later in this chapter. But his collocation of the symbolist poet and critic, de Gourmont, with Symons, the author of *The Symbolist Movement in Literature*, is in itself significant. It points to the fact that important "classical" elements were to be found in a movement that it has been fashionable to regard as a "second wave" of Romanticism. Ezra Pound, Eliot's friend and fellow literary revolutionist, said flatly: "De Gourmont prepared our era; behind him there stretches a limitless darkness." Despite the fact that he had his beginning "in the symbolistes," de Gourmont becomes for Pound a restorer of "the light of the XVIIIth century." [6]

II

IN THIS general connection one ought to mention another conspicuous champion of the classical virtues, T. E. Hulme, who was a companion of Pound's in London during the years before the first World War, in which Hulme was to die in 1917. When Pound launched "Imagism" in 1912, one of his prime exhibits was a group of five short poems, devised by Hulme to illustrate a point in a literary discussion, and published by Pound half-jokingly as "the complete poetical works of T. E. Hulme." Between Hulme's critical theory and de Gourmont's there are numerous parallels, as René Taupin has shown; [7] and de Gourmont himself has commented upon the Imagist poets with special reference to their debt to the French symbolists:

> The English Imagists obviously proceed from the French Symbolists. One sees that first of all in their horror of the cliché, horror of rhetoric and the grandiose, of every oratorical and facile manner with which the imitators of Victor Hugo have always disgusted us; the precision of the language, the nakedness of vision, the concentration of thought which they love to fuse in a dominant image. [8]

[5] *The Sacred Wood*, p. 13.
[6] "Remy de Gourmont: a Distinction followed by Notes" (1919), *Instigations* (New York, 1920), p. 169.
[7] *L'Influence du Symbolisme Français sur la Poésie Américaine, 1910–1920* (Paris, 1929), pp. 84–5.
[8] *La France*, May 5, 1915; quoted by Taupin, p. 87.

Hulme published very little in his short lifetime. His *Speculations* (the source of all the passages that we shall quote below) did not appear until 1924. Much of his influence upon his contemporaries has therefore to be referred to his lectures and conversations. (He and Eliot, by the way, had no personal contact.) It has been argued that Hulme's actual influence upon his immediate generation was much slighter than our present-day reading of *Speculations* would suggest.[9] Yet the parallels between his position and Eliot's are striking.

Hulme, like Eliot's Harvard teacher, Irving Babbitt, referred romanticism to Jean Jacques Rousseau's notion that "man was by nature good, that it was only bad laws and customs that had suppressed him." In the Romantic view man is "an infinite reservoir of possibilities" and not as in the classical view, a creature "intrinsically limited, but disciplined by order and tradition to something fairly decent." Hulme considered the classical view to be "identical with the normal religious attitude." [1]

The traditionalism of Hulme is thus much more thoroughgoing than that of Babbitt or of Arnold. It goes behind Babbitt's "Humanism" and Arnold's participation in the Victorian Compromise, and thus anticipates almost precisely Eliot's criticism of Babbitt and Arnold. Hulme wanted a return to orthodox doctrine. His concern with religion had nothing to do with recapturing "the sentiment of Fra Angelico."

> What is important, is what nobody seems to realize—the dogmas like that of Original Sin, which are the closest expression of the categories of the religious attitude. That man is in no sense perfect, but a wretched creature, who can yet apprehend perfection. It is not, then, that I put up with the dogma for the sake of the sentiment, but that I may possibly swallow the sentiment for the sake of the dogma.[2]

But the relation of such orthodoxy to Hulme's views about actual works of verbal art might not be hit at first guess by an uninitiated person. Unlike Babbitt and unlike Arnold, Hulme is not marshalling

[9] Ezra Pound, for example, writes: "Without malice toward T. E. H. it now [1938] seems advisable to correct a distortion which can be found even in portly works of reference. The critical LIGHT during the years immediately pre-war in London shone not from Hulme but from Ford (Madox, etc.) in so far as it fell on writing at all. . . . It detracts no jot from the honour due Hulme that he had no monopoly of London literary life and did not crowd out other interests. . . . Hulme's broadside may have come later as a godsend when published. I have no doubt that the bleak and smeary 'Twenties' wretchedly needed his guidance, and the pity is that he wasn't there in person to keep down vermin. . . ." (*The Townsman*, January, 1938). Quoted from *The Poetry of Ezra Pound*, by Hugh Kenner (Norfolk, Conn. 1951), pp. 307–9.

[1] *Speculations* (New York, 1924), pp. 116–17, by permission of the publishers, Harcourt, Brace and Company, Inc.

[2] *Speculations*, p. 71.

ethical or religious views as a frame for a didactic theory of literature. On the contrary the classicism of Hulme is a form of objectivism which insists upon clear distinctions between ethical or religious doctrine and poetic composition. Hulme thought that poetry ought to recognize its limitations. In order to compete with religion poetry has to try to lug in the infinite, and the infinite in poetic form may be somewhat less than satisfactory. We encounter here mainly the *emotions* "that are grouped round the word infinite." We enter the area of "spilt religion," a certain romantic "damp." ³ What Hulme is getting round to saying is that if ethics and religion themselves are firm, art too will enjoy its own kind of "dry hardness" ⁴—not as a vehicle for, or simple statement of, ethics or religion, but as a human artifact taking shape in the same universe where ethics and religion are sustaining principles. Certain corollaries of this basic view form a cluster of doctrines which we shall see interacting rather tightly in the logic of the neo-classic criticism.

(1) There is no such thing as a "poetic" subject matter. Hulme wants to knock out both Arnold's high seriousness and the romantic distinction between fancy and imagination. "It doesn't matter an atom," he says, "that the emotion produced is not of dignified vagueness, but on the contrary amusing." ⁵ The Coleridgean "fixities and definites" are apparently just what the poetic fancy *should* be occupied with. For "the great aim is accurate, precise and definite description." ⁶ Fancy would be the proper faculty for producing the "cheerful, dry and sophisticated" verse that Hulme predicted was to come.

(2) The business of the poet is not personal expression but craft. Hulme's version of this doctrine is, looking toward the reader, an objection to the "sloppiness" which "doesn't consider that a poem is a poem unless it is moaning or whining about something or other." ⁷ The proper aim of the poet is to "get the exact curve of what he sees, whether it be an object or an idea in the mind." ⁸

(3) Poetry is a matter of images, metaphors. That much is entailed in the advice about accuracy just given. "Visual meanings can only be transferred by the new bowl of metaphor; prose is an old pot that lets them leak out. Images in verse are not mere decoration, but the very essence of an intuitive language." ⁹ And so we are led to dwell on a distinction between prose and poetry, and, borrowing some logical terms from Henri Bergson, to explain the difference as a difference between the "extensive" and the "intensive." Prose—that is, the mode of intellectual exposition—the use of language properly made by writers of cook

³ *Speculations*, p. 118.
⁴ *Speculations*, p. 126.
⁵ *Speculations*, p. 137.
⁶ *Speculations*, p. 132.
⁷ *Speculations*, p. 126.
⁸ *Speculations*, p. 132.
⁹ *Speculations*, p. 135.

books and legal constitutions and scientific treatises—deals with "extensive manifolds." Prose makes "diagrams, and diagrams are essentially things whose parts are separate one from another. The intellect always analyses—when there is a synthesis it is baffled." But poetry deals with "intensive" manifolds, and "to deal with the intensive you must use intuition," [1] and hence "images," which "are the very essence of an intuitive language." [9]

(4) Finally, the complexity with which poetry deals is not mechanical but organic. Each "part" of a poem is "modified by the other's presence, and each to a certain extent is the whole." [1] Hulme is bound to remind us here of the German romantics and Coleridge rather than of any classical or neo-classical source. His central essay, "Romanticism and Classicism," indeed makes extensive reference to Coleridge. Still Hulme does emphasize the art object more cleanly than Coleridge. And as we have seen he has a positive distaste for that expansive "genius," or mind producing the art object, which was Coleridge's chief distraction. Hulme is guilty of a good many references to the poet's sincerity and to the zest which goes into his poetic activity—yet in the end he seems to refer these experiences to the actual poem and to want to find their validation there if anywhere. He is giving us on the whole the classical and objective version of organicity, which to be sure is what appears in the Schlegels and other German "romantics," if not in Coleridge.

III

HULME's training as a student of philosophy enabled him to provide a rather systematic account of the new classic reaction. By contrast, Ezra Pound's most vigorous and most influential criticism is *ad hoc* and occasional. It has often taken the form of practical advice to other writers. Pound has not aspired to system-building; he has rather been concerned to "discover" a new author; to help him find his appropriate idiom; to preside over the formation of taste (one of his books bears the characteristic title, *The ABC of Reading*); to assist in the final revision of particular poems. (The most celebrated of these was Eliot's *The Waste Land*, which is dedicated to Pound as *Il Miglior Fabbro*.)

Pound's special critical emphasis reveals itself in a letter that he wrote in 1915 to Harriet Monroe: "Poetry," he says, "must be *as well written as prose*," a sentiment to be echoed by Eliot in his Introduction to Samuel Johnson's *The Vanity of Human Wishes*. In the same letter Pound went on to specify the "prose" virtues that he had in mind:

[9] *Speculations*, p. 135.
[1] *Speculations*, p. 139.

There must be no book words, no periphrases, no inversions. It must be as simple as De Maupassant's best prose, and as hard as Stendhal's. . . . Rhythm MUST have meaning. It can't be merely a careless dash off, with no grip and no real hold to the words and sense.. . . .

There must be no clichés, set phrases, stereotyped journalese. The only escape from such is by precision, a result of concentrated attention to what [one] is writing. . . . Objectivity and again objectivity, and expression: no hindside-beforeness, no straddled adjectives (as "addled mosses dank"), no Tennysonianness of speech; nothing—nothing that you couldn't, in some circumstance, in the stress of some emotion, actually say." [2]

For Pound, content and expression are coterminous. In a good poem, where every word performs its function, there is no room for an idle ornament or a vague expression or a mechanical and irrelevant rhythm. Form is expressive of meaning: ideally, form *is* meaning.[3] "Great literature," Pound writes, "is simply language charged with meaning to the utmost possible degree." [4]

Pound's ideal poetry has the "simplicity" (the economy) of good prose; and it has the "hardness" of good prose—as opposed to the vague and imprecise feeling that he like Hulme associated with "romantic" poetry. But poetry has in addition its own characteristic devices for rendering its meanings. Principal among them is something which Pound connects with the method of the Chinese ideogram.[5]

Pound was fascinated with the concrete particularity apparently enjoined by the Chinese written character. In reading Chinese, it seemed to him that one was not attending to a mere "juggling [of] mental counters," but was "watching *things* work out their fate." How did the Chinese write "Man sees horse"?

> . . . the Chinese method follows natural suggestion. First stands the man on his two legs. Second, his eye moves through space: a bold figure represented by running legs under an eye, a modified picture of an eye, a modified picture of running legs but unforgettable once you have seen it. Third stands the horse on his four legs.[6]

[2] *Letters of Ezra Pound*, ed. D. D. Paige (New York, 1950), pp. 48–9, by permission of the publishers, Harcourt, Brace and Company, Inc. Compare Coleridge's amusingly similar remarks in his *Biographia Literaria*, Chapters I and XVIII.
[3] Cf. Croce's position, *ante* Chapter 23.
[4] "How to Read" (1929), *Polite Essays* (Norfolk, Conn., 1939), p. 167.
[5] By 1913 Pound had encountered the writings of Ernest Fenollosa and in 1919 edited Fenollosa's "The Chinese Written Character as a Medium for Poetry." This work was reprinted in *Instigations* (New York, 1920).
[6] *Instigations*, p. 363.

Whether in any workable language the discrete elements could retain so much of their original integrity may perhaps be questioned. A comparison with English (which is a manifold of dead metaphors that resist all but the most unremitting attempts to resuscitate them) will be hardly reassuring. But in any case the Chinese ideogram provided Pound with a screen upon which to make a vivid projection of his ideal for a poetic language.

In such a language, the grip upon concrete particulars remains firm. The language resists a tendency (to which Pound believes the modern Western reader is particularly prone) either to slip into woolly abstractions or to take abstractions to be themselves *things*. The ideographic method of juxtaposing picturable elements not only seemed to inhibit shallow and oversimple abstractions: it allowed a skilful artist to define with subtlety and precision what he wanted to say: not this, and not that, but precisely *this*.

Pound's ideographic method is, of course, metaphoric in essence and Pound acknowledges as much: "[The ideographic] process is metaphor, the use of material images to suggest immaterial relations." [7] But it is not hard to see why Pound would welcome a new term, one which would avoid the notions of refinement and decoration that adhere to the term *metaphor*, and which would allow him to stress function and structure. The ideograph is an arrangement of concrete particulars; there is a confrontation of these, yielding not a denatured abstraction, but a precise concrete experience. In constructing his ideograph, the poet is as "impersonal" as the scientist. "Poetry," Pound wrote in 1910, "is a sort of inspired mathematics, which gives us equations, not for abstract figures, triangles, spheres, and the like, but equations for the human emotions." [8]

IV

IT WAS Eliot, however, who brought this matter of impersonality squarely to the attention of his generation. In "Tradition and the Individual Talent" (1919), Eliot stated the position with almost shocking emphasis:

> the poet has, not a "personality" to express, but a particular medium, which is only a medium and not a personality, in which impressions and experiences combine in peculiar and unexpected ways. Impressions and experiences which are important for the man may take no place in the poetry, and those which

[7] *Instigations*, p. 376.
[8] *The Spirit of Romance* (London, 1910), p. 5.

become important in the poetry may play quite a negligible part in the man, the personality.[9]

Such an "impersonal" conception of art is almost belligerently "anti-romantic." It focuses attention, "not upon the poet but upon the poetry." It thus emphasizes the art object as such. It represents a return to something like Aristotelian theory. Hardly since the 17th century had a critic writing in English so resolutely transposed poetic theory from the axis of pleasure versus pain to that of unity versus multiplicity.[1]

The relations among the parts that make up the art work become the important matter for critical investigation. That relationship is conceived to be complex. Eliot even suggests that the work of art is to be regarded as an organism, alive with a life of its own. Thus, in the Introduction to the 1928 edition of *The Sacred Wood*, he writes:

> We can only say that a poem, in some sense, has its own life; that its parts form something quite different from a body of neatly ordered biographical data; that the feeling, or emotion, or vision, resulting from the poem is something different from the feeling or emotion or vision in the mind of the poet.[2]

Such an emphasis was bound to bring down upon Eliot the charge that he had reduced the poet to an automaton who secreted his poem in some unconscious and brainless way, and that he had thus committed himself to the most "romantic" theory possible. We shall notice some of these attacks upon Eliot's theory of art a little later in this chapter. But for the moment we are concerned to round out a little further Eliot's "classicism," particularly in its more general aspects. For Eliot, as for Pound, the essence of poetry is metaphor; but the special insights that he brings to metaphor come, not from Chinese picture writing, but from the French symbolist poets of the 19th century and from the English "metaphysical" poets of the 17th.

Eliot refused to be upset by the notorious "conceits" of a Donne or a Herbert; their admitted failures did not impugn their successes. As for Dr. Johnson's criticism that these poets "yoked by violence together" the "most heterogeneous ideas," Eliot remarked that "a degree of heterogeneity of material compelled into unity by the operation of the poet's mind is omnipresent in poetry."[3] He accepted the

---

[9] *Selected Essays, 1917–1932* (New York, 1932), p. 8. Cf. also from the same essay (p. 11) "The emotion of art is impersonal. And the poet cannot reach this impersonality without surrendering himself wholly to the work to be done," and (p. 10) "Poetry is not a turning loose of emotion, but an escape from emotion; it is not the expression of personality, but an escape from personality." René Taupin has pointed out (pp. 212–15) the derivation of these notions from Remy de Gourmont's *Problème du Style*.

[1] Cf. *ante* Chapter 7, p. 134.

[2] *The Sacred Wood* (1928), p. x.

[3] "The Metaphysical Poets," *Selected Essays*, p. 243.

incongruity of the elements as inevitable: the perennial problem of the poet was to unite what resists unification; the skilful poet was the poet who could turn to positive account the very resistances set up by his materials.

Eliot found in the bold and often strenuous figurative language of the metaphysical poets the necessary means for achieving "a direct sensuous apprehension of thought, or a recreation of thought into feeling." [4] He saw that the problem of "acceptable" metaphor was continuous with the general problem of poetic unity. Thus he writes:

> A thought to Donne was an experience; it modified his sensibility. When a poet's mind is perfectly equipped for its work, it is constantly amalgamating disparate experience; the ordinary man's experience is chaotic, irregular, fragmentary. The latter falls in love, or reads Spinoza, and these two experiences have nothing to do with each other, or with the noise of the typewriter or the smell of cooking; in the mind of the poet these experiences are always forming new wholes. [5]

This power to "amalgamate disparate experience" was not limited to the metaphysical poets. It was possessed by the great Elizabethan dramatists. Dante possessed it. And coming nearer to our own time, Eliot discerned in some of the French symbolist poets "a method curiously similar to that of the 'metaphysical poets'. . . . Jules Laforgue and Tristan Corbière in many of his poems, are," he declared, "nearer to the 'school of Donne' than any modern English poet." [6]

Any lapse of this power to "amalgamate" results in the separation of thought and feeling, the poetic and the unpoetic, form and content. As applied to figurative language, it has the effect of making metaphor non-structural, a mere echo of the thought (illustration) or emotional excess baggage (ornamentation). A high point of his praise of Andrew Marvell is that Marvell's best verse satisfies "the elucidation of Imagination given by Coleridge: 'This power . . . reveals itself in the balance or reconcilement of opposite or discordant qualities. . . .' " [7] In terms reminiscent of Hulme, Eliot speaks of Marvell's "bright, hard precision," which, as achieved by Marvell, does not render his poetry less but more serious. Marvell's poetry, with its serious wit, challenges Coleridge's distinction between the fancy and the imagination, for many of the devices in Marvell's poetry that Coleridge would have to range under

---

[4] *Selected Essays,* p. 246.
[5] *Selected Essays,* p. 247.
[6] *Selected Essays,* pp. 248-9.
[7] "Andrew Marvell," *Selected Essays,* p. 258. In the same essay Eliot remarks that "in the verses of Marvell . . . there is the making of the familiar strange, and the strange familiar, which Coleridge attributed to good poetry."

fancy are actually used to achieve effects that show the full power of the imagination.

V

ELIOT's thoughts about an impersonal art arrived at their most celebrated formulation in an essay entitled "Hamlet and his Problems" (1919). Eliot wrote:

> The only way of expressing emotion in the form of art is by finding an "objective correlative"; in other words, a set of objects, a situation, a chain of events which shall be the formula of that *particular* emotion; such that when the external facts, which must terminate in sensory experience, are given, the emotion is immediately evoked.[8]

The phrase "objective correlative" has gained a currency probably far beyond anything that the author could have expected or intended. With the advantage of hindsight, it is easy to see why; the notion of an objective correlative puts the emphasis firmly upon the work itself as a structure. Since the poet cannot transfer his emotions or his idea from his own mind directly to his readers, there must be some kind of mediation —"a set of objects, a situation, a chain of events." It is through these that the transaction between author and reader necessarily takes place. This is where "what the author has to say" is objectified, and it is with the shape and character of this object that the critic is properly concerned. For this object is the primary source of, and warrant for, the reader's response, whatever that may be; and it is also the primary basis for whatever inferences we may draw about what it is that the "author wanted to say."

Yet the doctrine of the objective correlative is a kind of summation of what Eliot, along with Hulme and Pound, derived from the theory and practice of the French symbolists. The symbolists had argued that poetry cannot express emotion directly; emotions can only be evoked. And their studies had canvassed the various means by which this can be done. Baudelaire maintained that every color, sound, odor, conceptualized emotion, and every visual image has its correspondence in each of the other fields. Mallarmé, insisting that poetry was made, not of ideas, but of words,[9] devoted himself to exploring the potentialities of words

[8] *Selected Essays*, pp. 124-5. This notion is perhaps anticipated by Pound's phrase "equations for the human emotions": cf. *ante* p. 664.

[9] Degas tried to write sonnets and complained to Mallarmé that he was unsuccessful, despite all the ideas he had. "You don't write poems with ideas, my dear Degas," said Mallarmé, "but with words." P. Valéry, 'Poésie et Pensée Abstraite,' in *Variété* V (Paris, 1945), p. 141.

conceived as gesture or as modes of emotive suggestion, and treated the interplay of words as a kind of ballet or a kind of "musical" organization. To name an object was to destroy three-quarters of the delight proper to a poetic evocation of it. Pound, in making acknowledgement of "the great gifts of 'symbolisme,'" mentions specifically "the doctrine that one should 'suggest' not 'present.'"[1]

The doctrine of the "objective correlative" places a thoroughly anti-Romantic stress upon craftsmanship; but Eliot, in the way in which he argues it, manages to involve himself in the language of expressionism. This expressionism and the "language of the emotions" have come in for a vigorous overhauling by the philosopher Eliseo Vivas.[2]

Eliot has implied that Shakespeare knew in advance the particular emotion for which *Hamlet* was to be the "correlative," and has implied further that the reader (or auditor) ought to feel this particular emotion too, if the play is to be considered successful. But Vivas contends that in fact the poet only discovers his emotion through trying to formulate it in words. What the poet "really felt could only be expressed precisely in and through the poem, which is to say that he had to discover it through the act of composition."[3] It is impossible that the reader should ever feel the same emotion as the poet did, and there is no reason why he should. A poem expresses *less* than the emotion with which the poet began, but it also expresses much more. It expresses "all that which the poet presents objectively in it for apprehension."[4] Among the elements making up the poem-object,

> there are some that we find easier to denote. . . . through the terms which we use to denote emotions. But I see no reason to assume that all else in the poem is put there merely to arouse an emotion in us or to bring about its objective denotation. Surface, formal, and ideational elements are all in their own right of intrinsic interest. And while the emotion expressed is also of interest, it is not, and it should not be, of chief or exclusive interest to the reader.[5]

Vivas is confident that such objections have "devastating" consequences for Eliot's "critical approach"; and with special regard to the theory about *Hamlet*, that judgment may well be correct. As regards Eliot's general position, however, Vivas' criticism is a pruning operation that lops off excrescences but can hardly affect the main branches of the theory set forth in "Tradition and the Individual Talent." "Poetry is

[1] *Make It New* (New Haven, 1935), p. 187.
[2] "The Objective Correlative of T. S. Eliot," *The American Bookman*, Winter, 1944; reprinted in *Creation and Discovery* (New York: The Noonday Press, 1955). Reprinted by permission of the author.
[3] *Creation and Discovery*, p. 184.   [5] *Creation and Discovery*, p. 188.
[4] *Creation and Discovery*, p. 188.

not a turning loose of emotion. . . . it is not the expression of personality, but an escape from personality." [6] "Honest criticism and sensitive
appreciation are directed not upon the poet but upon the poetry." [7]
Eliot is at times inconsistent, but he seems never to subscribe seriously
to the notion that the poet's main job is to hand over to the reader
some determinate content, whether an emotion or an idea, or that
the poet's effectiveness is to be measured by the success of this transaction. On the contrary, the weight of Eliot's prestige has been thrown
behind a quite antithetical conception: an anti-Romantic, "impersonal"
art, in which the claims of the art-object, with all their complexity and
indeterminacy have first consideration. A less vulnerable statement of
the objective correlative might be found in another of Eliot's essays, that
"On the Metaphysical Poets": "[The metaphysical poets] were, at best,
engaged in the task of trying to find the verbal equivalent for states of
mind and feeling." [8] The phrase "states of mind and feeling" has the
merit of minimizing the notion of some pure emotion, personal to the
poet, with which the reader is to be directly infected.

VI

OTHER attacks on Eliot, notably those of Ransom and Yvor Winters,
have rested upon more fundamental disagreements. Ransom found Eliot's
criticism too psychologistic, too much concerned with affective experience and too little cognitive. [9] Eliot's classicism, in short, was not classical
enough. This was in part Winters' criticism; but Winters' classical reaction, which harks back to that of Irving Babbitt, has in it a strong
ethical ingredient. Winters castigates romanticism not merely for its
murky indefiniteness but for its moral delinquency. Indeed he regards
one as an aspect of the other. [1]

In the first place, Eliot's acknowledgement that the poem has in
some sense a life of its own seems to Winters a concession that goes
far toward making the poet merely an automaton. [2] And this is very bad
for poetry.

> The artistic process is one of moral evaluation of human experi-
> ence, by means of a technique which renders possible an evalua-
> tion more precise than any other. The poet tries to understand
> his experience in rational terms, to state his understanding, and

[6] *Selected Essays,* p. 10.
[7] *Selected Essays,* p. 7.
[8] *Selected Essays,* p. 248.
[9] Cf. *ante* Chapter 27.
[1] Compare the position of Tolstoy: see *ante* Chapter 21.
[2] Ransom makes the same point: "This is very nearly a doctrine of poetic
automatism" (*The New Criticism,* p. 152).

simultaneously to state, by means of the feelings which we attach to words, the kind and degree of emotion that should
properly be motivated by this understanding.[3]

Since the poet is making an evaluation, he must remain fully in control
of his poem; there must be no French-symbolist nonsense about letting
the reins lie loose upon the horse's neck, allowing him to find his own
way. Eliot trusts Pegasus too far when he writes: "I do not deny that
art may be affirmed to serve ends beyond itself; but art is not required
to be aware of these ends. . . ."[4] The poet must be aware of where he
is going; it is not enough for him merely to try to "find the verbal
equivalent of states of mind and feeling." Those states of mind and feeling
must be judged and evaluated.

Winters charges that Eliot was too often content merely to reflect
the disorder and incoherence of the age. Instead of mastering his experience and judging it, he simply mirrors it. To do this is to fall into
what Winters has called the "fallacy of expressive, or imitative, form;
the procedure in which the form succumbs to the raw material of the
poem."[5] The modern poet would justify the formlessness of his poem
by saying that he is writing about a chaotic and disordered age. But on
the basis of such reasoning as this one could argue that the proper way
to write a poem about madness is to make the poem itself insanely
irrational, and the proper way to write about dulness is for the poet to
make his *Dunciad* as dull and sleep-provoking as possible.

Winters has urged his indictment relentlessly. Eliot's *Waste Land*
betrays in its "limp" rhythms Mr. Eliot's own "spiritual limpness."[6]
Likewise Pound's "Hugh Selwyn Mauberly," St. John Perse's *Anabase*,
and Joyce's *Ulysses*—all are found guilty in some degree or other of the
fallacy of imitative form. Even a poet like Marianne Moore, whom Winters credits with "unshakeable certainty of intention"[7] as distinguished
from the romantic ironist's "moral insecurity," reveals in her poetry some
of the weaknesses of imitative form.

Fortunately, one does not have to endorse Winters' applications of
his principle in order to endorse the principle itself. Winters is clearly
right in pointing out that confusion cannot be rendered by confusion;
the negative, by the presentation of a slice of negation. This insight has
allowed him to put with special cogency several questions having to do
with the structure of poetry: what is the minimum coherence required
of a poem and by what structural methods is that coherence to be attained?

[3] *In Defense of Reason*, p. 464.
[4] "The Function of Criticism," *Selected Essays*, p. 13.
[5] *Primitivism and Decadence* (1937), included in *In Defense of Reason*, p. 41.
[6] *In Defense of Reason*, p. 22.
[7] *In Defense of Reason*, p. 71.

The poem must have a rational structure, for it is the rational structure that controls the emotion. The rational statement made by the poem is the "motive" for the emotion. Winters, to be sure, does not demand that the poem have an *explicitly* logical organization: it is enough that it be "implicitly rational." The test is whether the poem "can be paraphrased in general terms." [8] The last phrase does a great deal to remove the rigor from Winters' prescriptions. If the terms of the paraphrase be general enough, then any poem that "makes sense" can be paraphrased, including many poems to which Winters would deny a rational structure. Ezra Pound, for instance, has denied Winters' charge that he has abandoned "logic in the Cantos." Much depends upon what person is to apply the test of paraphrasability.

The rational statement that the poem makes—however necessary in Winters' scheme—is not the essence of the poem. Winters himself cites a poem in which the rational content as such says quite the reverse of what the poem taken as a whole "says." [9] The "moral attitude" that Winters insists the poem shall present is defined not by the "logical content alone" but by the feeling as well, and "the feeling is quite specific and unparaphrasable." Yet however indirect the influence of rational structure, it has its final importance, and Winters' censure of Eliot boils down to the charge that he gives "primacy . . . to the emotions." [1]

Certain structural methods yield poems that cannot be paraphrased. Many of our modern poets, laying aside such time-honored methods for organizing a poem as Repetition, Logical Method, and Narrative, have used what Winters calls "Pseudo-reference" and "Qualitative Progression." Pseudo-reference pretends to rational coherence (by retaining the "syntactic forms and much of the vocabulary of rational coherence") [2] but it is not really coherent. Qualitative Progression goes further and abandons even the pretence of rational progression. It is an attempt to build poetry out of the "connotative" (i.e., the suggestive) aspects of language alone, and it actually results in merely a blur of "reverie."

In Qualitative Progression, the transition from image to image is governed by mood: the principle of coherence is that of feeling. Qualitative Progression occurs in traditional poetry, to be sure, but only as an ancillary to the basic method of progression, not as the basic method itself. For example, in Shakespeare

> the qualitative progression . . . is peripheral, the central move-
> ment of each play being dependent upon . . . the psychology
> of the hero, or narrative logic, and so firmly dependent that oc-

---

[8] *In Defense of Reason*, p. 31.
[9] See his discussion of Allen Tate's "The Subway," *In Defense of Reason*, pp. 19–20.
[1] *In Defense of Reason*, p. 469.
[2] *In Defense of Reason*, p. 40.

casional excursions into the rationally irrelevant can be managed
with no loss of force, whereas in [Eliot's] *The Waste Land* the
qualitative progression is central: it is as if we should have a
dislocated series of scenes from *Hamlet* without the prince himself, or with too slight an account of his history for his presence
to be helpful. The difference between Mr. Eliot and Mr. Pound
is this: that in *The Waste Land*, the prince is briefly introduced
in the footnotes, whereas it is to be doubted that Mr. Pound
could manage such an introduction were he so inclined.[3]

Beneath Winters' polemics lurks an important distinction that de-
serves a clear restatement: emotions may be presented in one of two basic
ways. The poet can give the reasons for his hero's emotion, "motivating"
the emotion by giving us the events which produced it, or the poet can
define the emotion through a symbol or a series of analogies. One method,
of course, does not exclude the other. Shakespeare can give us the series
of dramatic events that prompt Hamlet's puzzled disgust with himself,
but he can also, and does, allow Hamlet to find an analogy for his feelings:
"O what a rogue and peasant slave am I!" Winters censures the modern
poet for relying too exclusively upon the second method: he moves in
an aimless and random reverie from image to image with only a kind of
stream-of-consciousness connection between the images. The result is
vagueness and obscurity. "The great discovery of the French symbolists,"
remarks the author of a recent book on Pound, "was the irrelevance,
and hence the possibility of abolition, of paraphrasable plot."[4] It is just
this abolition that Winters censures.

VII

WINTERS has defined a third structural method that he regards as rep-
rehensible. He calls it progression by Double Mood (i.e., by ironic
qualification). He regards Lord Byron as the first poet to use this method
on a "pretentious scale," but Jules Laforgue and Tristan Corbière yield
striking instances of it in modern poetry. In this kind of progression,
the poet alternates moods: he "builds up a somewhat grandiloquent effect
only to demolish it by ridicule or by ridiculous anticlimax."[5] Such a
method is "the formula for adolescent disillusionment: the unhappily
'cynical' reaction to the loss of a feeling not worth having."[6]

The deflation of the positive mood is accomplished by irony—ro-

[3] *In Defense of Reason*, p. 59.
[4] Hugh Kenner, *The Poetry of Ezra Pound*, p. 91.
[5] *In Defense of Reason*, p. 65.
[6] *In Defense of Reason*, p. 67.

mantic irony,[7] Winters calls it, carefully distinguishing it from the classical irony of a Dryden or a Pope, who was "perfectly secure in his own feelings"[8] and whose irony was used to attack someone else.

The romantic ironist is not morally secure and his irony is thus a reflection of his confusion or of his moral flabbiness or of his lack of concern to focus his poem. It amounts to "an admission of careless feeling, which is to say careless writing." Winters therefore recommends "the waste-basket and a new beginning."[9] For the poet cannot legitimately say: my confused and uncertain poem simply reflects the confusion of the situation which happens to be my subject matter. That would be to embrace the fallacy of imitative form.

Winters' bias toward the logical, the definite, and the unequivocal gives him a certain corrective value. He has refused to be imposed upon by misty and vague meanings, and he has been able to put his finger on tendencies toward incoherence that have escaped the notice of many other modern critics. But one may doubt whether Winters leaves sufficient room for what was once attributed to the superventions and ministering grace bestowed by the Muse. Winters assumes that the poet knows (or ought to know) how to "adjust feeling"[1] to the rational structure of his poem, and that his failure to do so is a kind of moral failure. Thus, he places a great burden upon the poet's conscious intention, more perhaps than it can sustain. For as Vivas, for instance, has pointed out (see p. 668 above) the poet often *discovers* what he has to say in the process of saying it. Furthermore, Winters perhaps needs to be reminded of Mallarmé's dry observation that poetry is written not with ideas, but with words. The poet has to take into account not only the complexities of experience but the recalcitrant qualities of language; he must always depend, to some degree, upon implication and indirection.

Eliot's suggestion that a poem "has its own life" acknowledges its resistance to direct control by the poet. So do Eliot's reiterations that all poetry, even a lyric from the Greek anthology, is *dramatic*.[2] There may be some significance in the fact that Winters defines poetry as a *statement*. (He regards it as a statement of a special kind, to be sure, but a statement, nevertheless.) Winters never quite escapes, nor apparently does he wish to escape, the consequences of this term.

A curious passage in *Primitivism and Decadence* illustrates Winters' suspicion of "dramatic" presentation. He quotes with approval a student's

[7] Winters borrows the term from Irving Babbitt (cf. *ante* Chapter 20), whose use of the term was influenced by his unsympathetic response to the German critics' development of irony: cf. *ante* Chapter 17.
[8] *In Defense of Reason*, p. 70.
[9] *In Defense of Reason*, p. 73.
[1] *In Defense of Reason*, p. 367.
[2] "A Dialogue on Dramatic Poetry" (1928), *Selected Essays*, p. 38.

remark that "Laforgue resembles a person who speaks with undue harshness and then apologizes; whereas he should have made the necessary subtractions before speaking." [3] A considered *statement* does indeed require that one make the "subtractions" first, but the mode of *drama* undertakes to give us the very process by which the final attitude is reached: the "subtractions," the conflicts between rival attitudes, the ironic qualifications, the various stages in the dialectic—all of these are of the essence of dramatic presentation. For Winters, however, the issue comes down to this: "the question of how carefully one is willing to scrutinize his feelings and correct them." [4] So it does, and Winters is right in demanding that the poet refrain from "careless feeling, which is to say careless writing." That is to say, the poet should not correct his poem in public as it goes along. For such botching, Winters' recommendation is surely the proper one: "instead of irony as the remedy for the unsatisfactory feelings," the "wastebasket and a new beginning." But it can be argued that irony has other and more respectable functions.

Once the dramatic character of poetry is admitted, we make room for a very different conception of irony. Irony becomes a recognition of the incongruities with which poetry has to deal. It acknowledges the pressure of the total context upon the individual word or image, the slight warping of signification continually made by the poet as he shades the word to its precise meaning in his context. It registers the tensions set up between the disparate elements of the poem which are being compelled into unity. It concedes the element of compulsion.

If one insists in finding in this structural irony an index of the poet's attitude, that attitude is not necessarily one of carelessness or cynicism or moral slovenliness. The irony might rather point to his humility, to his sense of the limitations of the human mind and of the complexity of experience. Such a poet is willing to qualify his more sweeping generalizations and to undercut his more fervent enthusiasms. [5]

Most of what Eliot has had to say on this specific topic occurs in his essay on Marvell under the rubric "wit." Marvell's wit is "a tough rea-

[3] *In Defense of Reason*, p. 72.
[4] *In Defense of Reason*, p. 72.
[5] Much turns here upon whether one accepts the view that some measure of indirection is enjoined upon the poet by the very nature of poetry. To the man habituated to the motorboat of logic, the manoeuvers of a sailing vessel forced to tack against the wind will seem wasteful and silly. He may even accuse the skipper of drunkenness or of moral vacillation.

T. E. Hulme definitely found in his "classical" poetry a manifestation of the poet's humility and of his sense of his own limitations. Hulme wrote that even in "the most imaginative flights" of the classical poet, there is "always a holding back, a reservation. The classical poet never forgets this finiteness, this limit of man. . . . If you say an extravagant thing which does exceed the limits inside which you know man to be fastened, yet there is always conveyed in some way at the end an impression of yourself standing outside it, and not believing it, or consciously putting it forward as a flourish" (*Speculations*, pp. 119-20).

sonableness beneath the slight lyric grace"; it "implies a constant inspection and criticism of experience";[6] it provides for his poetry an "internal equilibrium."[7] But R. P. Warren will provide a good instance of the tendency of critics influenced by Eliot to use the term irony itself as a structural principle. In an essay from which we have already quoted he tries to answer the argument that poetry ought to be eloquently simple without ironic tension:

> Poets *have* tried very hard, for thousands of years, to say what they mean. But they have not only tried to say what they mean, they have tried to prove what they mean. The saint proves his vision by stepping cheerfully into the fires. The poet, somewhat less spectacularly, proves his vision by submitting it to the fires of irony—to the drama of his structure—in the hope that the fires will refine it. In other words, the poet wishes to indicate that his vision has been earned, that it can survive reference to the complexities and contradictions of experience. And irony is one such device of reference.[8]

VIII

BUT though Winters seems distrustful of "dramatic" presentation, because of its reliance upon implication and the consequent relinquishment of the poet's control over his "statement," his choice of the term *motive* ("rational statement . . . is . . . motive to emotion")[9] actually points toward the mode of drama. For if the emotions are "motivated," the emotion can only be *inferred* from the context of situation and action. It cannot be stated directly, and the paraphrasable matter that "motivates" it is not so much a "statement" as a dramatic situation—a narrative, or a plot.

Indeed it is possible to interpret Winters' criticism as a powerful reassertion of the importance of plot. One might even compare it to Matthew Arnold's "classical" protest against romantic "confused multitudinousness" and "exuberance of expression."[1] But Eliot's concern with metaphor and symbol and even with irony represents a like "classical" reaction. For these, as Eliot treats them, are all aspects of a dramatic presentation as distinguished from the *personal* expression of the poet. The distinction is crucial: once we have dissociated the speaker of the lyric from the personality of the poet, even the tiniest lyric reveals itself as drama. A

[6] *Selected Essays*, p. 262.
[7] *Selected Essays*, p. 263.
[8] "Pure and Impure Poetry," Stallman's *Critiques*, p. 103.
[9] *Anatomy of Nonsense*, p. 13.
[1] Cf. *ante* Chapter 20.

poem is not a "statement about" something, but, as Aristotle said of tragedy, an *action*. Even metaphor is an action is this sense. It is a presentation of discrete entities, and the role of interpreting their relationship is forced upon the hearer or the reader. Since the identification asserted by a metaphor is *literal* nonsense, the interpretation, by implication, directs attention to the situation, the character of the speaker, and the occasion.

If the smallest lyric can be regarded as a drama, conversely the most formidable tragedy can be regarded as symbolic. *Macbeth* is perennially interesting to us, not as a historic incident (even if the history in that play were undistorted history), but because Macbeth is universal; he is in some sense ourselves. If his emotions are "motivated" by the events presented in the play, they are also meaningful symbols of our own emotions. Otherwise we should feel that Macbeth's emotional reactions were indeed "unmotivated": he would seem perverse or incomprehensible.

A realization that Winters' conception of poetry, like Eliot's, is ultimately "dramatic" need not impugn the useful distinction between motive (the reason for an emotion) and objective correlative (the symbol of an emotion). (The perception may indicate, however, why it is difficult to maintain the absolute distinction, especially with reflexive and highly allusive poetry.) It suggests further that Winters' "motive" is itself a kind of objective correlative. If the poet is to "control" emotion by providing "motives" for it, he is indeed compelled to make use of "a set of objects, a situation, or a chain of events." These are objective and can be presented; and since the emotion is generated by these objects and actions and, in so far as it is controlled, is controlled by the selection and rearrangement of these objectified elements, they may fairly be called the "correlative" of the emotion. For whether their "relation" to the emotion is that of cause or of symbolic equivalent, their *cor*relation with the emotion is evident.

IX

THE concern for the poem as an objective thing is the special highlight of the classicism of Eliot. We have mentioned Eliot's observation that the poem possesses a life of its own, and his insistence on the poet's need to extinguish his personality in the poem. Though such remarks as these can be interpreted as an abdication of the poet's proper responsibility, they need not be. Indeed, Eliot's metaphor about the poem's "life" and his suggestion that the poet's primary task is to foster and nurture that life are not incorrigibly irrational. It is possible to argue that the poem, like a growing plant, naturally grows toward the light and unless interfered with tends to grow straight.

This notion that the developing poem furnishes the poet with certain norms for its own nurturing (along with the further implication that poetry gives us a special kind of knowledge) has been spelled out by Allen Tate a little more fully than by Eliot. Tate, rejecting Winters' conception of a poem as a *statement* about something, would define it as an action rendered in its totality. This action is not prescriptive of means (as science is) nor of ends (as religion is). The reader is left to draw his own conclusions: (". . . the vision of the whole," as Tate says, "is not susceptible of logical demonstration.") [2] There can be no *external* verification: the reader grasps it by an act of the imagination or not at all. (The didactic poet, the rhetorician in the service of a cause, the advertising man—all do appeal to some "truth"—some authority, scientific or unscientific—as proof of the case being made.)

But though the poem is not a statement that can be proved, Tate will not allow that it is a whimsical, subjective "projection." He reprehends metaphors and similes that are "imposed upon the material from above," for they should "grow out of the material." [3] The implications of the last clause are significant: the poet, it is implied, does not fashion statements to a prearranged formula. He does not impose his formulas upon experience but reveals the patterns inherent in experience.

As an instance of adequate metaphor Tate adduces "Ripeness is all," as spoken by Edgar in *King Lear*. This figure is not imposed upon the experience "as an explanation" of it. Rather

> the figure rises from the depths of Gloucester's situation. . . .
> Possibly *King Lear* would be as good without Edgar's words;
> but it would be difficult to imagine the play without the passage
> ending in those words. They are implicit in the total structure,
> the concrete quality, of the whole experience that we have
> when we read *King Lear*.[4]

One must be careful in assigning very precise meanings to phrases like "grow out of the material" and "implicit in . . . the whole experience," which are themselves figurative. But surely they seem to discountenance the view that the imagination is merely whimsical. They suggest that the imagination obeys laws implicit in the human psyche. They even seem to demand the assumption that all human experience is finally one.

Tate, it is true, never states these assumptions in so many words, and one supposes that he would have to resist the view that this ultimate

[2] "Three Types of Poetry" (1934), *On the Limits of Poetry* (New York, 1948), p. 113.
[3] *On the Limits of Poetry*, p. 92.   [4] *On the Limits of Poetry*, p. 93.

oneness of the human psyche can be formulated in a set of laws which could then be used to determine the goodness or badness of particular poems. But the assumption that man exists and that his fundamental oneness transcends the innumerable differences that set apart individual men and set apart men of various cultures and periods of history seems implicit here. Perhaps it should be brought to light and stated quite flatly. For it may be the necessary assumption if we are to undertake to talk about poetry at all. Unless we can assume it, we necessarily abandon any concept of an aesthetics of poetry in favor of a tabulation of various kinds of social and personal expressions.

SUPPLEMENT

. . . Among the things that dramatic action must burn up are the author's opinions; while he is writing he has no business to know anything that is not a portion of that action. Do you suppose for one moment that Shakespeare educated Hamlet and King Lear by telling them what he thought and believed? As I see it, Hamlet and Lear educated Shakespeare, and I have no doubt that in the process of that education he found out that he was an altogether different man to what he thought himself, and had altogether different beliefs. A dramatist can help his characters to educate him by thinking and studying everything that gives them the language they are groping for through his hands and eyes, but the control must be theirs, and that is why the ancient philosophers thought a poet or dramatist Daimon-possessed.

—W. B. Yeats to Sean O'Casey, *Letters*, ed. Allan Wade (New York, 1955), p. 741, by permission of the publishers, The Macmillan Company.

. . . even Hulme, who, as an anti-romantic, explicitly leads away from the Coleridgean imagination, must, as I shall show, end by returning to a markedly similar theory of poetic creativity.

Hulme feels that the essence of romanticism is located in its idolatry of the individual who, for the romantics, should have unlimited aspirations since he has unlimited powers. . . . For the classicist, according to Hulme, sees man as an extremely limited being who needs all kinds of severely imposed disciplines if he is to function as he should in his proper sphere. Thus Hulme, defending the view of the classicist, rejects a concept of imagination which would substitute a monism for Christian dualism and would make of man a god. For the attribution to man of the power to create absolutely, *ex nihilo*, could mean little less. Thus Hulme explicitly calls for a poetry of fancy rather than the poetry of unbounded imagination which he feels contaminated English verse in the nineteenth and early twentieth centuries. He calls for a poetry that is formally precise and whose pretensions are limited to simple and vivid description. One might say that he calls for a return to a theory of imitation and opposes the reigning theory of expression, the introduction of which was so largely Coleridge's responsibility.

But there is also a quite different side of Hulme. In his essay on Bergson, in which he expounds sympathetically the aesthetic of his master in philosophy, there is a description of the poet's activity that seems nearly as transcendental as Coleridge's. Here Hulme distinguishes between intuition and stock perception and characterizes artistic creativity as the former. It is only the artist, he claims, who can break through the mere static recognition of the world about us which practical life demands; he alone can see through to the dynamic flux which characterizes essential reality. And as artist he makes this vision available to others who, without the artist, could never see beyond the stereotyped world of practicality.

This conception gives the poet a far higher and more romantic function than Hulme has assigned him in his severe "Romanticism and Classicism.". . . For while Hulme, as influenced by Bergson, still wants the poet to be descriptive, he adds a metaphysical dimension to this objective. He would have the poet describe the world about him not merely as it seems to be but rather as it really is behind the veil which hides it from most of us. The poet must not give us as the world "the film of familiarity and selfish solicitude" (note how apt this Coleridgean phrase is here) which our senses normally allow to us; rather he must give us the rare world beyond, which he somehow intuits. Now this is a handsome objective; and the intuitive faculty which is to fulfill it for Hulme seems not far removed from the imagination invoked by Coleridge. Surely we may doubt the power of fancy to operate at these profound levels.

—Murray Krieger, *The New Apologists for Poetry* (Minneapolis, 1956), pp. 33-4, by permission of the University of Minnesota Press.

At this point I shall venture to generalize, and suggest that with this disappearance of the idea of *Original Sin*, with the disappearance of the idea of intense moral struggle, the human beings presented to us both in poetry and in prose fiction to-day, and more patently among the serious writers than in the underworld of letters, tend to become less and less real. It is in fact in moments of moral and spiritual struggle depending upon spiritual sanctions, rather than in those 'bewildering minutes' in which we are all very much alike, that men and women come nearest to being real. If you do away with this struggle, and maintain that by tolerance, benevolence, inoffensiveness and a redistribution or increase of purchasing power, combined with a devotion, on the part of an elite, to Art, the world will be as good as anyone could require, then you must expect human beings to become more and more vaporous.

—T. S. Eliot, *After Strange Gods* (London, 1934), p. 42

[Melville's] letter to Mrs. Hawthorne acknowledging her symbolic interpretation of *Moby-Dick* is remarkable both for what it says and for what it assumes:

> But, then, since you, with your spiritualizing nature, see more things than other people, and by the same process, refine all you see, so that

they are not the same things that other people see, but things which while you think you but humbly discover them, you do in fact create them for yourself—therefore, upon the whole, I do not so much marvel at your expressions concern'g Moby Dick. At any rate, your allusion for example to the "Spirit Spout" first showed to me that there was a subtle significance in that thing—but I did not, in that case, *mean* it. I had some vague idea while writing it, that the whole book was susceptible of an allegoric construction, & also that *parts* of it were—but the speciality of many of the particular subordinate allegories, were [*sic*] first revealed to me, after reading Mr. Hawthorne's letter, which, without citing any particular examples, yet intimated the part-&-parcel allegoricalness of the whole.

This is the full-blown doctrine of aesthetic impersonality.

> —Charles Feidelson, Jr., *Symbolism and American Literature* (Chicago, 1953), p. 176. Published by the University of Chicago Press, and copyright 1953 by the University of Chicago.

Augustine puts this [argument concerning evil] as succinctly as Pope does: As bad men use to ill purpose the goods of the world, God, who is good, uses bad men to good purpose. The painter knows where to place black in the scheme of his picture, and God knows where to place wicked men in the scheme of his world. (*Sermon* CCCI, 5)

All these abstract pieces of his argument Pope [in the *Essay on Man*] catches up like his predecessors in the metaphor of harmony-from-discord that has influenced Western thinking for more than twenty centuries. It may be that the ultimate appeal of this metaphor has lain in giving imaginative configuration to the average human being's sense that he is, and yet is not, at home in a world he never made. At any rate, it has had the special virtue for theodicy of recognizing the fact of evil while restricting its significance. It enabled one to take account of the observed heterogeneity and conflict of things, but reconcile them; as, for example, in the thought of Heraclitus, its probable inventor, who asserted that the universal discord—"everything happens by strife"—was the ground of the universal union—"as with the bow and the lyre, so with the world: it is the tension of opposing forces that makes the structure one." Thus the image brought together in one perspective man's present suffering and his faith, the partial and the whole views; and in such a way that even its commonest linguistic formulations (*concors discordia rerum*) dramatized the triumph of cosmos over chaos, and its commonest analogies (the world as picture, play, poem, building, etc.) all suggested, like the parent image, that in some higher dialectic than men could grasp the thesis and antithesis of experienced evil would be resolved: "All discord, harmony not understood."

> —Maynard Mack, ed. Alexander Pope, *An Essay on Man* (Twickenham Edition, London, 1950), Introduction, pp. xxxiv–xxxv, by permission of Methuen and Co., Ltd.

CHAPTER 30

FICTION AND DRAMA: THE GROSS STRUCTURE

§ *Henry James's concern for the novel as an art form in its own right: his debt to Turgenev and Flaubert—II. the novel conceived as an organic and dramatic structure: the action "rendered" rather than "told"—the problem of the narrator and the point of view—the problem of sequence in time, and of the "time-shift" as theorized by Conrad and Ford Madox Ford—III. the connection between this conception of fiction and the Eliot-Pound conception of poetry: an organic and "impersonal" quality shared by both, with differences only in scope and strategy —IV. the reassertion of the claims of plot as made by some recent critics—Francis Fergusson's denial that drama is "primarily" a composition "in the verbal medium": his definition of "action"—V. his indictment of a "lyric" conception of drama, and his appeal for a return to an Aristotelian theory of "imitation"—Elder Olson's "Aristotelian" poetics of the lyric—Henry James's views on objective values and the organic structure of fiction—VI. Eliot on the relation of poetry and drama—the general problem of the genres—VII. "cold-blooded" critics of poetry and "warm-blooded" critics of fiction §*

THE CONCEPTION OF THE NOVEL AS A SPECIAL ART FORM COMES relatively late. Henry James could complain in 1888 that the English novel "had no air of having a theory, a conviction, a consciousness of itself behind it—of being the expression of an artistic faith, the result of choice and comparison."[1] The French novelist, to be sure,

---

[1] "The Art of Fiction," in *Partial Portraits* (London and New York, 1888), reprinted in *The Art of Fiction and Other Essays by Henry James*, ed. Morris Roberts (New York, 1948), p. 3.

did regard writing as a craft and applied himself to the novel as an art form. But even in France the consciousness of fiction as a craft was relatively new, and James was separated by only one generation from the men whom he regarded as the first serious theorists of the art of fiction to be found anywhere—Ivan Turgenev and Gustave Flaubert. Guy de Maupassant, another of James's conscious artists, was seven years younger than James himself. As a young man James had talked with all of them, and in 1912 he could regard himself as the "last survivor of those then surrounding Gustave Flaubert." [2]

James was willing to concede that the English novel was not "necessarily the worse for" the fact that it proceeded from no special theorizing. But the English novel was "*naif*"; and James was himself too much the artist to rejoice in the "comfortable, good-humoured feeling" so widely held that "a novel is a novel, as a pudding is a pudding, and that our only business with it could be to swallow it." [3] The novel was or ought to be a work of art, and its special potentialities as a form needed to be explored. Flaubert was, for James, "the novelist's novelist," [4] and Flaubert became, especially for novelists like Joseph Conrad and Ford Madox Ford, who derived their theories from James as well as from the 19th-century French novelists, a fountainhead. James disliked, to be sure, the vision of the world that he found in Flaubert and Balzac and Zola. All three saw life as more dreary, more sordid, more mean and limited than James believed the facts to warrant. But whereas Zola conceived himself to be a kind of scientist and Balzac thought of himself as a historian, Flaubert, for all the solidity of his report of human circumstance, had shown himself to be an artist. At any rate, James believed that he could learn from Flaubert's work the principles of fictional construction.

"A novel," James declared in his essay on "The Art of Fiction," "is in its broadest definition a personal, a direct impression of life." [5] It is not clinical and "scientific," since it depends upon the individual artist's imaginative perception; and it is *direct*—not mediated through formulae or general ideas about life. A novel is also to be conceived as an organic thing—"all one and continuous, like any other organism." [6] How fully

---

[2] *The Letters of Henry James*, ed. Percy Lubbock (New York, 1920), II, 258.
[3] In a letter to Hugh Walpole, dated May 19, 1912, James wrote: "Tolstoi and D[ostoevsky] are fluid pudding, though not tasteless, because the amount of their own minds and souls in solution in the broth gives it savour and flavour, thanks to the strong, rank quality of their genius and their experience. But there are all sorts of things to be said of them, and in particular that we see how great a vice is their lack of composition. . . ." See *The Selected Letters of Henry James*, ed. Leon Edel (New York, 1955), p. 171.
[4] "Gustave Flaubert," *The Art of Fiction*, p. 153. He applied the same epithet to Turgenev.
[5] *The Art of Fiction*, p. 8.
[6] *The Art of Fiction*, p. 13.

organic James found Flaubert's best novels to be is well illustrated from a passage in which he discusses Flaubert's attention to the exact phrase:

> It was truly a wonderful success to be so the devotee of the phrase and yet never its victim. Fine as he inveterately desired it should be he still never lost sight of the question Fine for what? It is always so related and associated, so properly part of something else that is in turn part of something other, part of a reference, a tone, a passage, a page, that the simple may enjoy it for its least bearing and the initiated for its greatest.[7]

James praises Turgenev by saying that his work does away with "the perpetual clumsy assumption that subject and style are—aesthetically speaking or in the living work—different and separable things."[8]

II

A VIEW of art so thoroughly organic as this implies as a corollary an impersonal art; that is, that the work grows in accordance with some inner principle of its own being, and is not merely the creature of the writer's ego, either as an expression of his feelings as a man or as an assertion of his opinions. Ford Madox Ford records a conversation in which James said: "There are things that one wants to write all one's life, but one's artist's conscience prevents one. . . . And then . . . perhaps one allows oneself. . . ."[9] James was speaking of one of his failures, "The Altar of the Dead"; and Ford goes on to comment that the bitter lesson that the artist has to learn is "that he is not a man to be swayed by the hopes, fears, consummations or despairs of a man. He is a sensitized instrument, recording to the measure of the light vouchsafed him what is—what *may* be—the Truth."[1]

For the novelist, the problem of securing impersonality for his art has a special connection with management of the point of view. How does the narrator avoid intruding himself into the work? How, when there is information to be conveyed, can he avoid seeming to lecture his reader? How can he avoid spoiling a powerful scene by seeming to bob up before the reader like a prompt-clerk? These were questions that concerned James. But these also were the questions which Ford, and according to Ford, Joseph Conrad, with whom he collaborated on two or three novels, were to give particular attention.

They wished to make the reader forget the writer altogether so

---

[7] "Gustave Flaubert," *The Art of Fiction*, pp. 143-4.
[8] *The Art of Fiction*, p. 120.
[9] *Thus to Revisit* (London, 1921), p. 49.
[1] *Thus to Revisit*, p. 49.

that the story would seem to tell itself and develop with its own life. The novelist was not to "tell the reader" about what happened but to *render* it as action. Moreover, the action was not to be rendered with photographic fidelity but as it would make its impression upon a human observer. Hence Ford's name for the new art, Impressionism. As Ford put it, "Conrad found salvation not in any machined Form, but in the sheer attempt to produce in words life as it presents itself to the intelligent observer." [2] Or as Conrad himself put it (in his Preface to *The Nigger of the Narcissus*): "before all, to make you see."

The general tendency was back toward drama with the emphasis upon direct presentation rather than the mediation of a special expositor, and with a concomitant reliance upon the reader's power to infer, in Henry James's words, "the unseen from the seen, to trace the implication of things, to judge the whole piece by the pattern." [3]

Percy Lubbock, whose scholarly handbook *The Craft of Fiction* (1929) gives what may be regarded as the standard exposition of the tenets of the Flaubert-James school, distinguishes between panorama (the long-range view of the action) and scene (the close-up view), and describes the design of a novel in terms of the presentation of the action through scenes and panoramas, and the proper disposition of these in relation to each other.

It follows that two matters of special concern for critics of this school were those of the narrator and the point of view from which he "sees" the action. The narrator of the story is frequently a character, whose knowledge is limited to what he himself could have seen and heard, and this narrator may be either a major or a minor character. And even when the narrator is omniscient, possessed of all that the author himself knows about the story, he is scarcely to be thought of as merely the author speaking in his own right. Thus Lubbock interprets the celebrated impersonality of Flaubert's art to mean only "that Flaubert does not announce his opinion in so many words. . . . [The impersonality] of Flaubert and his kind lies only in the greater tact with which they express their feelings—dramatizing them, embodying them in living form, instead of stating them directly." [4]

The question about point of view is, of course, not a new one. In some sense it is as old as literature. Ezra Pound remarks: "I have . . . found also in Homer the imaginary spectator, which in 1918 I still thought was Henry James' particular property." [5] But since Flaubert's time the

[2] *Thus to Revisit*, p. 46.

[3] *The Art of Fiction*, p. 11. James is actually referring in this passage to a power of the novelist, but it is a power which in some measure any writer using a dramatic method must also demand of his reader.

[4] *The Craft of Fiction* (London, 1921), pp. 67–8.

[5] *The ABC of Reading* (1934), reprinted by New Directions (Norfolk, Conn., 1951), p. 43.

problem has come in for more conscious examination than perhaps it had ever received before.

The handling of time sequence is another such problem that comes in for special treatment by these theorists of fiction. Again, it is an old problem, and one that has received very sophisticated practical solutions in the past, including devices so different as the folk-balladist's abrupt juxtaposition of little discrete scenes without intermediate narration and the classic epic-writer's beginning *in medias res*. But such theorizing as it has received in the past has had to do principally with the drama, and under the rubric of the unities of time and place. In the modern novel, the problem, for obvious reasons, arises with special force.

The modern fiction writer's concern with time goes further than the making of a series of scenes and deciding the relative emphasis to be placed upon each of them. The novelist has frequently found it desirable to alter the chronological arrangement of events, sometimes describing an earlier event *after* portraying a later event, and he has sometimes attempted to achieve an effect of simultaneity of events. Flaubert, in discussing the famous incident of the *comices agricoles* in his *Madame Bovary*, wrote:

> Everything should sound simultaneously; one should hear the bellowing of the cattle, the whisperings of the lovers and the rhetoric of the officials all at the same time.[6]

But, as Joseph Frank points out in his "Spatial Form in Modern Literature,"[7]

> since language proceeds in time, it is impossible to approach this simultaneity of perception except by breaking up temporal sequence. And this is exactly what Flaubert does: he dissolves sequence by cutting back and forth between the various levels of action in a slowly-rising crescendo until—at the climax of the scene—Rodolphe's Chateaubriandesque phrases are read at almost the same moment as the names of prize winners for raising the best pigs.

This device of incongruous juxtaposition became the "Time-shift" developed by Conrad and Ford. Ford likened the effect of simultaneity gained by the time-shift to the effect experienced by a person looking out of a window "through glass so bright that whilst you perceive through it a landscape or a backyard, you are aware that, on its surface it reflects a face of a person behind you."[8] Joyce, of course, exploited the device to the limit in his *Ulysses*. But it is by no means confined to

---

[6] Cited by Joseph Frank; see footnote 7.
[7] *The Sewanee Review*, LI (Spring, 1943); reprinted in *Critiques*, p. 322.
[8] "On Impressionism," *Poetry and Drama*, I (June, 1914), 174.

modern fiction. Frank finds it throughout modern poetry—in Pound's *Cantos* and in Eliot's *Waste Land*, where the poet makes use of a "deliberate disconnectedness" and "superimposes one time scheme upon another." [9]

III

THAT modern poetry and fiction should make use of similar devices and should exhibit what is essentially the same kind of organization is not surprising. For the theorists of fiction we have been discussing were the associates of Hulme, Pound, and Eliot—and in the instance of Flaubert and James, moreover, they were sources from whom Hulme, Pound, and Eliot derived much of their theory. Like the theorists of poetry discussed in the preceding chapter they too display, in reaction against romantic inspirationalism, a concern for craftsmanship, and a stress upon form as opposed to the exploitation of privileged "poetic" materials. Indeed theirs too might be called an "impersonal" art. Even those aspects of it which might be thought of as exclusively "fictional"—*e.g.*, concern with point of view and with time sequence—are aspects of dramatic presentation—of the process of *rendering* as distinguished from *telling*. The time-shift also, with its potentiality for incongruous juxtapositions, finds its corresponding devices in the ironic confrontations characteristic of the poetry of Pound and Eliot.

There is no need to claim too much here. Fiction is set off sharply enough from lyric poetry to preclude any serious danger of our ever confusing the two. Fiction, for example, has an appetite for richness of circumstance, for sheer concretion, that sets it well apart from any lyric. Even short stories so far tilted over toward the lyric sensibility as James Joyce's "Clay," "Araby" and "The Sisters" do not seriously challenge this statement. Yet the lyric shares with the novel a common fictionality. If "character" and "sequence of action" seem to be especially the problems for the novelist, a little reflection will reveal that they confront the poet too. Eliot's Prufrock is a character, and Pound's "Mauberley" involves the problem of handling a sequence of time. Both Eliot's poem and Pound's differ in scope and scale, of course, from any novel. But like any novel, they too are organic structures, and they are forced to exploit to the limit such resources as a smaller compass affords—and because it is smaller, demands. Yet the general principle governing the relation of individual word to the total work is not changed simply because these are poems and not novels. As one writer on James remarks:

James's concern for form in the novel "implies an elaborate art, often close to poetry, the aim of which is the maximum of expression." [1]

[9] Stallman, *Critiques*, p. 321.
[1] Morris Roberts, Introduction to *The Art of Fiction*, p. xix.

IV

A CONCERN for "character" and "action" as they occur in poem or novel has not always, of course, been complemented by an adequate concern for craftsmanship. (In *Thus to Revisit*, Ford Madox Ford comments with amusement and sometimes bitterness on the slovenliness of the English novel of the 19th century.) Matthew Arnold[2] was confident that if one chose a "fitting action" and allowed oneself to become "penetrated" with "the feeling of its situations," then "everything else [would] follow." This prescription for composing a work might even be described as an implicitly "organic" theory inasmuch as Arnold's basic assumption seems to be that details of style and structure must be consonant with, being dictated by, the larger governing principle: these details, that is, have no merit in themselves but only in virtue of giving substantial form to the entelechy of the whole. About the soundness of this principle, neither Ford nor James could possibly have quarreled, though they might have wondered that Arnold should so scant the intricate problem of working out the details of style and structure, and though they might have been puzzled as to how one could be sure that one had chosen a "fitting action" until one had "fitted" it to words.

Arnold, as we have seen, was asserting the primacy of subject matter and plot against what he felt to be an overemphasis upon lyric sensibility and a preoccupation with the verbal medium as such. In our own times, the criticism stemming from Hulme and Eliot has provoked similar reactions and counterclaims for the primacy of plot. One of a group of critics writing recently at the University of Chicago notes that "the criticism of the last two centuries . . . has . . . been marked by a subsidiary interest in plot and its needful agents."[3] Plot and character delineation, so the argument of this group runs, have been slighted and neglected; the tendency has been to reduce literature to the verbal element.[4] Such counterclaims typically derive from the Aristotelian *Poetics* with its focus upon drama and its stress upon plot as "the soul of

[2] Cf. *ante* Chapter 20.

[3] Norman Maclean, in *Critics and Criticism, Ancient and Modern*, p. 414.

[4] A similar conflict occurred in the 17th century, with Thomas Rymer as the worthy champion of plot, "the foundation," as he termed it, in dealing with which the English dramatists had been defective. Dryden conceded the point but argued that they had been able to attain the end of tragedy through complementary means, namely, through their excellent treatment of the "superstructure" (characters, thoughts, and words). See Frank L. Huntley, *The Unity of John Dryden's Dramatic Criticism* (Chicago, 1944).

Charles Gildon also disparaged the critic who reaches "no farther than Words and Sentences; dealing in the very Scraps of Poetry; a Couplet, an Expression is the utmost he pretends to. But for a Design, or a complete Poem, to meddle with it, he accounts Pedantry, or Imposition" (*The Complete Art of Poetry*, 1718).

tragedy." Such also is the general derivation of a book from another quarter, Francis Fergusson's *The Idea of a Theater* (1949), which is one of the most engaging of these reassertions of the primacy of plot.

Fergusson does not regard drama as "primarily a composition in the verbal medium." Drama is a mixed art to which the actor and even the stage designer make their contributions. Yet the presence of such elements as these does not constitute the real basis for Fergusson's separation of drama from fiction and poetry. Remembering Aristotle, who, though naming "song" and "spectacle" as parts of tragedy, yet spends very little time in discussing them,[5] Fergusson gives scant attention to acting and stage effects as such. He is in search of something more ultimate; he is looking for "that dramatic art which, in all real plays, underlies these as well as the more highly developed arts of language."[6]

His basic direction is indicated in his assertion that whereas the lyric is a composition in the verbal medium, in drama "the words result . . . from the underlying structure of incident and character."[7] But it is not clear upon what kind of substructure the words of a lyric are supposed to rest. What supports *them* or do they simply float on the air? If the question should turn out to be a bogus question—like the ancient question as to what the earth rested upon, upon the back of an immense tortoise, or upon that of a fabulous elephant—its unintelligibility might call in question the distinction that Fergusson makes between lyric poetry and the drama. To this possibility we shall have to recur.

At any rate, Fergusson's search for a "dramatic art" that underlies all the "arts of language" takes him down to a stratum deeper even than plot, for he insists that plot itself rests upon "action." But action is something that Fergusson acknowledges it is difficult to define, and which cannot be "abstractly defined"[8] at all. It seems to be both inside and outside the drama, and thus Fergusson sometimes seems to be talking about an element within the play; at other times, about something outside the play which is to be located in the historical culture—a myth, for example. In considering a concrete instance, the action in *Oedipus Rex*, he is willing to describe the action as a theme: he calls it a quest—the search for the culprit in order to purify human life. He goes on to say:

> Sophocles must have seen this seeking action as the real life of the Oedipus myth. . . . Moreover, he must have seen this particular action as a type, or crucial instance, of human life in

[5] "The 'visual aspect of the staging' [*opsis*], despite its emotional appeal, is the least artistic of all the elements and has least to do with the art of poetry. . . . moreover the production of scenic effects lies more in the province of the 'costumer and stage-manager' [*skeuopoios*] than of the poet." *Poetics* VI: *Aristotle*, trans. Philip Wheelwright (New York, 1951), p. 299.
[6] *The Idea of a Theater* (Princeton, 1949), p. 9, by permission of the publishers, Princeton University Press.
[7] *Idea of a Theater*, p. 8.   [8] *Idea of a Theater*, p. 230.

general; and hence he was able to present it in the form of the ancient ritual which also presents and celebrates the perennial mystery of human life and action. Thus by "action" I do not mean the events of the story but the focus or aim of psychic life from which the events, in that situation, result.[9]

The *Oedipus Rex* is regarded as the expression of a total culture. "The perspectives of the myth, the rituals, and of the traditional *hodos*, the way of life of the City—'habits of thought and feeling' which constitute the traditional wisdom of the race—were all required to make this play possible."[1] The myths and rituals which were Sophocles' heritage and the heritage of the audience for which he wrote were "actions" upon which the dramatist could draw. Such resources are not available to the dispossessed and alienated modern artist. He must rely merely on his *art*—an observation which helps explain Fergusson's curious remark that Racine and Wagner were "purer artists than Sophocles, as the best modern critics have taught us to understand that idea."[2] The implication would seem to be that great art is not *merely* art but something else (art plus religion?).

V

FERGUSSON has made it clear that the "best modern critics" have been concerned with subtle verbal analysis, to the *neglect* of "action." Certain passages in his book, however, suggest that those qualities of drama that the lyric does *not* possess are outside the bounds of art altogether or at least are outside those of "pure art." They would seem to be cultural elements shared by the artist with his fellow citizens and thus would be mythic, ritualistic, religious, and even philosophical patterns.

In discussing the "action" upon which great drama has been based, Fergusson shows a great concern for what was *available* to a Sophocles and to the audience that saw his plays. T. S. Eliot, in his *Dialogue on Dramatic Poetry* (1928) had a speaker remark that

> Aristotle did not have to worry about the relation of drama to religion, about the traditional morality of the Hellenes, about the relation of art to politics . . . he did not have to read the (extremely interesting) works of Miss Harrison or Mr. Cornford, or the translations of Professor Murray, or wrinkle his brow over the antics of the Todas and the Veddahs. Nor did he have to reckon with the theatre as a paying proposition.[3]

[9] *Idea of a Theater*, p. 36.   [2] *Idea of a Theater*, p. 3.
[1] *Idea of a Theater*, p. 32.   [3] *Selected Essays*, p. 32.

But these are just the topics about which Fergusson feels that he must worry. The remark of Eliot's speaker, he says, is wistful because "we cannot escape the unanswerable questions which Aristotle did not have to ask. The analysis of the art of drama leads to the idea of a theater which gives it its sanction, and its actual time and place. And when the idea of a theater is inadequate or lacking, we are reduced to speculating about the plight of the whole culture." [4] Precisely. And Fergusson realizes that much of his book is just such a speculation. He is too intelligent to chide the modern author for what he cannot help. The problem is communal, and the artist can fairly be asked nothing more than that he should recognize that he is alienated and rootless and try to set his own lands in order.

Fergusson also would persuade the modern artist to abandon idealistic expressionism in favor of some theory of art based on "imitation." But the modern artist, "after three hundred years of rationalism and idealism, with the traditional modes of behavior lost or discredited," [5] finds it difficult to imitate or even to "see" any action other than that of his own subjectivity. Eliot, for example, approaches the drama from the standpoint of lyric poetry, and thus begins "with the Idealistic conception of art as formally prior to the theater itself." [6] Fergusson, on the other hand, would "extend Aristotle's definition to subsequent forms [of the drama]," for it presupposes an objective world, knowable but outside the mind that knows it. The "lyric" conception is hopelessly idealistic and subjective. Fergusson admits that

> The phrase "objective equivalent" [for the poet's feeling] seems to support Eliot's announced classicism. Yet it refers, not to the vision of the poet, but to the poem he is making; and it implies that it is only a *feeling* that the poet has to convey. . . . The emphasis on the poem and its form, to the exclusion of what it represents, recognizes only one of the instincts which Aristotle thought were the roots of poetry in general, the "instinct for harmony and rhythm." [7]

In brief, Fergusson, sensing the tendency of theories of symbolic form to become monistic, urges the counterview that the poet's vision must be objective. Sophocles, he says, "must have believed in the objective reality of the human situation which the tragic theater enabled him to mirror and celebrate." [8] Sophocles was not merely expressing himself but imitating something outside himself.

The question as to whether Eliot's objective correlative is merely

[4] *Idea of a Theater*, p. 226.   [7] *Idea of a Theater*, p. 240.
[5] *Idea of a Theater*, p. 239.   [8] *Idea of a Theater*, p. 236.
[6] *Idea of a Theater*, p. 8.

expressionistic has come in for some attention in Chapter 29 (*ante*, p. 668). But in any case, one may wonder whether the only way to avoid the extreme of subjective expressionism is to adopt a theory of "imitation." Fergusson is properly cautious in his speculations as to Sophocles' actual beliefs, and he has to admit that Euripides, though inheriting the "theater of Sophocles," did not believe in the Greek myths at all.[9]

One may come at the matter from the other direction. Fergusson's account of the "action" suggests that it is not an element peculiar to drama but is to be found in all literature, including lyric poetry. For he says action is "the focus or aim of psychic life from which the events . . . result." But every piece of literature is about psychic life in some sense, and the briefest lyric, if it is really a poem and not an aimless farrago, has a focus or an aim. Moreover, though one does not mean to collapse the useful distinction between the song and the drama, the analogies are there. The most fragile lyric has at least one character, that of the implied speaker himself, and it has a "plot"—an arrangement of psychic incidents, with a development, at least of mood.

What Fergusson and Eliot hold in common is the belief that the work of art is an organic whole, and this view of the art work is in some sense more important than the decision to fix our criticism upon the diction or upon the action—upon the "actualization" of the work or upon the "soul" of the work. In an organic work, one implies the other, and we can work from "inner" soul to "outer" manifestation, or *vice versa*. For if the work be truly organic, then each element of structure is a necessary or probable consequence of the larger principle of the whole. But if we do work backwards from the words to the characters who speak them and from the characters on back to the plot in which the characters are involved, small wonder that the final and fundamental governing principle, Fergusson's "action," should prove so difficult to define. Indeed, our only clues to it are its "actualizations," that is, the text of the play itself. If "action" is held to be the most important thing in the work, it yet remains an inference, a hypothesis constructed by the reader. The "action" resembles the Aristotelian *substance*, which is known only through the *accidents* that inhere in it. The *raison d'être* of Fergusson's action would seem to be to provide a ground in which

[9] Fergusson thinks that "Sophocles might well have taken myth and ritual as literally 'fictions,' yet still have accepted their deeper meanings—trope, allegory, and anagoge—as valid" (p. 35). This guess may well be correct, but if so, one wonders what to make of the difference between the ancient poet, buoyed up by myth and ritual, and the alienated modern who, "with the traditional modes of behavior lost or discredited," is unable to "see" any action but his own, and is thus unable to "imitate" it. Even William Butler Yeats, it can be claimed, accepted "the deeper meanings" of his *Vision*—"trope, allegory, and anagoge" as "valid." One could claim at least as much, presumably much more, for the symbols of T. S. Eliot's later poetry.

the "accidents" of the play (speeches, characters, gestures) may subsist.

Elder Olson has shown how arbitrary the use of terms taken from an imitative theory of art can be. The occasion is his adjustment of the Aristotelian terms to a poetics of the lyric. Olson arrives at his poetics by remodeling, or perhaps it would be more accurate to say, truncating, the Aristotelian poetics of tragedy. Whereas Aristotle found six parts in a tragedy, Olson requires four in order to deal with the lyric—or rather, to observe his own precision, "that species [of lyric] to which Yeats's *Sailing to Byzantium* belongs." [1] The four necessary parts are choice, character, thought, and diction. "For choice is the activity, and thought and character are the causes of the activity, and diction is the means. The choice, or deliberative activity of choosing, is the principal part for reasons analogous to those which make plot the principal part of tragedy. Next in importance comes character; next thought; and last, diction."

Yet one might argue for "plot" as a fifth necessary part—or at least as a substitute for "choice." Yeats's poem actually has a plot. The speaker in this poem pictures himself as having made the voyage to Byzantium and in excited reverie imagines his visit to St. Sophia and his vision of the holy sages and the prayer that he will utter to them. Conversely, one could argue that the four parts might be reduced to three: *e.g.*, that the term *thought* might be omitted altogether, since there can be neither character nor choice without thought. To conclude, the "four parts" would seem to be more or less convenient terms under which to discuss the poem—not the inevitable and necessary elements of the poem.

The doctrine of imitation has great virtues of its own, and it avoids a difficulty into which expressionist doctrines so easily slip: that of turning the whole work into the subjective fantasies issuing out of the poet's private consciousness. But the doctrine of imitation has its own difficulties. Aristotle himself did not make the artist's "imitation" a literal mirroring. It is in some sense a transformation as well. Fergusson's "action" seems to be at once inside and outside the work of art: sometimes it seems to be the primal structural principle of the drama but, at other times, it is an "aim of psychic life" with mythic antecedents.

Henry James, who was a good enough "Aristotelian" to believe that in his novels he was giving a picture of a real and objective and external world and to declare that "the soul of a novel is its action," faced this problem in his "Art of Fiction." His common sense is refreshing. He writes:

> I cannot see what is meant by talking as if there were a part of a novel which is the story and part of it which for mystical reasons is not. . . . "The story," if it represents anything, repre-

[1] *Critics and Criticism,* p. 563.

sents the subject, the idea, the *donnée* of the novel; and there is surely no "school" . . . which urges that a novel should be all treatment and no subject. There must assuredly be something to treat; every school is intimately conscious of that. The sense of the story being the idea, the starting-point, of the novel, is the only one that I see in which it can be spoken of as something different from its organic whole; and since in proportion as the work is successful the idea permeates and penetrates it, informs and animates it, so that every word and every punctuation-point contribute directly to the expression, in that proportion do we lose our sense of the story being a blade which may be drawn more or less out of its sheath.[2]

We have cited James and Eliot as champions of an organic theory of literature, and we have drawn the inference that for them and their schools the differences between poetry and fiction and drama tend to become less sharp and less radically deep. Whatever the author may owe to an idea as a "starting-point" or to a story as a "subject," informing idea and actualized story become something else in the work itself: they are no longer separable from the work.

VI

But it may be only fair to notice that on occasion Eliot himself can write as if poetry and drama were radically different forms. In *Poetry and Drama* he writes:

I laid down for myself the ascetic rule to avoid poetry which could not stand the test of strict dramatic utility: with such success, indeed, that it is perhaps an open question whether there is any poetry in the play at all.
. . . the self-education of a poet trying to write for the theatre seems to require a long period of disciplining his poetry, and putting it, so to speak, on a very thin diet. . . .[3]

But the stylistic problem described in these passages is precisely that described by Ford Madox Ford in his account of the wrestle with style that went on in his collaborations with Conrad.

[2] *The Art of Fiction*, pp. 17–18.
[3] *Poetry and Drama* (Cambridge, Mass., 1951), pp. 39–40, by permission of the publishers, Harvard University Press. In a recently reported interview, Eliot seems to make a distinction between "pure, unapplied" poetry and dramatic poetry as "applied" poetry. Perhaps we may wonder how much we are allowed to press distinctions made in apparently informal conversation. See *The New York Times Book Review*, November 29, 1953.

The trouble . . . with us was this: we could not get our own
prose keyed down enough. . . .

Our most constant preoccupation, then, was to avoid words
that stuck out of sentences either by their brilliant unusualness
or their "amazing aptness." For either sort of word arrests the
attention of a reader, and thus "hangs up" both the meaning and
the cadence of a phrase.[4]

Even in *Poetry and Drama* Eliot makes it plain that drama in verse
is the ideal. Prose dramatists, even the great prose dramatists, have been
"hampered in expression by writing in prose." There is a "peculiar range
of sensibility" that lies beyond prose but which "can be expressed by
dramatic poetry, at its moments of greatest intensity." [5] If we put this
late essay beside the earlier "Dialogue on Dramatic Poetry" (1928) we
get some such conception as this: poetry is essentially dramatic and the
greatest poetry always moves toward drama; drama is essentially poetic
and the greatest drama always moves toward poetry.[6]

The moral would seem to be that anyone, including Mr. Eliot,
speaking in a special and limited context, is likely to talk as if poetry
and drama were two very different things. For here we come up against
the ancient and vexing problem of genres. A recent discussion of genre
theory [7] indicates how confused and confusing some of these problems
are. The notion of genres, as Austin Warren points out, furnishes a principle of order. If, to borrow his phrase, we reduce lyric, epic, and drama
to "a common literariness," how shall we distinguish a play from a
story? Such reductions are in the interest of nobody. Yet it is proper to
glance at the other extreme: if we multiply the genres indefinitely, we
shall ultimately have to recognize a special genre for each art work,[8] and
if we make the larger genres watertight compartments, we shall end up
with at least three separate "literatures," not one.

[4] *Thus to Revisit*, pp. 52-3.

[5] *Poetry and Drama*, p. 43.

[6] "C: Do you mean that Shakespeare is a greater dramatist than Ibsen, not by
being a greater dramatist, but by being a greater poet? B: That is precisely what
I mean. For, on the other hand, what great poetry is not dramatic? Even the
minor writers of the Greek Anthology, even Martial, are dramatic. . . . E: [Archer]
was wrong, as you said, in thinking that drama and poetry are two different things."
Selected Essays, pp. 38-9.

[7] By Austin Warren, in Wellek and Warren's *Theory of Literature* (New
York, 1949). See pp. 235-47.

[8] A possibility less remote than one might think. Elder Olson writes that "the
beauty of a tragedy is not the same as the beauty of a lyric, any more than the
distinctive beauty of a horse is the same as that of a man," but then the beauty
of a lyric of "the species to which Yeats's 'Sailing to Byzantium' belongs" is evidently not that of a poem belonging to another subspecies of the lyric. Would
Yeats's "Among School Children" require the postulation of another subspecies?
And his Crazy Jane poems, still another? See *Critics and Criticism, Ancient and
Modern*, p. 563.

VII

CERTAIN academic critics, however, are not alone in their objection to a criticism that seems to deal "only with words" rather than with "character" and "plot." The more frequent objections come from those who care little for the niceties of genre theory and want only to distinguish "mere words" from "life." They often write as if words were a necessary evil—pale limp things, interposing themselves between the reader and the compelling stuff of experience offered him by the author.

Such objectors are by no means always literary journalists. At their best, one may say that these critics take the necessary mediation of words for granted and want to get on to the qualities in the author—his breadth of view, his compassion, his knowledge of the human heart—, or to an exposition of his views—his political sagacity, the relevance of what he says to the cultural situation, and the like.

At their most careless or most trivial, they express the typical Anglo-Saxon distrust of words. *Art* for them means the "artful" and probably also the "artificial." They frequently write as if the author could lay upon the page warm, quivering chunks of life, if he were only gifted enough, and if he only chose to. They are suspicious of any attempt to talk about words and their interaction.

The editor of *The Kenyon Review* has taken cognizance of the contemporary situation in the following terms:

> So in an age of unusual critical achievement we have managed to arrive rather quickly at an excruciating impasse: with cold-blooded critics of poetry working away at what sometimes appear to be the merest exercises with words; and warm-blooded critics of the critics of poetry [he has already said that these are likely to be "critics of fiction"] reproaching their exercises, and perhaps about to reproach their poetry too.
>
> How confidently, twenty years or so past, were some of us offering a new "understanding of poetry"! I will not say, How brashly; for the innovation was real, it was momentous; but it was not complete, and now it has bogged down at a most embarrassing point.[*]

The protest of the warm-bloods is scarcely new; something like it, we have noted, was to be heard in early Victorian England. John Henry Newman and his friend John Keble, author of *The Christian Year*, expressed this same sort of distrust of "art," technique, and execution. Like the modern warm-blooded "critics of fiction," Newman and Keble as-

[*] John Crowe Ransom, *The Kenyon Review*, XIV (Winter, 1952), p. 159.

sociated the difference between cold calculation and warm spontaneity with the difference between "plotted" narrative and the plotless lyric.[1] But Newman and Keble just reversed the modern correlation: with them "plot" is associated with cold-blood; the lyric utterance is warm and effusive. This reversed alignment of the contrasted elements reinforces the deeper commitment that both Victorian and modern warm-blooded critic share: a distrust of art and technique—whether the concern in question is that of poet or critic. As for the impasse apparently reached by modern criticism, we are disposed to offer a different metaphor, not that the caravan "has [now] bogged down at a most embarrassing point" in new and unexplored country, but rather that the hunt has circled and that some of the hounds are once again baying on the trail of the Longinian fox.

SUPPLEMENT

She was largish and of a French figure, that is with a noticeable waist and a more noticeable rear, and she had heels too high for her balance in a spurting bus. . . . She had much trouble getting the two fares in the box, and considerably more trouble getting herself from the box down the aisle, hauling from seat to seat by their shining handles against the momentum of the bus, lurching, as she had to, in all directions save the right one. During the whole business—and this is what I am getting at—she managed by sniffs and snorts, by smiles, by sticking her tongue out very sharp, by batting her very blue eyes about, and generally by cocking her head this way and that, she managed to express fully, and without a single word either uttered or wanted, the whole mixed, flourishing sense of her disconcertment, her discomfiture, her uncertainty, together with a sense of adventure and of gaiety, all of which she wanted to share with her companion behind me, who took it I was sure, as I did myself, all smiles. . . .

That is an example of the gesture that comes before language; but reflecting upon it, it seems also an example of the gesture which when it goes with language crowns it, and so animates it as to make it independent of speaker or writer; reflecting upon it, it seems that the highest use of language cannot be made without incorporating some such quality of gesture within it. How without it could the novelist make his dialogue ring? how could the poet make his cry lyric, his incongruity comic, or his perspective tragic? The great part of our knowledge of life and of nature—perhaps all our knowledge of their play and interplay—comes to us as gesture, and we are masters of the skill of that knowledge before we can ever make a rhyme or a pun, or even a simple sentence. Nor can we master language purposefully without re-mastering ges-

[1] Cf. *ante* Chapter 20.

ture within it. Gesture, in language, is the outward and dramatic play of inward and imagined meaning. It is that play of meaningfulness among words which cannot be defined in the formulas in the dictionary, but which is defined in their use together; gesture is that meaningfulness which is moving, in every sense of that word: what moves the words and what moves us.

—R. P. Blackmur, *Language as Gesture* (New York, 1952) pp. 5–6, by permission of the publisher, Harcourt, Brace and Company.

But who am I to offer such a diagnosis of fiction's ailment? Four years of instruction under the greatest faculty in English, philosophy and history that Harvard, or any other American university ever assembled, must have taught me nothing, because the constitutionally academic critics dismiss my kind as mere journalists, just as they dismiss any writing with the juice of life in it as mere journalism. The best I can wish for some of these gentlemen is that they might be exposed for a brief period of their careers to the bracing winds of human sympathy and understanding which blow through every newspaper office.

One trouble with literary criticism in this country today is that too much of it has been taken over by a group of impenetrably insulated bookworms. What they have to say about literature interests neither the intelligent public nor those writers who are worth their salt. Yet they exercise a corrupting influence because many of them are in a position to foist their ideas upon unformed, immature minds.

—J. Donald Adams, *The New York Times Book Review* (September 5, 1954). Reprinted by permission of the author and the publishers.

Also, I would hold that a "dramatistic" placement of the lyric is to be arrived at "deductively" in this sense: one approaches the lyric from the category of *action*, which Aristotle considers the primary element of the drama. And then by dialectic coaching one looks for a form that will have as its primary element the moment of *stasis*, or *rest*. We are admonished, however, to note that there are two concepts of "rest," often confused because we may apply the same word to both. There is rest as the sheer cessation of motion (in the sense that a rolling ball comes to rest); and there is rest as the end of action (end as finish or end as aim), the kind of rest that Aristotle conceived as the *primum mobile* of the world, the ground of motion and action both. It is proper for the physical sciences, we would grant, to treat experience nondramatically, in terms of motion, but things in the realm of the social or human require treatment in terms of action or drama. Or rather, though things in the realm of the human *may* be treated in terms of motion, the result will be statements not about the intrinsic, but about the extrinsic (as per our remarks on an "incongruous" science of the personality).

A treatment of the lyric in terms of action would not by any means require us merely to look for analogies from the drama. On the contrary, the *state of arrest* in which we would situate the essence of the lyric is not analogous to dramatic action at all, but is the dialectical counterpart of action. Consider as an illustration the fourteen Stations of the Cross: The concern with them in the totality of their progression would be dramatic. But the pause at any one of them, and the contemplation and deepening appreciation of its poignancy, in itself, would be lyric.

A typical Wordsworthian sonnet brings out this methodological aspect of the lyric (its special aptitude for conveying a *state* of mind, for erecting a moment into a universe) by selecting such themes as in themselves explicitly refer to the arrest, the pause, the hush. However, this lyric state is to be understood in terms of action, inasmuch as it is to be understood as a state that sums up an action in the form of an attitude.

Thus approached, an attitude is ambiguous in this sense: It may be either an incipient act or the substitute for an act. An attitude of sympathy is incipiently an act, for instance, in that it is the proper emotional preparation for a sympathetic act; or it may be the substitute for an act in that the sympathetic person can let the intent do service for the deed (precisely through doing nothing, one may feel more sympathetic than the person whose mood may be partially distracted by the conditions of action). In either case, an attitude is a state of emotion, or a moment of stasis, in which an act is arrested, summed up, made permanent and total, as with the Grecian Urn which in its summational quality Keats calls a "fair Attitude."

—Kenneth Burke, *A Grammar of Motives* (New York, 1945), pp. 475–6. Reprinted with permission of the publishers, from *A Grammar of Motives* by Kenneth Burke. Copyright, 1945, by Prentice-Hall, Inc.

CHAPTER 31

MYTH AND ARCHETYPE

§ *The increasing modern interest in the symbolization of primitive man: Vico as a pioneer in this field, and modern contributions from anthropology and psychology—Ernst Cassirer's* Philosophy of Symbolic Forms: *the origin of language and the origin of myth, the identification of subject and object in the symbol—II. Cassirer's view of what poetry expresses and of its relation to the language of science—W. M. Urban's* Language and Reality: *metaphysics as a symbolic language mediating among such other symbolic languages as those of science and art—III. Mrs. Langer's* Philosophy in a New Key *and her* Feeling and Form: *the "import" of art as a "pattern of sentience," her account of lyrics and of more complicated poems—the strengths and limitations of the doctrine of symbolic form—IV. the distinction between poetry and myth as maintained by Cassirer and Langer: the assimilation of poetry to myth made today by the new "myth" critics—Northrop Frye and the elevation of literary criticism to a social science—Richard Chase and the equation of poetry and myth—Leslie Fiedler and the return to the poet's biography—V. other applications of myth study to literature: Maud Bodkin and W. H. Auden—VI. Carl Jung's influence upon modern literary criticism: his conception of "purposive" myths and dreams, his application of a "cognitive" criticism to myths and dreams—VII. Jung's distinction between the dream and the work of art—his specification of what the psychologist can contribute to the study of literature—Yeats and the uses of myth* §

ONE CONSEQUENCE OF THE SYMBOLIST DEVELOPMENT IN LITERATURE [1] has been an increasing respect for the symbolism of primitive man, and specifically for the myths and legends through which he characteristically expresses himself. If, as Kant argued, the mind is no passive mirror, merely giving back the world reflected in it, but is

[1] Cf. *ante* Chapter 26.

rather an active force that affects the very shape of reality as perceived by us, then the symbolizations of primitive man are not necessarily childish and absurd, but have their own interest and perhaps make their own contribution to "truth." As we have seen in an earlier chapter,[2] J. G. Herder, who was a younger contemporary of Kant's, boldly derived language from the mythic process and made the special character of poetry reside in the fact that poetry preserves the dynamic quality of myth. Even earlier in his *Scienza Nuova*, the Neapolitan scholar Giambattista Vico had elaborated the theory that myth was a kind of poetic language, the only language that man was capable of in his primitive stage of development, and yet, for all that, a genuine language with its own principle of structure and its own logic.

Vico conjectured that language first began with gesture, then developed through the stages of myth and figurative language to the clarified and ordered language of modern polite societies. Yet if Vico dignified poetry by regarding it as a form of knowledge—and, for the historian of primitive times, an indispensable mode of knowledge—he regarded it as an inferior knowledge which had been superseded as civilization developed.

Vico had very little influence upon the thinkers of his own day. René Wellek writes that "the attempts to prove his influence in France, England, and Germany during the 18th century, especially in aesthetics, have all failed."[3] In our own time, however, Vico has come to exert a very powerful influence. Our modern studies of primitive man have confirmed some of Vico's insights and have, in any case, compelled recognition of his position as a brilliant pioneer. Even some of his more questionable observations find their parallels in those of present-day critics. If, for example, Vico was unable to distinguish poetry from myth, we find modern critics like Richard Chase insisting that myth is only poetry. It is interesting, however, to note that a modern philosopher like Croce, whom Vico influenced directly, displays very little interest in the sort of anthropological speculation in which Herder indulged in the 18th century and of which today Vico is to be regarded as the great pioneer. In spite of his acknowledged debt to the historical empiricism of Vico, Croce developed a rigorous philosophical idealism.

The philosopher of our day who has pushed furthest the concern for the origin of language and the laws that govern the development of primitive ritual and myth is Ernst Cassirer. His *Philosophy of Symbolic Forms* (1923–29) is Kantian in its general orientation, but Cassirer pays high tribute to Herder, calling him "the Copernicus of history."[4] He quarrels, however, with Herder's attempt to derive language from myth,

---

[2] Cf. *ante* Chapter 17.
[3] *A History of Modern Criticism*, I, 135.
[4] *The Philosophy of Symbolic Forms* (New Haven, 1953), I, 41.

insisting that neither is derivable from the other. We are rather to think of language and myth as "two diverse shoots from the same parent stem,"[5] springing from the same impulse of symbolic formulation. This impulse Cassirer calls "a concentration and heightening of simple sensory experience." Cassirer's association of primordial language with intense emotional experience is a matter of some importance for his conception of poetry. We shall return to it. But first it is important to sum up what Cassirer seems to say about the relation of language to reality.

Some of Cassirer's comments promise a great deal. Symbols, he holds, are shaped by man's needs and purposes. The symbol is not an aspect of reality: it *is* reality. In the symbol there is a thoroughgoing identification between subject and object:

> . . . in place of a more or less adequate "expression," we find a relation of identity, of complete congruence between "image" and "object," between the name and the thing.[6]

Indeed, Cassirer insists that we falsify the issues when we describe the symbol as a "meeting-place" of subject and object, for the very concept of the ego and non-ego belong to what is a relatively "late development" of language. Primitive man, Cassirer conjectures, knew no such duality. The distinction between the apprehending self and the apprehended thing required for its recognition the development of the power of reflection and of logic.

In an earlier chapter[7] we remarked upon Coleridge's yearning for the discovery of a realm in which the distinction between words and things should be abolished. But that realm actually exists, Cassirer declares—it exists in the world of the savage mentality. In the mind of primitive man, the flickering mythic perceptions—the "momentary gods" that are generated out of the savage's more vivid experiences—are, through the medium of words, stabilized and given a relative fixity. The word is no mere surrogate. "Often it is the *name* of the deity," Cassirer has observed, "rather than the god himself, that seems to be the real source of efficacy."[8]

Indeed, for Cassirer a local habitation and a name remains even to-day of the utmost importance; lacking a name, human experience cannot be "stored and stabilized." Only through the habitation afforded by a name can the psychic energy pass over into something like substance— a deposit of meaning that can be contemplated on later occasions, and linked with and related to other such deposits of meaning. The ability

---

[5] *Language and Myth*, trans. Susanne Langer (New York, 1946), p. 88, by permission of the publishers, Harper and Brothers.
[6] *Language and Myth*, p. 58.
[7] Cf. *ante* Chapter 26.
[8] *Language and Myth*, p. 48.

to make and use such symbols is what renders man a human being: man is the symbol-making animal—the only such animal.[9]

II

BUT as logic and discursive thought develop, language loses its emotional charge; its quality of concreteness is attenuated; and it approaches the state of the language of science. The process is, on the whole, one of deprivation: language is reduced to "a bare skeleton." There remains one area, however, in which, even for sophisticated modern man, language "recovers the fullness of life."[1] That is the realm of "artistic expression," where the original creative power of language is not only "preserved" but "renewed." Poetry expresses, Cassirer writes,

> neither the mythic word-picture of gods and daemons, nor the logical truth of abstract determinations and relations. . . . The world of poetry stands apart from both, as a world of illusion and fantasy—but it is just in this mode of illusion that the realm of pure feeling can find utterance, and can therewith attain its full and concrete actualization.[2]

Cassirer makes it plain that the "pure" feeling that art expresses is not merely the personal emotions of the poet. The lyric poet, he tells us, is not "just a man who indulges in displays of feeling." This realm of pure feeling has its own claim to objectivity. Since we can know reality only through symbolic forms, art constitutes one of the perspectives by which to view reality. Art is no mere entertainment, no mere divernon, no mere act of play. It is a revelation of a genuine aspect of our life.

> What would we know of the innumerable nuances in the aspect of things were it not for the works of the great painters and sculptors? Poetry is, similarly, the revelation of our personal life. The infinite potentialities of which we had but a dim and obscure presentiment are brought to light by the lyric poet, by the novelist, and by the dramatist. Such art is in no sense mere counterfeit or facsimile, but a genuine manifestation of our inner life.[3]

Cassirer seems to conceive of art as in some sense a counterpoise to science. Art gives us a special knowledge of our "inner" life, as science presumably does of our "outer" life. It restores the dimension of emotion

[9] "Hence, instead of defining man as an *animal rationale*, we should define him as an *animal symbolicum*." *An Essay on Man* (New Haven, 1944), p. 26.
[1] *Language and Myth*, p. 98.
[2] *Language and Myth*, p. 99.
[3] *Essay on Man*, p. 169.

and emotional response and thus offsets the attenuation and abstraction necessary to science. One wishes that Cassirer were somewhat clearer on this matter of the relation of one kind of language to another, and specifically with reference to the relation of art to science. He has, to be sure, some interesting and suggestive passages in which he says that language "moves in the middle kingdom between the 'indefinite' and the 'infinite,' " [4] and that the effort to realize a truly *pure* treatment of either being or of self would necessarily take us outside the realm of language altogether into "a world of silence." He tells us too that since we can know reality only through symbolic forms, the question of what reality is apart from such forms becomes irrelevant. The basic philosophical question, he says in his *Language and Myth*, has to do with the "mutual limitation and supplementation" [5] of myth, art, religion, and science— that is, with a mediation among the various accounts of reality given by the various kinds of language.

But by making science the "last step in man's mental development," by frankly calling it the "highest and most characteristic attainment of human culture," [6] Cassirer seems to give it a priority over the other kinds of language. Though he defends the objectivity of the other kinds of language, he leaves the suggestion that science, by paring away the personal and emotional elements that are so much a constitutive part of the languages of myth, religion, and art, does actually give us a wider and deeper aspect of reality—that in some sense, in spite of his general argument, science does have some very superior access to reality. On the whole, therefore, one must agree with a recent critic who writes that:

> Although Cassirer represents poetry as the regeneration of the creative power of the word. . . , he is ultimately loyal to reason. Truth is the province of the "conceptual sign," and poetry, however valuable, is "a world of illusion and fantasy." [7]

Wilbur Urban, who shares many of Cassirer's fundamental views, has been careful to repudiate any implication that art and religion use more "primitive" languages than do science and philosophy. In his *Language and Reality* he points out that all three are relevant to man, and to modern man. [8] He is also concerned to present them as not merely meaningful but true. That is, Urban is concerned to relate to one underlying reality what is "said" by all the kinds of languages. Urban's way

[4] *Language and Myth*, p. 81.
[5] *Language and Myth*, p. 9.
[6] *Essay on Man*, p. 261.
[7] *Symbolism and American Literature*, p. 55. Cf. René Wellek on this aspect of Cassirer, *Rocky Mountain Review*, IX (Summer, 1945), 195.
[8] *Language and Reality* (New York, 1939), *passim*. On pp. 469-70, he writes that it is a fallacy to view the aesthetic symbol "as a mere stage of, or imperfect substitute for, scientific and philosophical knowledge." Reprinted by permission of the publishers, The Macmillan Co.

of solving Cassirer's problem of "mutual limitation and supplementation" is to set up metaphysics as the special discipline whose function it is to interpret what art, religion, and science have "to say" about reality and to mediate their varying "statements."

In a loyal adherence to the doctrine of symbolic form, Urban has to dismiss any hope that we can discover "hypothetical 'pure experience' . . . by stripping [it of] language." [9] But he thinks that there is an approach to some final truth and reality through understanding the "symbolic forms of language" and through becoming "more conscious of the formative principles embodied in these constructions." Urban's deepest difficulty is to penetrate a "symbolic" language fully while respecting the fact that it *is* symbolic. This difficulty comes out especially in his remarks on the problem of art. Like Croce, he holds that a poem is strictly untranslatable.[1] The artistic symbol is not "merely a surrogate for a concept" but is rather the way in which the ideal content is apprehended and expressed. Yet if one wishes to connect what art has to tell us about reality with what science or with what religion has to tell us about reality, one is apparently compelled to make some kind of translation:

> We are apparently faced with a dilemma. If we are to interpret the "sense" of the symbol we must expand it, and this must be in terms of literal sentences. If, on the other hand, we thus expand it we lose the "sense" or value of the symbol *as symbol*. The solution of this paradox seems to me to lie in an adequate theory of interpretation of the symbol. It does not consist in substituting *literal* for symbol sentences, in other words substituting "blunt" truth for symbolic truth, but rather in deepening and enriching the meaning of the symbol.[2]

The fact that Urban ventures such a solution throws some light on our general problem. The autonomy that is conferred upon poetry by a doctrine of symbolic forms is bought at a high price if it leaves that autonomous realm quite isolated from other autonomous realms such as that of science. Yet Urban's solution poses real difficulties; and Mrs. Susanne K. Langer, another philosopher of symbolic form, has had to reject Urban's attempt to "interpret" artistic symbols as not only unsatisfactory but as quite inconsistent with Urban's general position.

III

Mrs. Langer's view appears first in *Philosophy in a New Key*, 1942. The title suggests something of the excitement with which her book is written. She considers that the concept of symbolic transformation, for which

---

[9] *Language and Reality*, p. 374.   [2] *Language and Reality*, pp. 434-5.
[1] *Language and Reality*, p. 490.

she gives special credit to Cassirer, strikes a new key in philosophy, a key into which all the great questions of our age must now be transposed.

The end of a philosophical epoch, she argues, comes "with the exhaustion of its motive concepts." [3] Now once more the springs of "philosophical thought have run dry." [4] In our own otherwise arid landscape, the principle of symbolic transformation represents a fresh fountainhead, a generative force providing us with new motives and problems. Activities of our day apparently so diverse as symbolic logic and Freudian psychology reveal themselves to be in fact related when one reflects that each has discovered in its own way the importance of this power of symbolization.

Like Cassirer, Mrs. Langer regards myth as the "primitive phase of metaphysical thought, the first embodiment of *general ideas.*" [5] In due course mythic conception gives way when discursive language has been developed. The civilization then moves into a rationalistic period, though Mrs. Langer concedes that a day may come in which, ideas having been "exploited and exhausted, there will be another vision, a new mythology." [6] But Mrs. Langer, though she seems to connect poetry and the arts generally with mythic thinking, is not willing to concede that art is a mere passing phase in man's mental history. On the contrary, art is a "new symbolic form" which is able to live on "side by side with philosophy and science and all the higher forms of thought." [7] Here, of course, Mrs. Langer follows closely Cassirer's statement that poetry presents us with a "world of illusion" in which "the realm of pure feeling can find utterance." In *Philosophy in a New Key* music was her primary example. Music, she says, is "our myth of the inner life—a young, vital, and meaningful myth, of recent inspiration and still in its 'vegetative' growth." [8] In *Feeling and Form*, 1953, she applies her theory of symbolic transformation in detail to the other arts.

All art has meaning, or more precisely, something called "import." Music, for example, has articulated form; it represents an intuition simple or complex, on the part of the composer. It has

> *import*, and this import is the pattern of sentience—the pattern of life itself, as it is felt and directly known. Let us therefore call the significance of music its "vital import" instead of "meaning," using "vital" not as a vague laudatory term, but as a qualifying adjective restricting the relevance of "import" to the dynamism of subject experience. [9]

[3] *Philosophy in a New Key* (Cambridge, Mass., 1942), p. 9.
[4] *Philosophy in a New Key*, p. 13.   [6] *Philosophy in a New Key*, p. 202.
[5] *Philosophy in a New Key*, p. 201.   [7] *Philosophy in a New Key*, p. 202-3.
[8] *Philosophy in a New Key*, p. 245.
[9] *Feeling and Form* (New York, 1953), pp. 31-2, by permission of the publishers, Charles Scribner's Sons.

A vase, a painting, even an abstract design has its import. We are presented not with actual feeling but with "ideas of feeling" and through art we come to recognize and know the "life of sentience."

Since the life of feeling is a stream of tensions and resolutions, and since all vital tension patterns are organic patterns, any work of art must be essentially organic. But Mrs. Langer warns us not to confuse this illusion of the life of feeling with anything so crude as a direct copying of feelings. Indeed, since the artist does not give us a direct copy, he need not have experienced in actual life the feelings that his work expresses. He may, in articulating the work, even discover new possibilities of feeling. "For, although a work of art reveals the character of subjectivity, it is itself objective; its purpose is to objectify the life of feeling." [1]

Mrs. Langer's position is in general a sensitive and highly sophisticated exposition of the symbolist view of art. Her highest praise of a poem is that it should be "entirely expressive"; and in fact her critical position scarcely allows her to offer more in the way of praise. This fact is clearly revealed in the detailed analyses of poems which she gives us in *Feeling and Form*. She is much more convincing when writing on the short lyrics than on more complicated poems. She is, for example, quite excellent in discussing a relatively simple and lyrical poem like William Blake's "The Echoing Green," which she takes to be a symbol "of life completely lived." "Here," she writes, the artistic form is "completely organic, and therefore able to articulate the great vital rhythms and emotional overtones and undertones." [2]

But her observations on Wordsworth's "Intimations Ode" suggest some of the embarrassments to which she is exposed by a poem of greater complexity. This "philosophical" poem, she points out properly enough, is not really a very formidable piece of philosophizing. The poet could not have "elaborated and defended his position." He evidently did not really believe in the doctrine of Platonic anamnesis to which the poem seems to commit him. The logical structure "of the thought is really very loose." [3] What the poem expresses is

> essentially the experience of having so great an idea [as that of transcendental remembrance], the excitement of it, the awe, the tinge of holiness it bestows on childhood, the explanation of the growing commonplaceness of later life, the resigned acceptance of an insight. [4]

The poem expresses what it feels like to have so great an idea. But what of greatness? If the idea seemed trivial to the reader, would

[1] *Feeling and Form*, p. 374.   [3] *Feeling and Form*, p. 220.
[2] *Feeling and Form*, p. 227.   [4] *Feeling and Form*, p. 219.

that fact not make a real difference? It would have been possible for Mrs. Langer to argue that only two things are required: first, as she has actually argued, that the idea should have appeared great to the poet, and second, as her general theory of art implies, that the poet should have been sufficiently competent as a poet to make the idea seem great to us; that is, Mrs. Langer might have argued that the poet's failure could only be the failure of inexpressiveness.[5] But the circular nature of such an argument scarcely needs pointing out: for the reader to whom the idea has been rendered great, it *is* great—that is, within the relevant frame of reference, the experience of the poem.

Mrs. Langer expresses some dissatisfaction with T. S. Eliot's "purer" poems, and she is rather impatient of some of his literary methods, particularly his use of literary allusions. Her reference to Eliot's "desperate nostalgia for a vanished culture,"[6] makes one wonder, however, whether her dissatisfaction has to do merely with literary techniques and not also with Eliot's ideas—which may not seem "true and important"[7] to her even though one assumes they must have seemed so to the poet. Yet one may question whether, in terms of her general theory, she is entitled to say more than that Eliot's poems are sometimes inexpressive. For elsewhere in *Feeling and Form* she makes such remarks as these: "Materials [for a poem] are neither good nor bad, strong nor weak";[8] "Where a theme comes from makes no difference; what matters is the excitement it begets, the importance it has for the poet";[9] and "There is nothing the matter with an ardent moral idea in poetry, provided the moral idea is used for poetic purposes."[1]

On the negative side, Mrs. Langer's presentation of the doctrine of symbolic form is admirable. She puts cogently the warning that we must not impose our preconceptions on the poem; nor wrench out of context any "statements" that may be imbedded in the poem; nor demand that it be a political or philosophical document answering to our own political or philosophical notions. But as another "answer to science" the doctrine of symbolic form, even as developed by Mrs. Langer, risks claiming at once too little and too much.

It risks claiming too little in stressing as the essential pattern of poetry the "life of sentience." Mrs. Langer is much more sophisticated than, say, Max Eastman. She carefully distinguishes between the pattern of feelings as articulated in the poem and the poet's own outpouring of emotions; she avoids the notion that the poet is simply projecting a subjective experience. But on close scrutiny there actually may be little to differentiate her account of what poetry expresses from Eastman's. He opines that

[5] *Feeling and Form*, p. 234.   [8] *Feeling and Form*, p. 406.
[6] *Feeling and Form*, p. 248.   [9] *Feeling and Form*, p. 254.
[7] *Feeling and Form*, p. 219.   [1] *Feeling and Form*, p. 5.

George Meredith made poetry of happy passion in "Love in the Valley," and of unhappy pain in "Modern Love," and though he was very intellectual, he had nothing to say to us about either one of them [i.e., those feelings] that we have been able to remember, except that there they were.[2]

At the same time, the doctrine of symbolic form risks claiming too much. Even in Mrs. Langer's treatment, and not merely in the obviously extravagant treatments of an Emerson or a Whitman, there is this risk. If all the cards in the deck are "wild" and can be counted as belonging to whatever suit and constituting whatever value we care to assign them, then the game ends. The possibility of conflict disappears. Perhaps Wordsworth's "great idea," Mrs. Langer has argued, was required only to generate the emotion for Wordsworth's poem, as a grain of sand within the oyster is required to generate a pearl. But the power of the idea to excite the poet's awe is not so easily separated from its ability to elicit the reader's awe: for to assume that the poet could have done quite as well with *any* idea that appealed to him is to conclude that ideas do not matter at all or—what amounts to the same thing—to assume that the poet is a kind of god, capable of making up his meanings out of whole cloth. In either case we are back to Emerson's symbolistic monism. If Mrs. Langer avoids this kind of monism, as on the whole she does, it is because in practise she uses more referential criteria than she is perhaps aware that she is using and more than her theory strictly entitles her to use.

IV

THOUGH both Cassirer and Mrs. Langer are, as we have seen, much interested in the relation of poetry to myth, and though they both levy upon myth to illustrate the theory of symbolic form, they are scrupulously careful to distinguish myth from poetry. Mrs. Langer writes, for instance, "Legend and myth and fairy tale are not in themselves literature, they are not art at all, but fantasies; as such, however, they are the natural materials of art." [3] But many of the critics of our time have, more boldly (or shall one say less scrupulously) seized upon the connection between myth and literature as providing a new key to criticism.

These new "myth" critics, now to be discussed, tend to be more conversant with psychology than with philosophy. They have also been heavily influenced by the anthropological studies of the last fifty years. They have been tremendously impressed by the discovery—or the rediscovery—that myth, ritual, and poetry are to be found at the begin-

[2] *The Literary Mind*, p. 148.   [3] *Feeling and Form*, p. 274.

nings of every culture. The specifically human estate begins, it has been persuasively argued, with these forms of human expression, and it develops under their influence. The modern myth critic has probably been even more powerfully impressed by the evidence that primitive man still lurks within each of us, and that the 20th-century citizen who dutifully drives to work each morning in an automobile, transacts business by telephone with a firm three thousand miles away, and gets himself ready for sleep by watching entertainment relayed to his living-room by the electronics industry, recreates nightly in his dreams the primordial symbols of ancient myth. Seen in these terms, myth seems to offer to poetry an inviolable refuge against the incursions of a hostile science.

Myth suggests a fresh means by which to study the "laws of the imagination." Mrs. Langer herself is willing to agree that, since these laws are "really just canons of symbolization," the "systematic study of them" may be justly said to have been "first undertaken by Freud."[4] The critics who hope to find in myth the key to artistic creation make much of the number of characteristics that poetry shares with dream. The process that Freud calls the "dream-work" shows startling similarities with "poetic work." In both there is "condensation" (the combining several images in one image), "displacement" (the vesting in some apparently unimportant element the underlying significance of the whole), and "overdetermination" (several quite different significances focused upon the same element so that it bears more than one meaning). In both poetry and dream, logical relationships are frequently evaded or transcended by the mere juxtaposition of images.[5] Not only Freud, but notably among other psychologists Carl Jung, and the cultural anthropologists in general are regarded as having furnished positive and specific directives for the study of poetry. Some of our recent critics, under the stimulus of such studies, write with the excitement of men who have suddenly envisaged a whole new hemisphere.

For Northrop Frye the discovery points to the possibility of turning literary criticism for the first time into a true science. No true science, he argues, can be content to rest in the structural analysis of the object with which it deals. The poet is only the *efficient* cause of the poem, but the poem, having form, has a formal cause that is to be sought. On examination, Frye finds this formal cause to be the archetype.[6]

What Frye calls "total" literary history moves from the primitive to the sophisticated, and so Frye glimpses the possibility of envisaging lit-

---

[4] *Feeling and Form*, p. 241.

[5] Cf. *ante* Chapter 28 for parallels in the modern "semantic" study of poetic language.

[6] "My [Critical] Credo," *The Kenyon Review*, XII (Winter, 1951), pp. 92–110. "Archetype," borrowed from Jung, means a primordial image, a part of the collective unconscious, the psychic residue of numberless experiences of the same kind, and thus part of the inherited response-pattern of the race.

erature as the "complication of a relatively . . . simple group of formulas that can be studied in a primitive culture." [7] In the light of this possibility, the search for archetypes becomes a kind of "literary anthropology, concerned with the way that literature is informed by preliterary categories such as ritual, myth and folk tale." [8] Since the quest-myth is central to ritual and myth—and thus to literature—all the literary genres may be derived from it. Groupings under the rubrics of the four seasons emerge. That of spring will illustrate what Frye has in mind:

> The dawn, spring, and birth phase. Myths of the birth of the hero, of revival and resurrection, of creation and . . . of the defeat of the powers of darkness, winter and death. Subordinate characters: the father and mother. The archetype of romance and of most dithyrambic and rhapsodic poetry. [9]

Frye not only envisages criticism's taking its place "among the other social sciences." He has suggestions for bringing this about through what amounts to a production-line technique. The literary specialists who will deal with the text in question are disposed as follows: first the editor ("to clean up the text for us"), then the rhetorician and philologist, the literary psychologist, the literary social historian, the philosopher and the historian of ideas, and finally at the end of the line, the literary anthropologist. Frye consistently refers to the work of art as a "product," an organic commodity that is capable of being sorted, classified, and graded—a notion that receives some support from the way in which Frye chooses to suggest how a poem comes into being:

> The fact that revision is possible, that the poet makes changes not because he likes them better but because they are better, means that poems, like poets, are born and not made. The poet's task is to deliver the poem in as uninjured a state as possible, and

---

[7] *Kenyon Review*, XII, 99.

[8] *Kenyon Review*, XII, 99–100.

[9] *Kenyon Review*, XII, p. 104. Joseph Campbell's *The Hero with a Thousand Faces* (Bollingen Series, XVII, 1949), is one of a number of recent books that treat the quest-myth. Campbell too feels that his mission is to proclaim the new dispensation. He tells us that the "great coordinating mythologies . . . now are known as lies" (p. 388), yet the problems with which they purported to deal remain. We shall solve these problems, he predicts, by learning "to recognize the lineaments of God in all the wonderful modulations of the face of man" (p. 390). Still more extravagant claims for the benefits to spring from our knowledge of the universal myth are made by James K. Feibleman in his *Aesthetics* (New York, 1949). He argues that the future of modern literature is immense: Though we moderns have no legends like that of Troy nor myths like that of the House of Atreus, we do have an extensive knowledge of the master myth, "the myth of the year god" (p. 426). The possession of this myth gives our artists an even greater opportunity than that afforded the Greek artist of the fifth century B.C., for the modern artist not only knows a *greater number* of myths he knows much more about the very nature of myth!

if the poem is alive, it is equally anxious to be rid of him, and
screams to be cut loose from his private memories and associations, his desire for self-expression, and all the other navel-strings
and feeding tubes of his ego. The critic takes over where the
poet leaves off. . . .[1]

In this lively analogy the poem is evidently the babe, the poet the
mother, and the critic the midwife and nurse, who ties off the cord,
tells the mother the infant is a boy or girl, washes it up for presentation
to the outside world, and presumably gives it an anthropological classification and takes its Bertillion measurements. Yet Frye's analogy fails to
cover what must finally be the crucial question of whether the poem is
still-born and inert, or alive. He merely alludes to this question with the
cautionary "if the poem is alive." In some sense this has always been
the primary question with which criticism has had to concern itself: is
the poem "alive," or is it merely a document, wooden, dead, lifeless, a
mere "exhibit," without literary merit? Frye's midwife-critic, in none of
the special roles portioned out to him as textual editor, historian of ideas,
or even literary anthropologist, can answer that question, and in none of
the many roles that Frye assigns him does he need to answer that question. The inert and valueless "document" will submit to the kind of
classification that Frye specifies just as well as a valuable poem. The
promise that by such means criticism may take its place among the other
social sciences justifies pressing the question suggested by Frye's analogy. For it is a matter of some consequence whether criticism, once it
has become a social science, will become as chary of making evaluations
and rendering normative judgments. In short, is the aim to make criticism a purely descriptive, value-free social science? That eventuality
would prove to be simply a new variant on the old historicism.

In the position developed by Richard Chase in *The Quest for Myth*,
the term "myth" is clearly a value term. A poem that is vibrantly alive
is mythic and vice versa; for Chase absolutely identifies poetry and myth.
"Myth," he writes, "is only art."[2] The adverb *only* in this context is
rather curious. One wants to ask whether Chase is attempting to debunk
myth, on the assumption that myth has close affiliations with religion;
or whether he is striving to enhance art by suggesting that the important
function claimed for myth in past cultures is actually still available
through art for our scientific civilization. A reading of Chase's book
indicates that he means to do something of both.

Poetry and myth, he argues, arise out of the same human needs,
represent the same kind of symbolic structure, succeed in investing experience with the same kind of awe and magical wonder, and perform

[1] *Kenyon Review*, XII, 97-8.
[2] *The Quest for Myth* (Baton Rouge, 1949), p. 110.

the same cathartic function. The last phrase, however, is strictly a
misnomer. Here Chase substitutes for Aristotle's metaphor of purgation
a figure of his own that has to do with animal taming. We have been
made, he says, whether we like it or not, the trustees "of inhumanly
powerful forces which were once caged and domesticated by the ap-
paratus of the Christian religion." That cage has been broken and the
beasts have escaped and now lurk in the depths of man's unconscious.
Ghosts such as haunt the hero in Henry James's "The Beast in the
Jungle"

> are terrible and destructive just because they are inadequately
> projected by their victims. . . . We must do with "the beast"
> what James himself did: flush it from the jungle so that it may
> be captured in the texture of aesthetic experience and bent to
> our will.[3]

The artist is evidently the hound that flushes the beast from the
jungle; his art is the cage that holds him when captured, and also, one
supposes, the kitchen-chair and whip which the artist lion-tamer uses to
force him to take his stand on the pedestal and sit quietly, obedient to
the trainer's will. But the complications of Chase's image need not obscure
at all the function which he assigns to poetry. It is substantially the role
that Matthew Arnold assigned to poetry. The strength of art is that it
does not rest upon dogma, and therefore can survive the breakup of
dogma. If myth once upon a time tamed the destructive forces within
man, and if myth is only art, then art ought to be able to tame them for
us now.

The parallel with Arnold will suggest why Chase is so hostile to the
proposition that myth originally implied belief. And here, of course,
Chase comes into sharp collision with philosophers of symbolic form
like Cassirer and Langer, who, as we have seen, firmly insist that in
the true "mythical imagination there is always implied an act of belief."[4] I. A. Richards once wrote of *The Waste Land* that Eliot had
effected a complete severance of poetry and belief, though Eliot himself
was to demur. Chase seems to be saying that there never was any effective relation between belief and myth (poetry). The claim is almost
heroically desperate. Yet it is easy to see why Chase has to insist upon
it. If it could be made good, it would constitute an answer to a question
that nowadays is certain to be raised by many voices: namely, how
modern man is to profit from the power inherent in myth if in fact no
intellectually respectable modern can any longer believe in myth? If,
however, myth is "only art," the day is saved.

For Leslie Fiedler, the new perspective now offered by myth leads

[3] *Quest for Myth*, p. 102.   [4] *An Essay on Man*, p. 75.

straight back into the study of message and consequently into the study of biography.[5] Fiedler reacts sharply against recent "formalist" trends in criticism: the emphasis upon an "impersonal art," upon the poem itself rather than the study of its background. He wishes to reaffirm the importance of the poet's personality and the relevance of the poet's "intention." It is easy to see why: the theories that he is attacking tend to minimize the ancient distinction between literary form and content. Fiedler is engaged in reasserting a full dualism. For the archetypal materials are really a privileged poetic subject matter in disguise. He argues that any great poem must be an acceptable rendition of this special poetic content.

At the same time, a study of the poet's response—of the way in which he expresses, and by expressing, stamps, his personal "signature" upon the archetype—forces the critic to take full account of the biography of the poet. For in Fiedler's conception, a poem is not an object to be known; it is rather a clue to an event in the poet's psyche. The poet's psyche is the arena in which *Dichtung* and *Wahrheit* become one: the poetic work itself is incidental to this important process:

> In deed as in word, the poet composes himself as maker and mask, in accordance with some contemporaneous *mythos* of the artist. And as we all know, in our day, it is even possible to be a writer without having written anything! [6]

Literature has come a long way since the day of Thomas Gray and his "mute inglorious Miltons." That our poets may be tongue-tied, or too busy with their psychic struggles to stop and put anything down on paper, may or may not endanger their status as real poets. But, of course, Fiedler expects them normally to put themselves on paper, for then the therapeutic benefits of the process of poetic objectification (compare Chase *ante*) become socially available:

> In the Mask of [the poet's] life and the manifold masks of his work, the poet expresses for a whole society the ritual meaning of its inarticulate selves; the artist goes forth not to "recreate the conscience of his race," but to redeem its unconscious. We cannot get back into the primal Garden of the unfallen Archetypes, but we can yield ourselves to the dreams and images that mean paradise regained.[7]

In the same essay Fiedler writes that the poet is able to take us back "to his unconscious core, where he becomes one with us all in the presence of our ancient Gods, the protagonists of fables we think we no

---

[5] "Archetype and Signature," *The Sewanee Review,* LX (Spring, 1952), 253-73. Reprinted by permission of *The Sewanee Review.*
[6] *The Sewanee Review,* LX, 261.   [7] *Sewanee Review,* LX, 273.

longer believe." [8] But never mind what we *think* on these occasions; do we or do we not believe? That will be the question that some readers will want to put. Can we, by taking a firm hold on our bootstraps, actually lift ourselves to a belief in what we do not "really believe"? Or is "believe" being used in a Pickwickian sense? One is aware that the question may not be easy to answer, but eventually it must at least be faced.

V

THE more literary question that is raised by Fiedler and by the myth critics in general may be put as follows: Have they found in their study of myth and the psychology of dreams an authoritative clue to the interpretation of poems? They certainly write with the excitement of men who have found such a key. Yet their claims are a little incoherent and at points contradictory.

The attempt to apply Freudian theory to poetry runs into a similar problem: Mrs. Langer points out that the peculiar weakness of Freud's theory as applied to poetics is that it tends to "put good and bad art on a par, making all art a natural self-expressive function like dream and 'make-believe.' " [9]

It is possible, of course, to argue that one poet uses a myth more "artistically" or more "powerfully" than another; or one may argue that some myths are more powerful or more significant than other myths and therefore yield greater poems. But to take either alternative would seem to reinstate the traditional critical problems in full force. For our attempt to show that Poem A uses Myth X artistically whereas Poem B does not, brings up what Frye has called the "problem of rhetoric." And so does our argument that Myth X is more significant (and therefore makes for a greater poem) than Myth Y. Considerations of this sort suggest that "mythic" and "archetypal" criticism, whatever other contribution it may make, provides no way of circumventing the basic problems of traditional criticism. [1]

In considering some of the recent "myth" criticism, we have seen how various it is in its emphases: with Frye we are asked to assign an almost monstrous "life of its own" to the poem; with Fiedler, on the other hand, the poem is important as an event in the life of the poet; and there is Chase's concern for the audience in his therapeutic emphasis. But the literary use of the study of myths *can* be centered firmly upon the poetic structure itself. Maude Bodkin's *Archetypal Patterns of*

---

[8] *Sewanee Review*, LX, 273.
[9] *Feeling and Form*, p. 240.
[1] Cf. Fergusson, *Idea of a Theater*, pp. 17, 77.

Poetry is an excellent demonstration of this possibility. Her archetypal patterns are the primordial images that occur in the poetry of both the past and the present. They are such images as that of the mysterious cavern, of the guilt-haunted wanderer, of the fountain, of the buried corn, and so on. She keeps specific passages of the poems that she discusses steadily in view. In her sensitive commentaries on particular poems, Miss Bodkin is for the most part filling out implications, suggesting comparisons between the symbols in the poem and symbols as they occur in tribal and religious life, and in general employing the special findings of psychology and comparative religion in the same way that she employs other fields of knowledge. Such work is always important, but it scarcely invokes a revolutionary technique—nor does Miss Bodkin regard it as doing so. Her very conception of archetypes implies that images endowed with such universal significance—images rooted so deep in the human psyche—must have yielded much of their significance to both poet and reader in the past. The work left to the modern psychologist can be no more than to make explicit in a particular way what was already in some sense intuited by the earlier reader.

> It is with the complete resources of our minds that we must appreciate, if appreciation is to be genuine. If, for instance, we have found certain elements in experience made newly explicit through the teaching of Freud, that new awareness will enter into our apprehension of *Othello,* or of *Hamlet,* though it was not present in Shakespeare's own thought, nor in the audience for whom he wrote.
>
> One can no more bind within the limits of the author's intention the interactions with new minds of a play or poem that lives on centuries after his death, than one can restrict within its parents' understanding the interrelations of the child that goes forth from their bodies to live its own life in the world.[2]

Thus, Miss Bodkin, refusing to allow the "author's intention" to tyrannize over the meaning of the work, recognizes the possibility of a growth of meaning in the constituent elements of a work and therefore a possible development in the meaning of the work itself. But she is as far as she can be from suggesting that a new "archetypal" criticism will now replace criticism as we have known it. Knowledge of archetypes may be regarded as an acquisition of new artistic materials or else as an enrichment of older artistic materials: it constitutes an enlargement of the poet's (and of the reader's) potential resources; but it is not a "new" method of organization or interpretation.

[2] *Archetypal Patterns of Poetry* (Oxford, 1934), p. 334, by permission of the publishers, Oxford University Press, Inc. Another excellent treatment of this sort of imagery is to be found in W. H. Auden's *The Enchafèd Flood* (1950).

VI

RECENT "myth" criticism, as previous allusions in this chapter indicate, owes more to Carl Jung than to any other man. It may be interesting, therefore, to examine his notions of the relation of the study of myth to literary criticism. There can be no doubt as to the serious role that Jung assigns to myth. One aspect of the seriousness with which he takes the function of myth in our psychic life is his insistence that one must discriminate very carefully among myths and even among dreams. He does not speak of dreaming "skilfully" or "eloquently," but he does assert that one can on occasion dream "significantly." He writes that he is compelled to admit "that the unconscious mind is capable at times of assuming an intelligence and purposiveness which are superior to actual conscious insight."[3] The implications of this statement are large. If the activity of the unconscious in dream and myth is not merely a symptom of psychic disorder but "at times" at least is an intelligent and purposive ordering, then all myths and dreams are not alike; some are evidently more purposive and significant than others. And this judgment, that some are more purposive and significant than others, implies a cognitive criticism and interpretation of myth and dream. Jung means too that the function of "purposive" myths and dreams is not merely or even primarily cathartic; it is knowledge-giving: dreams give us knowledge of ourselves.

This emphasis in Jung perhaps accounts for the fact that he has been more directly influential on recent literary criticism than Freud has been. Miss Bodkin has put the matter very well:

> The difference between the two schools [of Freud and Jung] lies in Jung's belief that a synthetic or creative function does pertain to the unconscious—that within the fantasies arising in sleep or waking life there are present indications of new directions or modes of adaptation, which the reflective self, when it discerns them, may adopt, and follow with some assurance that along these lines it has the backing of unconscious energies.[4]

It may not be too much to say that Jung (in contrast to Freud with his "psychiatric" analysis even of the poem) brings a cognitive criticism to bear even upon the dream.

> The "manifest" dream-picture is the dream itself, and contains the "latent" meaning. If I find sugar in the urine, it is sugar, and not a façade that conceals albumen. When Freud speaks of

[3] *Psychology and Religion* (New Haven, 1938), p. 45.
[4] *Archetypal Patterns*, p. 73.

the "dream-façade," he is really speaking, not of the dream itself, but of its obscurity. . . . We say that a dream has a false front only because we fail to see into it. We would do better to say that we are dealing with something like a text that is unintelligible, not because it is a façade, but simply because we cannot read it.[5]

Some of the dreams that he describes are very elaborate symbolic structures. Their parts are ordered in accordance with a "logic of the imagination" and are therefore, to the proper interpreter, coherent and intelligible. They are in some sense analogous to poems, and the role of the interpreter—if we are to judge from Jung's own procedure in his published analyses—is analogous to that of the literary critic. For example, Jung will write of a particularly elaborate dream that it "speaks of religion and that it means to do so. Since the dream is elaborate and consistent it suggests a certain logic and a certain intention." [6] Moreover the interpretation does not require a secret key: the symbols that it makes use of are remarkably "public" and traditional—not nearly so clandestine as one might have thought. The condensations, juxtapositions and symbolic ambiguities, as Jung interprets this dream, show a remarkable resemblance to those met with in much modern literary criticism.

"A great work of art," Jung writes, "is like a dream." And he specifies two ways in which it is: "for all its apparent obviousness it does not explain itself and is never unequivocal." That is, the poem is not prescriptive; neither the poem nor even the dream says "You ought" or "This is the truth." Moreover, like the dream, the poem requires us to make our own interpretation, for the poem presents an image "in much the same way as nature allows a plant to grow, and we must draw our own conclusions." [7]

VII

IN VERY important ways, Jung's conception of the poem parallels that of the symbolist theorist. A poem is organic; it is filled with implicit meaning; the relation of its parts may transcend that of rational arrangement—may indeed involve the reconciliation of apparent contradictions. This last parallel with certain modern theories of poetry becomes especially apparent if, following up Jung's claim for parallelism between poem and dream, we attribute to poetry on his view the kind of tension which he is emphatic in claiming for dream. Psychic energy in general, he

---

[5] *Modern Man in Search of a Soul* (New York, 1933), p. 15, by permission of the publishers, Harcourt, Brace and Company, Inc.

[6] *Psychology and Religion*, p. 31.   [7] *Modern Man*, p. 198.

tells us, involves "the play of opposites." The healthy growth of the mind involves a shattering of narrow states of consciousness through "the tension inherent in the play of opposites" and a building up thereby of a state of "wider and higher consciousness."[8]

We have thus far stressed the likeness between poem and dream. Jung in fact draws a very sharp distinction between them. The dream is shaped by the unconscious, but the poem, though it may draw upon the depths of man's being, is "apparently intentional and consciously shaped."[9] Moreover Jung is careful to distinguish the psychologist's study of the poet from his study of the poem:

> The truth is that [Freud's view of art] takes us away from the psychological study of the work of art, and confronts us with the psychic disposition of the poet himself. That the latter presents an important problem is not to be denied, but the work of art is something in its own right, and may not be conjured away.[1]

The psychologist, then, is able (if he wishes) to study the poem and not merely the mind of the man who made it.

If we ask what specific contribution the psychologist can make to the study of literature, Jung first offers us a distinction between two broad classes of literary work. There is what he calls "psychological" literature, which

> always takes its materials from the vast realm of conscious human experience—from the vivid foreground of life, we might say. I have called this mode of artistic creation psychological because in its activity it nowhere transcends the bounds of psychological intelligibility. . . .
>
> In dealing with the psychological mode of artistic creation, we never need ask ourselves what the material consists of or what it means.[2]

But this question does force itself upon us as soon as we come to the visionary mode of creation.

> We are astonished, taken aback, confused, put on our guard or even disgusted—and we demand commentaries and explanations. We are reminded in nothing of everyday, human life,

[8] *Modern Man*, p. 117.

[9] *Modern Man*, p. 175. The full context of Jung's discussion makes it quite plain that the intentionality is to be inferred from the work itself and not merely from some statement by the poet. In this matter Jung is emphatic, writing that "the truth is that poets are human beings, and that what a poet has to say about his work is often far from being the most illuminating word on the subject" (p. 186).

[1] *Modern Man*, p. 185.   [2] *Modern Man*, pp. 180-1.

but rather of dreams, night-time fears and the dark recesses of the mind that we sometimes sense with misgiving.[3]

Apparently, the literature of the visionary mode may require the services of the psychologist. What those specific services are, it remains to consider.

In the first place, according to Jung, the psychologist can show us that the kind of experience with which, say, a Dante or a Melville deals is, in spite of its "visionary" nature, important and to be taken seriously. The psychologist can point out that "we must take [the vision] at least as seriously as we do the experiences that underlie the psychological mode of artistic creation," experiences that "no one doubts . . . are both real and serious."[4]

In the second place, the psychologist can point out that however "dark this nocturnal world" with which the visionary artist deals may be, "it is not wholly unfamiliar."[5] The last clause is worth stressing. If what the visionary artist treated were *wholly* unfamiliar, that is, really private and eccentric, its expression might have value for the artist himself and might provide an interesting case-study for the psychologist, but it would cease to be a work of art. The fact is that the nocturnal world is in some sense the world of all of us, and this the psychologist can help us to see.

The work of the psychologist, *qua* psychologist, therefore, turns out to be not so much a work of interpretation as one of vindication. The artist is to be freed from the charge that his vision is merely a symptom of some personal psychic maladjustment and from the charge that his symbols are merely subjective distortions of that world fashioned by those whom Jung calls the "reason-mongers." Actually, as to specific "methods" of interpretation, Jung has in his later writings very little to say. But the clear implication is against the possibility of any special "method" by which the psychologist takes over from, and substitutes himself for, the literary critic. Jung has made it plain that "visionary" literature includes some of the most important literature that we have—*Moby Dick* and even the *Divine Comedy*. But he is careful also to include among instances of "visionary" literature such a work as Rider Haggard's *She*.[6] Jung does not indicate how we know that *She* is not so great a novel as *Moby Dick;* he simply takes it for granted that we do know it. But this judgment of relative literary value is clearly made by the critic, judging by whatever criteria a critic does judge, and not by the psychologist judging as psychologist.

To the question raised earlier as to whether the new "myth" criticism possesses a special key for literary interpretation, the answer of

[3] *Modern Man*, p. 182.   [4] *Modern Man*, p. 185.   [5] *Modern Man*, p. 188.
[6] Jung also says specifically that "Literary products of highly dubious merit are often of the greatest interest to the psychologist" (*Modern Man*, p. 177).

Jung would seem to be an emphatic no. The literary critic will obviously profit by all that he can learn about what human beings are, about how they behave, and especially about the way their minds work.[7] He will also find valuable whatever knowledge he can obtain about the languages in which men express themselves—not only Latin or French or Old Norse, but all those recurrent patterns of symbolism to which the modern anthropologist or the depth psychologist or the student of comparative literature direct our attention. By studying these symbolic languages he will learn again how various is man and yet how much the same man remains. In this area of knowledge Jung furnishes stimulating—even exciting—observations, but by his own confession, his contribution would seem to consist in having added to our knowledge about man's processes of symbolization and the great immemorial symbols—the archetypes—in which man tends to express himself.

So it is also with W. B. Yeats, surely the greatest of the recent poets who have tried to use myth as the basis of their own work. As we have indicated in an earlier chapter,[8] Yeats proposed in writing *A Vision* to create a living myth. But no one knew better than Yeats that this would be literally impossible. We find him saying, therefore, that no mere intellectual revolution can bring back the "old simple celebration of life tuned to its highest pitch." What might be possible for such a revolution to bring about would necessarily have to be "something more deliberate . . . , more systematized, more external, more self-conscious, as must be at a second coming."[9]

Just so. Yeats's own "myth" as embodied in *A Vision* is more fully systematized, more deliberate, more external than any genuine myth can be. *A Vision* is in part a theory of history; in part a psychology of creation, in part—and perhaps most importantly—a dictionary of public and semi-personal symbols—a kind of logbook of the symbols that Yeats had used and was in the future to use in his own poetry. *A Vision* contains some prose wrought almost fully up to the pitch of poetry; and it throws light upon Yeats's own development as a thinker and an artist. But the finest of Yeats's poems do not depend upon it. They transcend it, making use of the "natural" and traditional symbols that he discusses in *A Vision*, or at times ignoring that body of symbols altogether and creating their own symbols. They are poems and their symbols are poetically effective, not because Yeats was a maker of myths but because he was a poet. And we for our part recognize his poems to be poems by whatever means we have for recognizing poetry.

---

[7] "Psychology and the study of art will always have to turn to one another for help, and the one will not invalidate the other" (*Modern Man*, p. 177).

[8] Cf. *ante* Chapter 26.

[9] *Wheels and Butterflies*, 1934 (New York, 1935), pp. 65-6.

PART FIVE

CHAPTER 32

EPILOGUE

§ retrospect: from Plato through the Middle Ages—II. the Renaissance and neo-classic eras—III. the romantic and post-romantic, to about 1940—IV. the historical method as a study of the audience, criticism of gross structure, myth and ritual origins, the century of the common man—V. the correct view of Plato's rhapsode? the critical problem of values and emotions, subject and object, relative and universal, the role of words, accent on experience, light refracted through a crystal, reality of external values, the "naive"—VI. aesthetic emotion and real life, tension and reconciliation, tragic and comic, Plato's Philebus, pure and impure pleasures, aesthetics of "significant form," 18th-century dismal feelings, opposed to analysis of wit and irony, problem of pain and destruction, material concreteness, division, conflict, evil in literature, problem of moral commitment, Manichaean dualism, human substance vs. philosophic melodrama—VII. irony as metaphoric structure, "form," the metaphysical metaphor, metaphor as universality and concreteness, metaphor and historical information, multiple perspectives, Aristotelian mimetic, Ricardian affective, Crocean expressionistic and linguistic, metaphor in criticism, status of the literary "kinds," various focuses—VIII. values sensory, spiritual, and aesthetic (representative and non-representative), reduction up or down, opposing and reconciling terms, "speculative," "practical," "doing," "making," "useful," "fine," various simplifications, the difficult alternative: "A theory of poetic or fine art must keep asserting in various idioms, by various stratagems, in accord with the demands of the dialectic of the time, the special character of poetry as a tensional union of making with seeing and saying" §

THE HISTORY WHICH WE HAVE JUST BROUGHT TO ONE OF ITS MOMEN-
tary conclusions in the modern theory of mythic archetypes had
one of its remote formal beginnings, we remember, in a Platonic
dialogue where an ironic dialectician compelled a naive professor and
reciter of poetry, a rhapsode, to make some damaging admissions about
the kind of science or wisdom which either the rhapsode or his authority the poet might lay claim to. The upshot of the inquisition
appeared to be that neither poet nor rhapsode, so far as they were
simply poet or rhapsode, "knew" anything at all. They were prompted
to their marvelous utterance by a divinely irrational afflatus; they were
out of their minds with a power which came directly to the poet and
was passed on by him to the rhapsode and to *his* auditors by a kind of
magnetism.

The *Ion* was an early and simple preliminary to Plato's more elaborate attacks on the illusionistic and emotive power of poetry (and of
rhetoric) in the *Republic*, *Phaedrus* and other mature dialogues. Aristotle in his *Poetics* answered that a workout of painful emotions is a
good thing, effecting a homeopathic purgation, and as for the allegedly
deceptive remove at which poetry stood from the universals, the tragic
or epic poem was actually a kind of ethical invention which came much
closer than the uncontrived chronicle of history to saying something
serious and philosophic and universal about the human protagonist. There
were hints about a certain blend of goodness and fault in that protagonist and his experience of disastrous results. A comic poem was more
abstract, less mythic, and the mistakes made were less painful and less
destructive. In his *Rhetoric* Aristotle made some remarks about verbal
tricks and heightened metaphoric ways of speaking, and about the character of a speaker and the emotions of his audience. These were inescapable dimensions of discourse, and as they might be used in one way
by the sophist, the honest orator had better look well to their opposite
use.

A few hundred years later in Augustan Rome we found the urbane
lyric and epistolary poet Horace still talking—in a tradition of Peripatetic codifications—about dramatic and epic poetry and speaking casually about Socratic wisdom as a sufficient source of poetic content. It
seemed important to him—or he spoke as if it seemed important—to
recognize certain well defined types of poetry, their metres, contents,
and rules of decorum. He said that correct usage in words was important and along with that a great deal of care and craft in putting
them together. Despite his formal textbook talk about tragedy and comedy (the genres a young aspirant would be expected to try his hand at),
Horace himself was a conversational, satiric, and epistolary poet—and
through this focus on poetry as a kind of skilled and gentlemanly ex-

ercise in talking he makes his shrewdest observations. But then at Rome less than a century later, we have, in the all but anonymous Greek man of letters who wrote the *Peri Hupsous*, almost the direct opposite of Horace. The *Peri Hupsous* is a celebration of ecstasy and inspiration; it now asserts in full earnestness and enthusiasm the view that was framed half playfully in Plato's *Ion*. The educational prestige of declamation and rhetoric was such in first-century Rome that the treatise of Longinus could not but be much preoccupied with certain technical entanglements, figures and kinds of diction and formulas for amplification. But the special and pulsing accent of Longinus is on the great and impassioned soul of the poet, his flashes and spurts of inspiration, the careless and plunging grandeur of his utterance, the bigness of the objects which inspire him, and the corresponding transport of his audience.

And that accent was something far from alien to the full Roman neo-Platonism which appears two centuries later with the metaphysician and visionary Plotinus. The difference is that whereas Longinus rests his case on the flash of inspiration, the quasi-divine illumination, Plotinus, systematic, meditative, profoundly metaphysical and brooding, would integrate the flash into a comprehensive philosophy of divine intelligence and life radiant through and immanent in all the universe and all human souls and minds. A special instance of that intelligence is the artist, who by some superior access to divinity gives us the better and brighter image of Zeus. The ambitious synthetic reasoning of Plotinus produces some interesting emphases, such as those on the beauty and simplicity of light, on the superiority of the ocular sense which meets and appreciates light, and on the likeness and union of knowing organ and subject with object. The same reasoning produces two such difficult problems as that of the double form (form upon form) in the carved stone, and the conflict between the divine principle of unity and the Stoic principle of beauty in the complexity implied by "symmetry." St. Augustine with a geometric and numerical emphasis on unity and harmony, and Aquinas (despite a nearly Platonic assignment of poetry to the area of sophistry) continue the Plotinian accent on order and radiance and on "connaturality" of subject and object.

The long course of the Christian Middle Ages acknowledges and develops without deviation the philosophy of intelligible unity, being, and beauty, with an accent now on numerical harmony, astronomy and music, now on a cosmological principle of visible radiance, and always on the vast and minutely detailed symbolism of God's illuminated book, the universe. Thus one kind of Platonic strain joins with and, from Patristic times on, helps to develop the ancient allegorical reading of poetry, which is freshly and with unprecedented vigor applied to the exegesis of the Hebrew and Christian Scriptures. The Middle Ages and later the Renaissance make a long period of all-out symbolic reading—though scarcely in the more fluid and "creative" sense in which "symbolism" has been understood in times closer to our own. Finally, the Middle Ages is a period of a certain kind of rhetorical poetics— *Poetria Nova* in the 13th century—which means Hellenistic prescriptions for how to use all the figures, and on what occasions.

II

DURING all that period Aristotle was not known as a literary authority, and there was no other authority. But with the 16th century in Italy Aristotle's *Poetics* had to be dealt with (perhaps for the first time directly as a dead system of partly cryptic notes), and Horace too, who became "fused" with Aristotle in a newly completed code. But meanwhile there was the luxuriance of vernacular literature from Dante to Ariosto to be coped with by the theoretical arbiters, vernacular problems of diction and of metrics, and of burlesque and "errant" romance forms of epic. There was the heroic love theme of Tasso, the pastoral mixture innovated by Guarini. Hence a series of denunciations and spirited defences. Romantic freedoms were won, but the classic professors were stout champions too—and from Scaliger and Castelvetro, though for different reasons, emerged the hyper-Aristotelian dramatic unities of action, time and place, destined to become for French dramatists of the next century and for Dryden a theoretical precedent and challenge of great meaning. During the later 16th century in Italy the question about levels of symbolism appears in somewhat simpler forms than in the Middle Ages, and there appears too the grand question, implied in the whole classical debate from Plato and Aristotle on, as to whether poetry is an "icastic" (or literal, or realistic) image, or whether it has some kind of warrant to be imaginative or "fantastic." *Aut prodesse aut delectare* too is much debated—and all possible combinations of the aims of pleasing and teaching are contrived, including in the French mid-17th century at least as early as the Abbé D'Aubignac's *Pratique du Théâtre*, 1657, the notion that poetry is to please *through* instructing —a notable, if somewhat cramped, anticipation of the later famous idea that aesthetic values are one kind of end in themselves. Sir Philip Sidney is the Elizabethan English man of letters who gives us the best epitome of all these continental themes, especially the didactic and moral. His phrase about the poet "ranging within the zodiac of his own wit" and his dictum that the poet "nothing affirmeth and therefore never lieth" are brilliant, if perhaps only incidental, announcements of poetic freedom and might. And beside these may be set Bacon's passage about science buckling and bowing the mind to reality, poetry "submitting the shews of things to the desires of the mind."

In the generation of the Jacobeans, Ben Jonson's more ruggedly assertive didactic and satiric classicism includes a surprisingly severe, almost agelastic, version of Aristotle's meager dictum that the comic is a form of the ugly. Jonson furnishes also a lively demonstration, through free and virile Englishing, how little the classic mind thought that previous realization of an idea could tarnish it.

The most long-lived, productive and important English critic of the 17th century is Dryden, who in his several phases—as the "new" English dramatic theorist against the French norms, as heroic dramatist, court wit and conversationalist, as Shakespearian critic, as satirist or refined executioner of dullness, as translator of the classics, as translator and appreciator of Chaucer—shows us the meaning of such gradually shifting neo-classic debates as those concerning the stage unities and rhyme in drama (matters of intensity and realization disguised as matters of verisimilitude), those concerning verbal decorum, the real, the marvelous and the heroic, and those concerning such various topics as "poetic justice," the serious aims of laughter, the rivalry between ancients and moderns, the possibility and the meaning of translation and imitation. The "heroic" focus (so far as it really was a theoretical focus) was a momentary juncture of Aristotelian ideas about the hero with inflational notions of grandeur and inspiration. Concurrently (in a confused alliance with the heroic) came the quieter and tougher revival of Horatian courtly urbanity—the kind of wit that was destined to succeed "metaphysical" wit (a thing uncelebrated in contemporary theory), the kind of poetry that would persist longest into the severe era of reason that was being ushered in.

The 17th century saw the end of Ciceronian and medieval and early Renaissance rhetorical culture; it was a century of decline in the prestige of words and the mysteries of auditory doctrine, of a soaring new prestige for seeing and diagramming, for the simplifying and classifying spirit of science. We have observed the variations in meaning of the index word "wit"—the gradual discountenancing of the metaphysical and imaginative meaning (one which might be used to describe the poetry of Donne, Herbert, Milton, or Shakespeare) and the evolution of the new concept of "true" wit as only judgment after all, propriety of thought and speech, "nature to advantage dressed"—until literary criticism centered in a highly ambiguous *new* key term. The term "wit" might now be either viewed suspiciously in its older poetic meaning, as by Locke or Addison, or applied in its safer new meaning (by reason of an ingeniously evasive submission to good sense on the part of the best English poets) in a deceptive way to current poetry.

In that crisis of the accomplished dissociation of sensibility, with Cartesian and Newtonian rationality running ahead to apparently limitless conquests of clarity, and with the verbal arts lavishing themselves

on patterns of oratorical trim, on repeated metaphorical recommenda-
tions of a lost sense—was heard the new accent on ocular and auditory
pleasure ("pleasures of the imagination"), on sensation, on the aesthetic,
on landscape, on supposed weddings of the arts in forms like oratorio,
song, and opera. And there was heard also, more and more plainly, the
new accent on feeling, on tender and sympathetic feeling, on the pleasures of painful feeling. The Platonic universal of Samuel Johnson and
Sir Joshua Reynolds was merged in the neo-Longinian sublime. Despite
much stalwart talk about norms and species, Johnson's classic garment
flies in tatters in the strong affective breezes. Yet classical precedents
were always invoked: for the sensational, the Horatian *ut pictura poesis;*
for the emotive, both Longinian ecstasy and sentimentalized versions of
Aristotelian catharsis. In the sublimity of awful and threatening natural
phenomena, in the physiognomy of emotive expressions, the aesthetic
of sensation and the aesthetic of emotion conclusively joined. The new
movement, for all its sources in antiquity, was headlong toward the
future and would be "modern" for at least two centuries to come. Add
the subtly pervasive principle of "association." This was first only a way
of breaking up traditional patterns of expectancy and of value. But in
a second phase (in conjunction with a new fondness for particularity
and especially for picturesque details of nature) it became a principle
of positive, creative, emotionally warm and plastic power—a principle
of imaginative "coalescence."

III

A CERTAIN kind of classicism persisted long in England under the name
and in the actuality of "poetic diction"—that curious species of glossy
ornament which was demolished by Wordsworth in the first phases of
his primitivism and simplism. After that the scene was clear for both
Wordsworth and Coleridge to proceed from "association" in its simpler
Hartleyan and mechanical phase to the more emotive and plastic notion
which, by pushing ahead only a slight distance and by showing in their
mature poems what the fullness of the doctrine could mean, they
established in the glorious (though momentary) status of "imagination." Coleridge added the deepening and fortification of German metaphysics—the epistemology of "object" and "subject," or the imaginative
reconciliation of these two opposites and along with them of art and
nature, emotion and thought, the universal and the particular, and other
satellites. Coleridge and Wordsworth show in a manageable landscape
vignette what the larger and more varied movement of German romanticism, the poetry and theory of Goethe and Schiller and Novalis,
the lectures of the Schlegels, the philosophy of Kant, Schelling and

Fichte, was in process of doing for the whole history of modern poetry and aesthetics in the West.

The romantic theory was in effect a highly ambiguous and double claim—a claim both for poetic freedom and for poetic responsibility. It was thus the cloud-capped starting point for certain quite opposite lines of poetic theory that came down through the 19th century toward our own day. One of these, moving from Kantian disinterest, formality and beauty, through French academic aesthetics and then early symbolist and Parnassian poetics, resulted in what we look back on as Art for Art's Sake—the end-of-the-century gilded celebration of autonomous poetic power. At the level of general aesthetics and linguistic, the philosophy of Benedetto Croce is the voraciously systematic expression of this view. Not so far removed from art-for-art's sake as we might wish to think, and in some phases part of it, was the thing, technically so much more subtle and more interesting to us, which came out of romantic "imagination" and "symbol" and became "symbolism." This seems to have come not so much directly from the German philosophers as through Coleridge and Poe, and Heine and Baudelaire, to the era of Mallarmé and the Wagnerians. Here was a more subtle "music" of "ideas" than the neo-classic theory of painting the passions had conceived—and a new quasi-spiritual reaction against the philosophy of science.

But those kinds of theory, both pure art and symbolism, were directly at odds with three other main kinds which developed the opposite accent of the romantic heritage—not that on autonomous privilege but that on moral and social power and evolutionary responsibility. Here were three versions of didacticism: one, the earliest and most fully romantic—what we may call the rhapsodic, the bardic, the prophetic, as it is brandished for instance in the *Defense of Poetry* by Shelley or the *Heroes and Hero Worship* of Carlyle; a second, the most nearly allied to a proper literary interest, the classical humanism, severity, and loftiness, both German and French in origin, which is fully expressed in English by Matthew Arnold; a third, owing much to Hegelian dialectic, getting under way more slowly, but more modern and more resolute, the Franco-Russian complex of ideas under the heads of the real, the natural, the social or sociological. This last was the most urgently didactic and the most confidently evolutionary of all. Tolstoy is the greatest literary artist who gave himself to this kind of theory. Tolstoy on what is true and telling in literature, on what is effete, jaded, hedonistic, and merely aristocratic, hits hard, and we may have to take him into account in a way that we do not have to take into account Zola on the novel as an experiment in a social science laboratory.

If we look around the critical scene and especially the American critical scene during the first decades of our own century, we see distinct aftermaths of all the 19th-century events which we have just been tracing: For one thing the exotic and flashy tail-ends of the art-for-art's sake tradition, the cosmopolitanism of the *Smart Set* and *Mercury* writers. For another, the continuation of Arnoldian humanism in the long influence of P. E. More and Irving Babbitt and the approximate end of that humanism in the twin detonations of the anthologies for and against it in 1930. There was also a strong socio-real tradition, under the names of naturalism, Responsibilities of the Novelist, and the uglier name of Muck-Raking, and also the coming of age of honest America, a matter of smoke and steel, the Prairie Schooner, and slabs of the sunburnt west. And then the most acutely didactic accent of all, in the Marxist criticism of the 1930's—rampaging until it becomes obvious to the literary intelligences connected with it that this kind of thing will never do.

One of the most novel strains of literary criticism produced by the 20th century has been that which we may roughly sum up under the name of psychologism. On the one hand, and perhaps most conspicuously: the Freudian kind, in the shape of new motivations drawn out of the unconscious for novels and poems, and literary biographies rewritten into case histories and ordeals. (Groping for tragic and comic motives in depth psychology and anthropology goes back through Freud to Nietzschean rhapsody and repose and Hegelian conflict of ethical substance.) And on the other hand: the quieter kind of affectivism, the equipoise, the beautiful harmony of impulses, promoted by Richards and his colleagues in the 'twenties. And this slips back through the exquisitely refined hedonism of Santayana to the affectivism connected with utilitarian ethics during the 19th century. J. S. Mill's two essays on poetry show how this 18th-century heritage could get into criticism. Mill echoes the way it had already done so in Wordsworth and Coleridge.

But by and large the literary discussion of the 19th century, unlike that of the 18th, had not been notable for any systematic affectivism. And when this romantic and aesthetic plea reappeared with Richards in the 1920's, it had so much to say about mere incipience of impulses and their equipoise that it was a new witness for something like a classical disinterest or detachment. With its up-to-date paraphernalia of verbal analysis, Ricardian aesthetic was readily available, or at least convertible, for purposes of cognitive literary discussion.

Richards connected readily enough with the "neo-classicism" which was represented in the same era by the conspicuous figures of Pound and Eliot. Twentieth-century "neo-classicism" derived attitudes from the intuitionist but classical philosopher T. E. Hulme, from the precise grammatical statements of Gourmont, and from the whole tide of the French symbolist and musically ironic poetics. (With Pound there was too the thing called "imagism," and at least a flourish of something supposed or pretended to be due to the fact of Chinese ideographic writing. But that can hardly be important.) Impersonality, craftsmanship, objectivity, hardness and clarity of a kind, a union of emotion with verbal object, a norm of inclusiveness and reconciliation and hence a close inter-dependence of drama, irony, ambiguity, and metaphor, or the near equivalence of these four—such ideas made up the neo-classic system as it worked its way into practical criticism about 1935 or 1940. And, however far short the system fell of being able to convince old-line historians or to demonstrate beyond appeal or cavil that this or that poem meant this much or that much or was excellent or not, the arrival of this kind of criticism did mean a new technical and objective interest in poetry.

IV

THE past fifteen years on the critical front have seen several new, or newish, large claims making headway. Let us move somewhat more slowly now for a few pages and let us restate and bring together certain themes which have appeared more or less separately in earlier chapters (21, 24, 31). The most academic of the new claims, the most profes-sional, the most scholarly, is that relatively new kind of graduate school study that seeks to substitute for the poem, not the author, as in former more romantic phases of historicism, but precisely and deliberately the audience for which the author may in any sense be proved to have written the poem. If we look back to the mid-18th century and the first clear start of the modern historical method in such documents as Thomas Warton's *Observations on the Faerie Queene*, Bishop Hurd's *Letters on Chivalry and Romance*, or even Samuel Johnson's *Preface to Shakespeare*, we note that their sympathy for the Gothic or the Eliza-bethan hesitates somewhat between a plea for tolerance of antique authors, despite the barbarous ages in which they wrote, and a plea for appreciation of the inspirational opportunities afforded by those very ages. But the decisive concept for the time was personal "genius." That is, criticism was on the side of Shakespeare in spite of his handicaps. In the 19th century, there were nationalism, folklorism, and cultural de-terminism, the race, milieu, and moment of Taine's *History*. But literary studies still tended to marshal such interests rather squarely behind the author. That is, they were important because they showed the mind of the author, what made him write the way he did. Sainte-Beuve's pro-fession of intense interest in the author's boyhood, his brothers and sisters, his parents and his grandparents, is an extreme yet typical in-stance of such Shandean depth in criticism. Despite the somewhat con-trary cultural massiveness of Courthope's *History of English Poetry*, it is mainly right to say that English and American literary research (following good continental models) continued until fairly recent years to be a pursuit of the author, his whole history, both internal and external, and his habitat. It requires perhaps only a tilt of the mirror to turn the habitat into the author's audience. And the audience had of course all along received attention. It was clearly one name for the socio-real focus. But to shift the accent of value in academic research (the accent on both the value of poetry itself and the value of research into poetic history) was yet another step, and it has been a fairly recent one. Until recently it was the normal aim of academic research to be able to announce: "And thus we prove what the author was trying to say," "thus we prove his learning and accuracy," "thus we prove his sincerity," or "thus we prove his deep feeling." But the new mode, one which is more comprehensive and difficult, and has yet advanced so little as to have perhaps a large and dangerous future, seems to entertain the aim of announcing: "And thus we prove that the author's poem was addressed to the audience of his day, or to the real audience, or to the audience that mattered." "Thus he knew what he was doing, and thus he was a good author." More and more articles in journals and books from university presses nowadays have titles referring to *Shakespeare's Audience*, to *The Social Mode of Restoration Comedy*, to *Paradise Lost and the Seventeenth Century Reader*, to *Box, Pit, and Gallery, The Theatrical Public in the Time of Garrick*, to the rise of a reading public, to the number of Victorian persons who bought Macaulay's *History of England* or Tennyson's *Maud*.

It is not difficult to suggest sympathies between the new kind of historicism turned toward the audience and a second recent critical trend, the bad conscience which has been developing in some critics with regard to nice verbal analysis. This is being expressed not only in direct misgivings about analysis, or pleas for a more "open" contextual reading, but also partly in the form of proclamations about the need for doing justice to the overall structures of stories and dramas, their motives, plots, actions, tragic rhythms, their deeper, wider, and more bulky symbolism, their bigger meaning—in short, all that part and aspect of them which may be supposed to be too massive and too important to be penetrated by the technique known as verbal criticism. This kind of conscience had a summary and rather impressive exposition about 100 years ago in Matthew Arnold's Preface to his *Poems* of 1853, where he repented of the inaction, or the suicidally limited action, of his *Empedocles*, appealed to the great serious action of the Greek tragedies, and thought that Shakespeare enjoyed such rhetorical virtuosity that he had been a bad influence on romantic poets, notably on Keats. (Keats, like a modern critic summoned before the bar in Chicago, was too much interested in words and images.) Arnold was giving Germanic and post-romantic moral resonance to an older classical plea—heard, for instance, in Rymer, with echoes by Dryden, and in Gildon—that Shakespeare was defective and not to be imitated in the fundamental matter of plot, and that a critic ought indeed to concern himself with the plot, with the whole poem, the grand design, and not be a "criticaster" of words, a "piece-broker." It was a theme heard in the classically severe Lessing too, whose ideas on drama were parallel to his Lockean and Cartesian notion that the colors of painting were unreal and hence inferior to the reality of sculptural mass and shape. The ideas of Arnold were part of his ambitious humanistic and moralistic program for literature. That, as we have been saying, was one branch of post-romantic didacticism. Later on there was a new criticism concerning prose fiction, not the criticism of Zola, but that of Flaubert, James and Ford, and this was not so far from the spirit of symbolist poetics. It does not appear that Henry James was much afraid of being caught in the mesh of words or of piddling away his effort on the texture or surface of things. If a woman put her hand on a table and looked at him in a certain way, that was for James, or for one of his characters, an event. And the event interlocked with every other event in the world. (The artist tried to conjure or pretend some kind of circle around it.) It is not in these great theorists of prose fiction that we find the scruple against dallying with the details of the medium.

But we do find it again more recently, and not only in the fortifications of a certain kind of academic neo-Aristotelianism but in more momentous campaigns under the standard of myth and the ritual origins. Here metaphor is action, and big action. For the first time since Dryden and Le Bossu the literary gist is supposed to be big enough and solid enough so that you would think it could be rendered essentially from one language to another. The rhythm of the tragic idea—the going out in quest, the confrontation and passion, the discovery or education—is the big thing. We have observed that the book which gives this theory the most persuasive articulation is Francis Fergusson's *Idea of a Theatre*. Here we have the most imposing of the several recent critical trends. Surely the hugest cloudy symbol, the most threatening, of our last ten or fifteen years in criticism is the principle of criticism by myth and ritual origins.

It is true that this new mythologism is not always associated with any strong mistrust of rhetorical inspection. Expression and symbolism can make a ready enough alliance with myth and ritual. For all four are theories of the creative imagination, the fiat of the human spirit as deity or as participating in deity. Herder and Schelling and Cassirer join Lévy-Bruhl and Frazer and the Cambridge classical anthropologists in the secularization of the spirit according to the philosophy of symbolic form. Philip Wheelwright's *Burning Fountain*, the most recent important book in the mythic mode, is a magnificent synopsis of relations between a special semantics on the one hand and on the other ritual anthropology interpreted by the darkness visible of depth psychology. The semantics states the difference between a scientifically bare "steno-language" and the "plurisignations," the trans-logical "depth-language" common to poetry, myth, religion, and metaphysics. The anthropology dwells on hereditary and "preconsciously rooted" symbols, symbols of the "threshold," the world view of primitive man, the death and rebirth of the vegetation god. (The *Fire Sermon* of Buddha, the *Oresteia* of Aeschylus, the *Four Quartets* of Eliot may be cited to define the infra-red range of illustration.) To a writer who participated strongly in the new yearning for a gross structural poetics Wheelwright's book might well look like a deplorable re-celebration of imagery and thematic "paraplots."

But myth and ritual are, as we have already said, patterns of action and of large action. In that way they can have their easy enough connection with an anti-verbal poetics. And both these interests involve a stress on what is important about poetry in a large and public way, what can give it religious and social dignity and didactic claims. The validation for the new myth philosophy is thought to lie in the primitive racial unconsciousness. Thus it eschews the risky appeal to objectivity, but plunges in the vast reservoir of racial and prelogical unconsciousness for an intersubjective base of universality. It arrives at the phase of apocalyptic and prophetic vision. Along with the Greeks and the Hindus (from whom Friedrich Schlegel also once drew inspiration), there is Milton, there is Blake, there is Melville, there is Yeats, there is Eliot, there is Joyce, and maybe there is Faulkner. The three main trends of recent criticism which we have just sketched—that toward the audience, that toward gross structure, and that toward myth—have in common a horizontal or folkways alignment (in contrast, for instance, to the vertical and aristocratic alignment of the neoclassic formalism). All three show to some degree the didactic and evangelizing interest which was prepared in the 19th-century socio-real tradition. Despite the fact that sociology does come out of the 19th century, the humanism and literary theory in English and French during that century were mainly inspirational, individualistic, and heroic. It is the present century, as we all know, which is the century of the common man. The literary trends we have named conceive man, whether common or elite, in large multiples, thinking and responding in classes. Plato's rhapsode makes a strong bid for the recovery of his weeping thousands.

V

WHAT is the real status, the correct status, of Plato's rhapsode and of the poet whose inspired representative the rhapsode is? After Aristotle and throughout antiquity—in the Peripatetic and Horatian tradition, in the Isocratean and Ciceronian tradition of wisdom in oratorical eloquence, in the emotive and mysterious phases of neo-Platonism, the poetic power enjoyed a certain fairly high prestige, perhaps we may say an approximately sufficient degree and kind of prestige. During the Middle Ages both for theological reasons and because of the growing, strongly implicit scientific aims of the whole scholastic effort, poetry went through an era of theoretically low esteem. The Renaissance was a rebirth exactly of the humanistic classical literary claim, though this was vastly complicated now by codifications drawn out of the authority of the ancient writings and by the dialectic engendered from literary practice in the emergent spirit of "romance." The waning of the Renaissance into the era of literary neo-classicism and the first centuries of modern science brought a decline in the prestige of verbal power comparable to what Plato, at least in moments of the *Republic* and in the *Ion*, would seem to have thought desirable. The reawakening or German romantic renascence of poetic power drew plentifully enough on the classical heritage, but was also in a new way emotive, subjective, associational, "imaginative," creative, the claimant of a markedly new kind of authority. Since the day of the high romanticizing, literary theory has included perhaps the whole range of possible claims for poetry: the autonomy of various expressionisms, and of art for art's sake, the biographical and environmental substitutions made possible by improved historical methodology, the deterministic and evolutionary aspects of sociological theory, and the varied didacticisms of the 19th century, reappearing in the claims of the 20th-century archetypal myth.

We can study the history of changes in opinion, writes T. S. Eliot in his short history of English criticism, "without coming to the stultifying conclusion that there is nothing to be said but that opinion changes." The present writers have not written this short history of literary opinion without seeing in it a pattern of effort pointed toward at least a certain kind of goal.

The most difficult moment, the most insistently recurring moment under the most varying forms, in the history and dialectic of literary theory is that which touches values and emotions—or what human beings like and dislike and the experience of their liking and disliking. And one of the most sustained trends of modern critical history—paralleling and shadowing the course of modern metaphysics and psychology—has been toward the reduction of values to subjectivity, that is, toward the doctrine that what human beings like and dislike is a question that refers precisely and only to the experience itself of their liking and disliking. It would be difficult, perhaps impossible, for a literary critic or a historian of literary criticism to contrive within the limit of his own idiom and decorum a sufficient account of the difficult metaphysics that make the problem of value. Yet a literary theorist ought to be at least moderately aware of the relation his thoughts may show to that problem.

The great variety of human tastes for pleasure and of emotive responses to experience, the variety even for a single person from moment to moment and under this or that condition, may at times cast a chilly light over our speculations about value. These facts are scarcely matters which the theorist of poetry can dispute as facts. He can scarcely re-verify or re-count them, or balance or redress them by fresh statistics. He may, however, have a deeper or a shallower perspective in the under-standing of such facts. A sense of order, of hierarchy, of unity in the uni-verse of our experience—a sense of purpose, if one may whisper the word —can do something to dispel the cold illusion of the neutral substrate, the opaque ground below good and evil.

Let us say first that the situation of the person confronting his world of values is a vastly complicated one. He confronts not any single type and grade of thing constituting an objectively insulated and external "value," but various objects in various kinds of relations to himself. In each value situation there is both an objective and a subjective aspect— but the accent falls now upon one and now upon the other of these, and with various degrees of weight. A man is hurt by a knife or a club, and he feels the hurt and the damage as something that happens to a part of himself—not as a quality of the knife or club, the inflicting external entity. He tastes salt or sugar, and the taste with the liking or disliking of it is a subtle union of that specific new entity from outside both with his own mouth and with whatever may just previously have been tasted. And then, at a third level, he views red or blue, and whatever any theory may tell him about the relation of light to his eye (whatever sophistica-tion in theory of vision he is equal to) he experiences the pleasant or un-pleasant quality as a quality outside himself. (Such at least is the "phe-nomenology" of the event.) He looks at a landscape, and the complexity of the visual pattern and of the meanings inevitably attached to it place the locus of value even more emphatically—and stereoptically—outside. (To tickle one's foot, to "tickle" one's palate, to "tickle" one's fancy— these three grades in the semantics of the word "tickle" will summarize the series of values which we have just sketched.) Finally, suppose that a given man sees or hears of a murder (a knife stuck in another man); here the value implicated exhibits a very distinct and superior kind of external firmness and objectivity—that of the ethical realm. And yet this value is rooted in the pain and destruction inflicted upon a certain subject. To say that a value is relative to a subject is not to say that the value is relative in the sense that anybody's opinion about it may be as correct as anybody else's. Or, to say that a value is not objective, or not purely and simply objective, is not to say that it is not *universal*, or valid in relation to all subjects. Some such term as *inter-subjective* may perhaps be invoked to describe the accent that falls on some universals. It is surely true, for in-stance, that any human subject whatever will suffer pain and damage from knife wounds—even though this truth is not sufficient to establish a property of evil intrinsic to the knife itself.

But here let us revert, with some insistence, to the fact that the present discussion is concerned not directly with knives and persons, with sensory pleasures or moral values, but with poetry and hence with words. The problem of value which we are sketching is made even more complicated for the poetic theorist—and perhaps a certain distance from the basic value problem is created for him—by the fact that poetry is composed of words. For words introduce a special kind of valuing "subject," the subject who not only responds to values with emotions or feelings but formulates and utters (if only to himself) his awareness of both value and response. Not that such persons are unusual, but by the very fact of utterance a person values in a special way.

And most likely he values in a very subtly mingled way:—by exclamations and by the rhythmic aspects of utterance achieving something like a direct expression at least of vaguer feeling; by the names of pleasures and pains and of emotions and of their correlative values (hate, anger, love, and joy, the good and the bad, the beautiful and the ugly) achieving a firmer if more abstract delineation; by the neutral-sounding names of all sorts of objects, qualities, actions, and relations (of man, animal, and stone, of color, shape, and movement) achieving a deeper substantiation. The words of the last category do not name either responses or values directly, yet in real contexts they may have intense emotive import. For the purpose of poetic criticism it would appear to be significant to divide this large group into two great parts: the names of objects and actions which are causes, or motives, of an emotive response (the characters and the plot of the poem), and the names of the large world of symbols and associations which, though not direct objects of emotion, often fortify emotive interpretation (the black, the white, the crow, and the dove). No one of these classes of words carries very far in creating the expression (or in promoting the contagion) of emotive experience. They operate always by a complex meshing and nowhere more than in the verbal constructions which are poems. The complexity of their operation forbids all the more extreme simplifications of poetic theory—both the simply mimetic (theories of either real or metaphysically ideal imitation of the objective world) and the simply emotive or sentimental (pure theories of emotive expression or pure theories of emotive result).

One of the main lessons of critical history would seem, indeed, to be that the stress of literary theory must fall on the *experience* (subjective and emotive) rather than on the *what*, the object of value so far as that is outside *any* experiencing subject. Yet, for reasons which we have been sketching, this lesson need not be interpreted as relegating the values of poetry to the realm of the whimsical and undebatable. A refraction of light through a crystal tells something about the light, something about the crystal; the refraction itself is a kind of reality, interesting to observe. Let us say that poetry is a kind of reality refracted through subjective responses. This refraction itself is an area of reality. Does the refraction tell us something unique and profound about the reality beyond itself? We need not actually say much about this for the purposes of a workable poetics. (Much will depend on what we conceive the ultimate character of that reality to be.)

The norm of wit and cunning word-play entertained by Horace and centuries later, with a stress on the imitation of gentlemanly polite conversation, by Boileau, Dryden, and Pope, was one version of this important truth:—that if poetry is to "imitate," it will imitate what is alive with the human spirit. And no less relevant to the same truth was the fully self-conscious, creative and expressionist romantic theory. The following resonant statement by Shelley has been partly quoted in an earlier chapter:

> . . . as the lyre trembles and sounds after the wind has died away, so the child seeks, by prolonging in its voice and motions the duration of the effect, to prolong also a consciousness of the cause. In relation to the objects which delight a child, these expressions are, what poetry is to higher objects. The savage . . . expresses the emotions produced in him by surrounding objects in a similar manner; and language and gesture, together with plastic or pictorial imitation, become the image of the combined effect of those objects, and of his apprehension of them. Man in society, with all his passions and his pleasures, next becomes the object of the passions and pleasures of man; an additional class of emotions produces an augmented treasure of expressions; and language, gesture, and the imitative arts, become at once the representation and the medium, the pencil and the picture, the chisel and the statue, the chord and the harmony.

In a more soberly grammatical passage of the *Biographia* (Chapter XXII) Coleridge wrote:

> Be it observed . . . that I include in the *meaning* of a word not only its correspondent object, but likewise all the associations which it recalls. For language is framed to convey not the object alone, but likewise the character, mood and intentions of the person who is representing it.

A capsule symbol of the situation for the theorist might be made out of the *Poetics* of Aristotle, which talks about *mimēsis* or the imitation (through words and music and scenes and an outward story) of certain objects, but the objects are characters, passions, and *praxeis*, that is, actions or farings, adventures, experience—objects of the inner realm of spirit.

Yet we have been implying, and let us now say more plainly, that to entertain such a theory of poetic value is not to *deny* the reality and the value of the outer realm, the *what* which is at various levels external to each valuing subject. The theory cannot make such a denial, even at what may appear the most superficial levels, without dissolving the grounds on which it hopes to talk about poetic experience. As we move into the inner moral and spiritual experience of man in search of our most clearly absolute, our most securely universal, concepts of value, it may seem that we leave behind, abandon to an uncertain and merely academic fate, the values, pleasant or unpleasant, which in a more superficial scheme we might assign to such external phenomena as the colors red and blue. Neither the poet nor the theorist, however, is in a good position to leave these behind. If there were nobody else at all—no metaphysician, moralist, or theologian—who cared to speak in defence of sensory values—yet the poet, in his indirect and obscure way, would have to go on confessing them, and his theorist would have to think about them. For they contribute the symbolic, the external, the phenomenological language by which the poet speaks about the inner and deeper realities of value. And if they did not constitute at least an inter-subjectively universal and reliable set of values, they could not be used as signs in the poet's communication. Most likely it is not necessary for the theorist of poetry to decide the nice metaphysical question as to the *locus* of each sensory value—*in* object or *in* subject. Perhaps the very question is illusory. But both poet and theorist can be sure of one minimum thing: that at least inter-subjective viability is required for poetic communication. It will not be enough for a reader to be instructed (by a theorist or by a historian) that once upon a time, here and there, this meant that, purple was royal, black meant death, Dorian was martial, Lydian erotic, flutes were sweet, thunder frightening. If a poem is actually experienced and valued, these things, no less than (and as a condition for) the deeper poetic meanings of spirit, must lie somehow within the range of experience.

"We see how . . . [Schiller] plagued himself," says Goethe, "with the design of perfectly separating sentimental from *naive* poetry. For the former he could find no proper soil, and this brought him into unspeakable perplexity. As if . . . sentimental poetry could exist at all without the *naive* ground in which, as it were, it has its root."[1] A theorist of poetry may be driven to be some kind of idealist about the nature of poetry itself or the area of its operation. But if he remains close to the objects of his scrutiny—that is, to actual poems—he will be equally driven to remain a realist in his conception of the universe in which the poetic area is contained and in which poetry finds its reasons. Theories of sheer affectivity and subjective valuing have suffered the paradox of promoting not enthusiasm for value but distance, detachment, cooling, neutrality. The sterner metaphysical, cognitive theories, talking about

[1] *Conversations*, November 14, 1823.

real right and wrong, real beauty and ugliness, are the theories which actually sustain value and make responses to value possible. For response cannot feed indefinitely on itself.[2]

VI

WHAT is the relation of the poetic or aesthetic emotion to the emotions of real or ordinary life? This difficult question has been implicit in the critical debate from ancient days, with the catharsis of Aristotle or the transport of Longinus, to the recent past, with the incipience and equipoise of Ricardian psychology or the Freudian varieties of worked-off inhibitions. If one has to make a stark choice between the simply realistic theory—that poetry deals with straight emotions of pity, fear, or erotic passion, and that is why we like it—and some theory of artistic modification—that poetry works some distinctive change in real-life emotions, and that is why we like it—one must clearly choose the latter. But then this alternative, the theory of modification, is itself perhaps susceptible of a puzzling refinement into alternatives. Is the emotion which is characteristic of poetry only a modification of real-life emotion (anger toned down, for instance, or anger caught or embodied in an expression), or is the modified and expressed real-life emotion the ground or object of some further distinct emotion, not anger at all, but precisely the aesthetic emotion? Something like the latter would seem to be required if we are to range poetry under the time-honored heading of the "beautiful"—or the aesthetic. The correct response to the beautiful or the aesthetic is presumably not anger, even in an ameliorated form. Yet that correct response is something that can hardly be the proper business of the critic or theorist of poetry, simply because it *is* an ultimate emotive response to the poetic object and not a part of that object. This correct response will have to take care of itself. If it *is* the aim of poetry, it is an aim beyond the direct aim, which is to make an utterance.

---

[2] The situation of the poet in general is well described in the following recent account of symbolism. "The conscious symbolist will find himself in a curious position. . . . Poetic form presupposes the rational world. . . . And the more thoroughly the symbolist conceives of language as symbol, the more likely it is that he will lose touch with language as sign; to the extent that he attains his aim, it would seem that his sense of direction must waver, since he cannot locate his work with reference to himself or an external world. Deliberate symbolism is hazardous in its quest for a pure poetry, for poetry can be pure only by virtue of the impurities it assimilates. In the degree that the poem shakes loose from the poet himself and from the world of objects, in the degree that the poetic world is free from logical bonds, poetry will be deprived of material; in performing its function, it will destroy its subject matter."—Charles Feidelson, Jr., *Symbolism and American Literature* (Chicago, 1953), pp. 70-1. Published by The University of Chicago Press and copyrighted (1953) by the University of Chicago.

We move thus from the epistemological problem—whether the value expressed by poetry is something objective or something subjective—to a kind of ontological problem arising perhaps precisely out of the specific mixed or half-way epistemology of the poetic act. For if we say poetry is to talk of beauty and love (and yet not aim at exciting erotic emotion or even an emotion of Platonic esteem) and if it is to talk of anger and murder (and yet not aim at arousing anger and indignation)—then it may be that the poetic way of dealing with these emotions will not be any kind of intensification, compounding, or magnification, or any direct assault upon the affections at all. Something indirect, mixed, reconciling, tensional might well be the strategem, the devious technique by which a poet indulged in all kinds of talk about love and anger and even in something like "expressions" of these emotions, without aiming at their incitement or even uttering anything that essentially involves their incitement. This problem has been touched on obliquely all through critical history —in all discussions of the tragic and painful and all hints about the comically defective and about the tragicomic—in all theories of irony, paradox, and reconciled opposites.

One part of the difficulty about the modern myth and ritual claims has all along been their solemnity:—the deep cathartic function and the vast canonical subject matters, the cycles of death and rebirth which they impute to or prescribe for the poetry of serious worth. These ideas may be called unhistorical. Like 18th-century Gothicists and Druidists, the myth critics want to push us back into some prelogical and hence pre-literary supposed state of very somberly serious mentality. And hence they are forgetting where they are in history and are overlooking at least two great types of lesson—the lesson of religion, especially that of the Hebrew and Christian religion—which is the lesson of genuine solemnity —and the lesson of accomplished poetry, in Homer, let us say, in Horace, Dante, Shakespeare, Pope—which is surely a different kind of lesson. Let us run the risk of seeming frivolous by saying that it is much less like a lesson of solemnity than a lesson of strife and fun. And to round out our pattern of competing principles, let us add a third modern lesson, that of abstract philosophy.

The ancient division of poetry into tragic and comic, while it is a division, is also an inclusion, and it involves a suggestion that the tragic and the comic may be complementary. On the other hand, there was Plato, in his *Republic*, complaining about the promotion of strife and division by poetry, the feeding and watering of the passions, and in his *Philebus* (or as the recent Cambridge version calls it, *Plato's Examination of Pleasure*) saying that both tragedy and comedy are impure pleasures arising from pain and certain kinds of triumph over pain (like life itself, which is at once tragic and comic), but that a better kind of pleasure is the pure kind arising, for instance, from the knowledge of geometric forms. We can see this kind of Platonism, the numerical and geometric, reappearing here and there down through the centuries, in Augustine and Boethius, for instance (where the orientation is musical), in 18th-century reasoners on order and harmony like Hutcheson (where the orientation again may be visual and geometric). During the early part of our own century the same thing, with frequent appeals to Plato's *Philebus*, has appeared in the aesthetic of "significant" form. The ideas of Bell, Fry, and Wilenski, or of Jay Hambidge, on painting and sculpture, have a clear enough resemblance to art for art's sake in the phase of Whistler and Wilde, and this whole school of formalism (intent on the "significance" of the cube, the "significance" of the cylinder, as well as on the porcelain nicety of certain French verse forms) has contributed a shade of meaning to the term "formalist" when it has been used in an unfriendly way during the more or less recent course of literary debate. Nevertheless, the school of significant form provides us with a sufficiently sharp contrast to the kind of "formalist" criticism which in recent years has been so much concerned with principles of tension, drama, metaphor, paradox, irony, and wit. Another early modern solution to the problem of evil in art was the opposite of the Platonic, and just as extreme. This was the 18th-century resolution by surrender to dismal or to tender feelings. The analysis of wit has been equally an opponent of that. Thus the authors of this history find little difficulty in explaining to themselves a strong sympathy for the contemporary neo-classic school of ironic criticism and for what it has in common with the theory that prevailed in the time of Coleridge and the Germans.

We have observed that the reconciliation of opposites as it was meditated by Schelling and Coleridge had a largely metaphysical bearing. How to get subject and object together and yet explain their distinctness; how to unify inner and outer, general and particular, thought and emotion, art and nature, or a longer series of almost any such opposites one might name—this was the speculation that preoccupied these deeply introspective, transcendentally minded men. An irony of a more darkly moral coloring, a sardonic self-transcendence, was known to Friedrich Schlegel and others. The 20th-century neo-classic irony of poetic inclusiveness, looking back to conversational ironic symbolism, and finding a theoretical hint in quotations from Coleridge by Eliot and Richards, has had a strongly emotive and at times moral accent. There is a direct concern with human affairs and human values here (human "interests"), good and evil, pleasure and pain, rather than with the mysteries of knowledge and creation, the activity of that "synthetic and magical power" the imagination. And so it seems to us that the recent ironists have put a hard problem very compellingly.

Pain and destruction are the two great components of the problem. You can show that pleasure is only an elusive and phantasmal by-product of things and qualities; it cannot be pursued in itself with any success; and you can subsume pleasure under the head of interest, which is the general affective counterpart of knowledge and objects. But pain is not like that; it can sometimes be avoided (that is, it does not always increase through flight; as pleasure diminishes through pursuit); and when it cannot be avoided, we wish it could be. It is one of the most positive experiences we have. (Pain has the two dominant aspects of being a thing we don't like and of being a kind of intensity. The artist, we may speculate, in achieving a certain distance from the aspect of what we don't like is able to take advantage of the intensity.) On the other hand, destruction is clearly enough negative, the termination of experience, being, and interest. The question here is: Why? There is a religious answer that speaks of patience and atonement. This answer is not at odds with poetry, but neither is it available to poetry as a formal solution to the poetic problem.

Of course the reflective and responsible theorist will say that he doesn't call evil itself, or division, or conflict, desirable things. He is sure, however, that facing up to them, facing up to the human predicament, is a desirable and mature state of soul and the right model and source of a mature poetic art. But again, with a certain accent, that may sound somewhat like telling a boy at a baseball game that the *contest* is not really important but only his *noticing* that there *is* a contest.

Let us say that we recognize the fact of material concreteness in human experience, and though matter itself be not evil (as in the Persian scheme), yet it does seem the plausible enough ground for some kind of dualism, division, tension, and conflict, the clash of desires, and evil and pain. Spirit and matter, supernatural and natural, good and evil, these tend to line up as parallel oppositions. Even so refined and geometric a material concept as that of symmetry has its danger for the concept of beauty through unity. How *could* symmetry be part of the definition of beauty? Think, says Plotinus, what that doctrine leads to. "Only a compound can be beautiful, never anything devoid of parts" (I, vi, 1). But parts and composition (and decomposition) seem to be inescapable in the human situation, and on the modern view, art, especially verbal art, confronts this fact. The theorist says that art ought to have the concreteness which comes from recognizing reality and including it. Art ought to have tension, balance, wholeness. Anybody will have to admit that there could never be any drama or story, either comic or tragic, without tension, without conflict, without evil. It may not be at first glance so obvious, but it is nevertheless true, that without some shade of these same elements there could never be any pastoral or idyllic retreat, any didactic or satiric warning, any lyric complaint—or, for that matter, any lyric rejoicing,[3] so far are the springs of human rejoicing buried in the possibility, the threat, the memory of sorrow, so far is human life an experience of mutation, of struggle, of stasis only momentarily and dynamically attained.[4] The great works and the fine works of literature seem to need evil—just as much as the cheap ones, the adventure or detective stories. Evil or the tension of strife with evil is welcomed and absorbed into the structure of the story, the rhythm of the song. The literary spirit flourishes in evil and couldn't get along without it.

The problem can be put succinctly in the following way: Is the unity and order of beauty (and poetry) something that comes about *in spite of* diversity of parts or only *in virtue of* such diversity? The obvious facts in tragedy and comedy and the less obvious facts in other poetic genres would seem to say that the kind of unity required can come about only in virtue of diversity—only in virtue of a certain strife. In certain arts of abstract visual design and perhaps even in some kinds of music, we can see the diversity necessary for the art appearing without much, or without any, idea of strife or painful emotion attached to it. There may well be certain Platonic forms of truly fine art—notably certain forms of drawing and carving, arts which Plato himself was apparently concerned to

[3]
> Yet if we could scorn
>   Hate and pride and fear;
> If we were things born
>   Not to shed a tear,
> I know not how thy joy we ever should come near.
>   —P. B. Shelley, *To a Skylark*

Shelley's brief statement concerning pain and poetry in his *Defense* (ed. Cook, p. 35) is much to the point. The following is one of many fine glimpses in Wordsworth's *Prelude:*

>   To fear and love,
> To love as prime and chief, for there fear ends,
> Be this [imaginative wisdom] ascribed; to early intercourse,
> In presence of sublime or beautiful forms,
> With the adverse principles of pain or joy—
> Evil as one is rashly named by men
> Who know not what they speak.
>   —(1850), XIV, 163

[4] Somewhat more extremely: ". . . it is not possible for imagination to acquaint us with any other world. . . . without the horror we should never focus the beauty; without death there would be no relish for life; without danger, no courage; without savagery, no gentleness; and without the background of our frequent ignominy, no human dignity and pride. (These are excellent and rather Hegelian commonplaces.) . . . there is provided traditionally, betwixt the residence of the soul in one world and its residence in another world, a Lethean bath to bring forgetfulness of that nature which the soul has just lived with; in order that it may adapt to whatever nature may be next in order" (John Crowe Ransom, "The Concrete Universal: Observations on the Understanding of Poetry, II," *The Kenyon Review*, XVII, Summer, 1955, 405–6; also in Ransom's *Poems and Essays*, New York 1955, Vintage Books, Inc.). The Nietzschean version of these commonplaces has been sampled *ante* Chapter 25, pp. 562–4.

purify in the geometric direction, and perhaps certain kinds of music. But as soon as we get into the realm of verbal art, we see the accent of strife in diversity very prominent, and in the major poetic forms, either narrative or dramatic, that element is unmistakable and unavoidable.

One might look on the concept of "poetry" as a kind of central locus where a pull for duality and conflict coming in from the direction of tragedy and comedy encounters and has its own kind of conflict with a pull for harmony coming in from the direction of general aesthetics, "beauty," and beyond that the philosophy of order, being, and the unity of God. "Human interest" confronts Kantian "disinterest" and Thomist "ipsa apprehensio."

Perhaps we face here some kind of problem concerning *The Marriage of Heaven and Hell*. If we take the relatively cautious course of saying that in poetry there has to be an ironic balance of impulses, rather than clear Fourth-of-July choices and celebrations, it will sound to a moralist as if we entertained only wavering beliefs and purposes, no moral commitments.[5] And if we talk more boldly about evil being "reconciled" in poetry, we may sound as if we were actually propitiating evil, giving some dark earth spirit its rightful place in the scheme of things. We may look like a set of Manichaean dualists, some kind of split personalities, or pagans trying to stand on tiptoe.[6]

The lineaments of a response to such difficulties may be discerned in the well-enough-known fact that poetic art is neither the comic-strip melodrama of good and evil as separate agents, hero and villain, nor any kind of philosophic melodrama, truth and falsity disguised as personages and fighting out their duel to one only canonical conclusion, the triumph of truth. For the theater of poetic conflict is human substance itself, ethical substance, as Hegel put it; the conflict is of man with himself or of good and evil in man. Even if the conflict is externally so simple as man against a flood or a forest fire, the poetic conflict is what happens inside the man fighting or the man observing the man fighting. The desire expressed by a few recent theorists for some kind of literary substance as opposed to either Platonic idea or Platonic semblance may be invoked here as a witness. We have alluded in an earlier chapter to what we may call the "no-angelism" of Allen Tate in his volume of "Didactic and Critical Essays" entitled *The Forlorn Demon*. And thus Miss Elizabeth Sewell:

> I have repeated one essential thing about what I conceive to be the true life of the imagination, that in it the life of the mind depends for its liberation upon a kind of submission to the life of the body (and the human), and that the two must live together, according to the way of man, and not of angels or demons.

[5] Cf. *ante*, Chapter 29, pp. 672–4, the view of Yvor Winters.
[6] Cf. H. M. McLuhan, review of D. E. S. Maxwell on T. S. Eliot in *Renascence*, Spring, 1955.

> This submission is, superficially, a scandal, but, more profoundly
> viewed, it is a way of freedom.[7]

Other writers in this vein have touched more emphatically on the intimacy
which obtains between human substance and the fact of evil both as
suffering and as division and destruction. Thus Father William Lynch:

> True tragedy has always been a sober calculation of the relation
> of human energy to existence. Such calculating has always re-
> quired profound honesty and the rejecting of the cheaper forms
> of mysticism. St. Paul himself had weighed the matter well and
> found it impossible to work out the equation. And he therefore
> cried out: "Who shall deliver me from the body of this
> death?" [8]

The patristic idea of the "Fortunate Fall," variously expressed by Am-
brose, by Augustine, by Gregory the Great, and in the liturgy ("*O felix
culpa, quae talem ac tantum meruit habere Redemptorem*") [9] is probably
a closer analogue to an adequate literary theory than such neo-Platonic
ideas as Augustine entertained about the beauty of the triangle or the
circle. The writers of the present history have not been concerned to
implicate literary theory with any kind of religious doctrine. It appears
to us, however, relevant, as we near our conclusion, at least to confess
an opinion that the kind of literary theory which seems to us to emerge
the most plausibly from the long history of the debates is far more difficult
to orient within any of the Platonic or Gnostic ideal world views, or
within the Manichaean full dualism and strife of principles, than precisely
within the vision of suffering, the optimism, the mystery which are em-
braced in the religious dogma of the Incarnation.

And let us say furthermore: that if verbal art has to take up the
mixed business of good and evil, its most likely way of success and its
peculiar way is a mixed way. And this means not simply a complicated
correspondence, a method of alternation, now sad, now happy (as in some
neo-classic theories of tragicomedy), but the oblique glance, the vertical
unification of the metaphoric smile. To pursue the ironic and tensional
theories in the way most likely to avoid the Manichaean heresy will require a certain caution in the use of the solemn and tragic emphasis. Dark
feelings, painful feelings, dismal feelings, even tender feelings move readily toward the worship of evil. And they have the further disadvantage
that they run readily into pure feeling itself, its indulgence and the theory
of that, as in the 18th century. There was a girl in Mrs. Thrale's set at

---

[7] "The Death of the Imagination," *Thought*, XXVIII (Autumn, 1953), 443.
[8] "Confusion in Our Theater," *Thought*, XXVI (Autumn, 1951), 359–60.
[9] Cf. A. O. Lovejoy, *Essays in the History of Ideas* (Baltimore, 1948), pp.
285–94, "Milton and the Paradox of the Fortunate Fall."

Streatham who could weep so prettily that she was sometimes called upon for a parlor demonstration.

It is true that pure laughter too has its limitations. It may be idiotic. There is a certain kind of optimistic writing that sounds like the result of laughing gas. But bright feelings and the smile go with metaphor and wit, and when playing on serious topics, wit generates a certain mimicry of substance which is poetry. There was another member of the Streatham set who in a *Preface to Shakespeare* noticed that "Shakespeare has united the powers of exciting laughter and sorrow not only in one mind, but in one composition." By this line of suggestion and by quoting further authorities of this tenor we might arrive at a theory that sounded too much like the homely formula "Grin and bear it," or perhaps like a prescription for *The Most Lamentable Comedy and Most Cruel Death of Pyramus and Thisbe*. But the theory also could be made to sound like a phrase in Aristotle's *Poetics*—the four words *anōdunon kai ou phthartikon* —not painful and not destructive, a description which Aristotle meant for the comic object as distinguished from the hideously suffering tragic object. But the phrase, even in Aristotle's system, can easily be lifted so as to operate not only at the level of poetic object but at that of poetic utterance, poetry itself, and then it will refer not only to comedy but to tragedy too.

VII

ONE apparently needs to insist nowadays that the term "irony" need not always be taken with a strongly emotive and moral accent. "Irony" may be usefully taken rather as a cognitive principle which shades off through paradox into the general principle of metaphor and metaphoric structure —the tension which is always present when words are used in vitally new ways. The ultimate advantage of the theory of irony and metaphor is that it is a theory that involves both poetic content and poetic "form" and demands the interdependence of these two. There are certain kinds of contentual meaning which can scarcely be discussed except under the aspect of technique, style, "form." These meanings are pre-eminently the ironic-metaphoric.

The term "form," perhaps it will be well to assert briefly at this point, is one which we have been content to use throughout this history in a provisional but convenient Renaissance and modern manner [1] to refer

---

[1] See, for instance, Gilbert, pp. 202, 470, 492, 500, Dante (*Letter to Can Grande*) and Tasso (*Discorsi*); Gregory Smith, I, 266, William Webbe; René le Bossu, *Traité du poème epique*, 1675, "Livre Second, De la matière du poeme. epique"; "Livre Troisième, De la Forme du poème epique"; and *ante*, Chapter 22, p. 484, Arnold on Wordsworth; p. 488-9, Gautier on *Emaux et Camées* and Wilde ("Form is everything"). And see Chapter 2, p. 33.

to all those elements of a verbal composition—rhythm, metrics, structure, coherence, emphasis, diction, images—which can more or less readily be discussed as if they were not a part of the poem's "content," message, or doctrine. "Form," as we have suggested by apposition just above, is technique and style. "Form" includes all those elements which an aesthete might conceive as justifying a view of art as pure, non-conceptual, non-didactic. It is all that the old rhetorical theory might call either "disposition" or "elocution." It is what Aristotle in the *Poetics* calls "medium" (diction and music) and "manner" (spectacle). Thus "form" is not identical, at first glance anyway, with *all* the character that a work may have, as in the radical view of monistic expressionism. "Form" in the sense implied by the last three or four hundred years of literary criticism is only a dim analogy of the Aristotelian idea or essence by which "matter" is *formed* into some kind of thing (stone into a statue, or something less identifiable than stone into stone itself). Only a dim or inferior analogy, we say. Yet it is at least as clear and good as the opposed more Platonic analogy (found in Scaliger and more recently in the Chicago critics) by which "matter" is the sheer meaningless phonetics, the physical sound, of words (if such a thing can be conceived) and "form" is the idea of the story or other meaning imposed upon the words. Our exposition has preferred to make use of the readily definable and widely understood convention that "matter" is the content or message of literary works, so far as that may be extricated from their dense formality, and "form" is all that complication and stylization which in past ages has in one way or another been looked on as extraneous to matter—a kind of ornament, recommendation, fortification, dress, or the like. Nevertheless our final view, implicit in our whole narrative and in whatever moments of argument we may have allowed ourselves, has been that "form" in fact embraces and penetrates "message" in a way that constitutes a deeper and more substantial meaning than either abstract message or separable ornament. In both the scientific or abstract dimension and in the practical or rhetorical dimension there *is* both message and the means of conveying message, but the poetic dimension is just that dramatically unified meaning which is coterminous with form. This is true both in the sense that all verbal discourse, no matter how unpoetic, has this poetic aspect, and in the more special sense that certain instances of verbal discourse are almost insusceptible of abstractive message reading, and these are poems (in verse and prose) in the most special and excellent sense.

Poetry is truth of "coherence," rather than truth of "correspondence," as the matter is sometimes phrased nowadays. We have heard Sir Philip Sidney say that the poet "nothing affirmeth and therefore never lieth." And Wilde, in the vein of wit peculiar to him: "After all, what is a fine lie? Simply that which is its own evidence."

A close internal relation exists of course between this kind of "form"

and the tension of values and emotions on which we were insisting a few
pages back. Such tension can occur at structural levels or in local detail of
symbols and metaphors. It can be read as metaphoric meaning here and
there in poems or as metaphoric character or dimension extending all
through poems and constituting their very "imitative" relation to the
world of reality which with their aid and in them we come to know.
For excellent reasons the *discordia concors* of the metaphysical metaphor or simile has seemed to some critics of our generation the very type
and acme of the poetic structure. Such a figure is at least a small-scale
model, a manageable miniature, in which a critic may more or less readily
scrutinize certain features: the non-literal confrontation of vehicle and
tenor, the pull of opposite values and feelings—the lovers, their sighs and
anguish, and the willed control, the restraint, the geometry and the com-
passes.

Let us speak briefly here in praise of metaphor. Let us observe that
metaphor combines the element of necessity or universality (the prime
poetic quality which Aristotle noticed) with that other element of concreteness or specificity which was implicit in Aristotle's requirement of
the mimetic object. Metaphor is the union of history and philosophy
which was the main premise of Sidney's *Defence*. And metaphor would
seem to be the only verbal structure which will accomplish this feat. We
can have our universals in the full conceptualized discourse of science and
philosophy. We can have specific detail lavishly in the newspapers and in
records of trials and revelations of psychiatric cases. But it is only in
metaphor, and hence it is *par excellence* in poetry, that we encounter the
most radically and relevantly fused union of the detail and the universal
idea. Detail in itself is contingent on information and it is the characteristic object of the historian's research. Still it gets into poems, and poems
start with it and from it, and the historian is in the happy position of not
necessarily renouncing criticism. Metaphor is the universal amber for the
preservation and enhancement of the scraps and trifles of historic fact.
"Pretty! in amber to observe the forms, Of hairs, or straws, or dirt, or
grubs, or worms! The things, we know, are neither rich nor rare, But
wonder how the devil they got there." For it is not a universal fact and
not universally admired that men should wear cork-heeled "shoon." But
joined with certain ideas of vanity and frivolity and with salt water (in the
ballad of *Sir Patrick Spens*), the shoes make a permanent and important,
a universally conceivable, human meaning. A "superannuated" British
warship of the year 1838 becomes by modern naval norms a highly
vulnerable smallish wooden tub. But in the high slant perspective, the
orange and bloody sunset, of Turner's illumination we still have *The
Fighting Téméraire*. Metaphors are poetry's permanent and necessary
conclusions drawn from variable and contingent premises. Other universals are abstract and to that extent *a priori*, even tautological. (A rose is a

rose. . . .) Metaphor is a substantive—or a mock-substantive—universal.

It is true that metaphor in poetry is not the same thing as metaphor in poetic theory. Yet a metaphoric theory of poetry is almost necessarily a theory of multiple focuses and hence a historic theory and a perspective theory. It entertains not historically separate and opaque conceptions but a translucent continuous view of history as vista and development. The theory implicit in our narrative sees three main focuses or three most radical ideas in the history of literary criticism, believes them interrelated and reconcilable, and aspires to discard no one of the three. Thus, we recognize: (1) the mimetic or Aristotelian, which does justice to the world of things and real values and keeps our criticism from being merely idealistic; (2) the emotive (as developed with most subtlety perhaps by Richards), which does justice to human responses to values and keeps criticism from talking too much about either ethics or physics; (3) the expressionistic and linguistic (*par excellence* the Crocean), which does justice to man's knowledge as reflexive and creative and keeps criticism from talking about poetry as a literal recording of either things or responses. Our account of critical history says that the second and the third of these radical ideas are present in Aristotle along with the first, though the third, the expressionistic, is surely the weakest of the three and least explicitly developed. It appears to us that these ideas can be made the main points of reference for an indefinitely variable criticism of *all* poems. That is, there are no poems which, as one academic school of our day would have it, are in some exclusively proper way "mimetic" and which hence should not be permitted an expressionistic or symbolic reading; and conversely, all "symbolic" poems, if they are real poems, are in some important sense "mimetic" and dramatic. It seems to us, finally, that metaphor is not only in a broad sense the principle of all poetry but is also inevitable in practical criticism and will be active there in proportion as criticism moves beyond the historical report or the academic exercise.

These observations imply the principle too by which we evaluate the history of the celebrated, perhaps notorious, "genres," literary "species," "types," or "kinds"—not wishing to adopt either these genres or any modification of them as authoritative points of reference or fixations in our scheme of literary valuing, nor on the other hand to follow the Crocean sweep in refusing to allow any worth at all to or make any use of such technically defined entities. The evolution of criticism has produced four, perhaps five, genre conceptions dominant enough in their eras to serve as focusses for the poetic whole. Each of these (with perhaps one exception) seems to have had its advantages; each has enabled a certain understanding not only of one literary genre but of the whole poetic structure and problem. Aristotle's view was dramatic, or more precisely tragic (with intimations of a twin comic view), and this had the great advantage of opening up the more broadly "dramatic," the ethically

problematic and tensional, aspect of poetry as a whole. *Peri Poiētikēs*—
On the Art of Fiction. Aristotle, if read rightly, has something to say
about all the poetic genres. The next basic view is that of Horace, conversational, epistolary, idiomatic, ironic, satiric—despite all the defunct
doctrines about drama which Horace manages to embalm in his gentlemanly wit. This view has the advantage of opening up the linguistic, the
idiomatic, the metaphoric and in that sense again the "dramatic" aspect
of all poetry. Next is the high, the grand, the ecstatic view of Longinus—
which on the whole opens up more dangers and confusions perhaps than
affective advantage, and is not a view according to literary species (but
just the opposite) unless we look on it as making a large contribution
(via Boileau) to the new genre of the "heroic" in the third quarter of the
17th century. Here was a perspective that was almost altogether inflation-
ary and bad, looking not into the realm of spirit and word, where poetry really is, but into a gigantorama of grossly direct stimulations, of
pageantry, drums, duels, warfare, spectres, loud protestations of lust,
honor, and valor. Meanwhile, in the same essays of Dryden which defend the heroic, a theory of courtly wit and ridicule is asserted, and by
the time of Pope and Swift, this can be considered a second focussing of
the Horatian conversational and satiric ideal. And in close liaison, appears the mocking genre of the anti-heroic or burlesque. (Both these, it
is true, are, as with the original Horatian satire, genre norms more by
the implication of prevalent and successful practice than by any clearly
enunciated theory.) Lastly, the cycle of genres is completed in the era
of the romantics with the now affectionately remembered lyric ideal and
its attendant opinion that a long poem is a contradiction in terms. This
had the advantage of exploiting a new view of "expression," a view of
subjectivity both as cognition and as feeling, and of metaphor as the
small-scale model and touchstone of the whole poetic business. After that
Copernican revolution, from dramatic, epic and satiric forms to the lyric,
there were no new genre theories.[2] Theories after that were returns ei-

---

[2] "Those forms which he [Friedrich Schlegel] finds appropriate to his own
taste and time and which are congenial, above all, to the reflective, ironic temper
of the modern mind are the fragment, the dialogue (*das Gespräch*), the rhapsody,
the arabesque, the ironic comedy, and the speculative, satirical, or polemical
aphorism. All these are 'mixed' forms ('All pure, classical forms,' he says in *Lyceum*
fragment 60, 'are now absurd'). . . . The lyrical soliloquy, so indicative of a later
and different sort of nineteenth-century romanticism, is for Schlegel an enviable
but certainly a primitive and inferior manner. Unlike these forms, which have at
least a sporadic historical character in common, the form of the novel is radically
new and certainly without a continuous history. The novel (*der Roman*) represents
for Schlegel the most significant invention of the modern analytical sensibility. It is
related by its philosophical and discursive purpose not to the classical epic but to
the didactic poem, whose greatest single specimen is the *Divine Comedy*. . . . the
novel is not a consistent art form; it is not, in a strict sense, a genre . . ." (Victor
Lange, "Friedrich Schlegel's Literary Criticism," *Comparative Literature*, VII, Fall,
1955, 299).

ther to the classic idea of bigness, as with Arnold, or to the romantic idea
of the lyrically intense moment, as with the imagists of the early 20th
century. Or they were more and more subtly and dialectically blended
obliterations of the old genre idea, as with the 19th-century dramatic
monologues and idylls, and then the varieties of symbolism, post-symbol-
ism, and latterly surrealism. The interlude of the porcelain verse genres
with the Parnassians scarcely counts.

VIII

ONE perhaps will look about for some comprehensive issue, some paradoxical junction, that will catch, if only in a precarious and momentary
stasis, the whole of the problem. This seems to appear nowadays in the
question so often asked or implied: whether a poetic theory should be
Platonic (concerned with meanings, even though only with analogical
meanings) or Aristotelian, concerned, some critics appear to suppose,
only with structures—structures of meaning which are somehow, in
themselves, as structures, devoid of any meaning and not a modification
or enablement of the meanings which are thought to be structured.
Which view should poetic theory lean toward? Or, perhaps better, why
should such a question be asked? The reason appears to lie in a kind of
three-story pattern of human values which may be expounded roughly
as follows: There is (1) easiest and lowest, the level of sensory pleasure
and pain, terminal in its own way, unexplainable, more or less opaque.
There is—to jump to the other extreme—(3) spiritual value, ethical and
religious, terminal too, in a different way, in the sense that there is no
higher appeal or sanction. And then in between there is (2) something
like what Kant saw (which made him close a gap in his system with the
Critique of Judgment). That is, there is aesthetic pleasure, pleasure of
art, and this divides into two kinds: (A) the non-referential and Platonic,
a form of sensory-intellectual pleasure (like wall paper and arabesques),
terminal again in its own way—and (B) the referential or symbolic, the
anti-Platonic art pleasure, especially the pleasure of poetry. But this kind
of aesthetic value is an unstable conception. It almost inevitably invites
being reduced—either up or down—to (1) sensory values, pleasure and
pain (the portrayal of flowers and perfumes in Eden, says Addison, is
more delightful than the portrayal of brimstone and smoke in Hell)—or
to (3) conceptualized ethical and religious values (poetry, says the old
didactic theory, is to teach correct lessons).

The grand problem for the theorist would appear to be how to evade
these temptations, or, perhaps better, how to embrace them both and thus
have a double or paradoxical theory. His best chance to do this, we have
suggested, is found in the curious fact of metaphor, which is a combi-

nation of concreteness and significance, a reconciliation or simultaneous embodiment of diverse emotive pulls, a way of facing and even asserting something serious while at the same time declining the didactic gambit which nature is always pushing forward—both to artist and to theorist.

A theory of art will not be able to get along without at least two key terms—to stand in partial opposition to each other and keep the theory from collapsing into tautology or into literalism. At the same time it will hardly be a theory at all unless it tries to bring these two terms into a reconciled and necessary relation, or to see each in and through the other. The two best critical terms, the most simple, inclusive, and unavoidable, are perhaps *making* and *saying* (if the latter be understood to include its expressionist complement the term *seeing*—"Always the seer is a sayer"). Or *Creation and Discovery*, as the title of an aesthetic philosopher's recent book has it. *Making*, the Aristotelian emphasis, and *saying-seeing*, the Platonic and romantic. The justification of this polar arrangement is the impossibility that the two can ever come completely together without the collapse and loss of poetry, and the equal impossibility of their being taken in strict dichotomy or separation without the same loss. Under these two complementary but opposed heads we can marshal an indefinite list of the antitheses that emerge in various phases of critical argument: drama vs. statement, metaphor vs. literal fact, concrete vs. abstract, whole vs. part, whole structure vs. Longinian or Crocean flash, inclusion vs. exclusion, pleasure *and* pain vs. pleasure *or* pain, Aristotelian *harmonia* vs. Aristotelian *mimēsis*, art in full vs. either romantic or classical art; finally, and again basically, the work vs. either the author or the audience. Art or poetry is the peculiar situation where we see each member of each pair only in or through its opposite: making through saying and saying through making.

Something can be learned, something perhaps ultimate, from the most abstract schemes of the philosophers. Let us take a concluding look at an Aristotelian and scholastic classification of human mental activities recently readvertised in the aesthetic writings of the neo-scholastic philosopher Jacques Maritain. Systematic mental activities (arts and sciences), says the tradition, are either speculative (like metaphysics and mathematics) or practical, and the practical are either concerned with doing (ethics and politics) or with making (arts), and then these activities of making are further divisible into useful arts and fine arts—the last being the category where we find poetry. Perhaps, though we will not urge this in a quarrelsome way against aestheticians of painting or music, poetry is *the* fine art. Mr. Maritain thinks that something he calls "poetry," a principle of subjective communion with objective reality, is the essence of all the fine arts. And indeed the verbal principle as it works in poetry more pronouncedly than in other arts does at least put a special emphasis on the relation of tension which holds between fine art (especially poetry) and the other arts and between art in general and the sciences. There is a doubling of art and fine art, in two stages, from their generic non-speculative direction back through the status of *making* (as distinct from doing) to the status of *fine* (as distinct from useful). This last, the status of *fine*, is one where acting takes on in a peculiar way the aspect of speculation (seeing-saying). Let us imagine a tabular arrangement as follows:

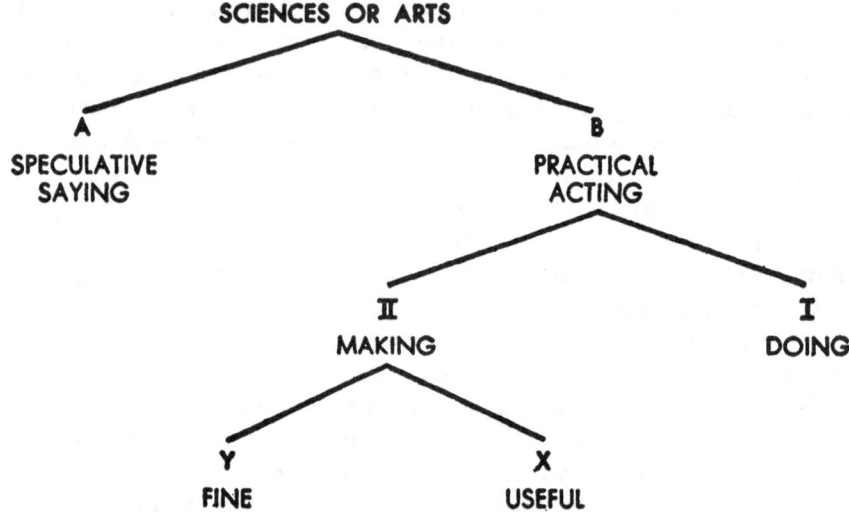

And let us recite thus the broadest lessons of critical history: (1) A pragmatic general philosophy collapses A and B, and hence there is no possibility that a problem about art can really arise. "When we look at a picture, or read a poem, or listen to music," says Richards, "we are not doing something quite unlike what we were doing on our way to the Gallery or when we dressed in the morning." [3] (2) Functionalism in art theory (even in a scholastic frame of general reference) collapses X and Y, echoing and complementing the general pragmatic reduction of A to B. "To make a drainpipe," says Eric Gill, "is as much the work of an artist as it is to make paintings or poems." [4] (3) Platonic versions of art and beauty (including perhaps the neo-scholastic theory of Mr. Maritain) and fully idealist versions of expressionism, like that of Croce, put a transcendental "beauty" somehow specially under Y, though by definition as a transcendental this beauty is also everywhere else and is hence the proper object of the most generalized speculative activity. "If an epigram be art," says Croce, "why not a simple word?" [5] (4) Didactic art theory, from Plato to the present day, completes too in its own way the motion of return (from right to left in our spatial representation) and rules art

[3] *Principles of Literary Criticism* (New York, 1934), p. 16.
[4] Eric Gill, *Art* (London, 1935), p. 4.
[5] *Aesthetic*, trans. Douglas Ainslie (London, 1922), p. 13.

by the straight norms of A, conceptual truth. Poetry, that is, becomes the art of *saying* something *correct* either about God or nature or about some human activity. Would a pilot or a poet know better, asks Socrates, how to steer a boat in a storm?

It remains that a theory of poetic or fine art must do something yet different. It must keep asserting in various idioms, by various stratagems, in accord with the demands of the dialectic of the time, the special character of Y (poetry) as a tensional union of making with seeing and saying.

INDEX

Index

For Product Safety Concerns and Information please contact our EU
representative GPSR@taylorandfrancis.com
Taylor & Francis Verlag GmbH, Kaufingerstraße 24, 80331 München, Germany

www.ingramcontent.com/pod-product-compliance
Lightning Source LLC
Chambersburg PA
CBHW051149030726
47504CB00004B/1116

* 9 7 8 0 3 6 7 6 9 2 2 9 2 *